Dedication

SHARON NELSON AND John Simek dedicate this book to our children, Kelly, Sara, Kim, JJ, Jason, and Jamie, and to our grandchildren, Samantha and Jordan, with many more to come, we hope!

Michael Maschke dedicates this book to his wife, family, and friends. Without their patience, understanding, support, and, most of all, love, the completion of this work would not have been possible.

The 2012 Solo and Small Firm Legal Technology Guide

CRITICAL DECISIONS MADE SIMPLE

Sharon D. Nelson, Esq., John W. Simek and Michael C. Maschke

INTRODUCTION BY ROSS L. KODNER, ESQ.

ABA LawPracticeManagementSection
MARKETING • MANAGEMENT • TECHNOLOGY • FINANCE

Commitment to Quality: The Law Practice Management Section is committed to quality in our publications. Our authors are experienced practitioners in their fields. Prior to publication, the contents of all our books are rigorously reviewed by experts to ensure the highest quality product and presentation. Because we are committed to serving our readers' needs, we welcome your feedback on how we can improve future editions of this book.

Cover design by RIPE Creative, Inc.

Nothing contained in this book is to be considered as the rendering of legal advice for specific cases, and readers are responsible for obtaining such advice from their own legal counsel. This book and any forms and agreements herein are intended for educational and informational purposes only.

The products and services mentioned in this publication are under or may be under trademark or service mark protection. Product and service names and terms are used throughout only in an editorial fashion, to the benefit of the product manufacturer or service provider, with no intention of infringement. Use of a product or service name or term in this publication should not be regarded as affecting the validity of any trademark or service mark.

The Law Practice Management Section, American Bar Association, offers an educational program for lawyers in practice. Books and other materials are published in furtherance of that program. Authors and editors of publications may express their own legal interpretations and opinions, which are not necessarily those of either the American Bar Association or the Law Practice Management Section unless adopted pursuant to the bylaws of the Association. The opinions expressed do not reflect in any way a position of the Section or the American Bar Association.

© 2012 American Bar Association. All rights reserved.

Printed in the United States of America.

13 12 11   5 4 3 2 1

Library of Congress Cataloging-in-Publication Data
The 2012 Solo and Small Firm Legal Technology Guide: Critical Decisions Made Simple. Sharon Nelson, John Simek and Michael Maschke: Library of Congress Cataloging-in-Publication Data is on file.

ISBN: 978-1-61438-187-7

Discounts are available for books ordered in bulk. Special consideration is given to state bars, CLE programs, and other bar-related organizations. Inquire at Book Publishing, American Bar Association, 321 N. Clark Street, Chicago, Illinois 60654.

www.ShopABA.org

Contents at a Glance

About the Authors	xv
Acknowledgments	xix
Preface to the Fifth Edition	xxi
Introduction	xxiii

Chapter 1: Computers	1
Chapter 2: Computer Operating Systems	13
Chapter 3: Monitors	19
Chapter 4: Computer Peripherals	23
Chapter 5: Printers	31
Chapter 6: Scanners	39
Chapter 7: Servers	43
Chapter 8: Server Operating Systems	55
Chapter 9: Networking Hardware	63
Chapter 10: Miscellaneous Hardware	73
Chapter 11: Smartphones	79
Chapter 12: Productivity Software	85
Chapter 13: Security Software	97
Chapter 14: Case Management	103
Chapter 15: Time and Billing Software	111
Chapter 16: Litigation Programs	121
Chapter 17: Document Management	123
Chapter 18: Document Assembly	127
Chapter 19: Cloud Computing and SaaS	131
Chapter 20: Collaboration	135
Chapter 21: Remote Access	141
Chapter 22: Mobile Security	147
Chapter 23: More from Apple	153
Chapter 24: Unified Messaging and Telecommunications	165

Chapter 25: Utilities	**173**
Chapter 26: Navigating a Minefield: Social Media and the Law	**191**
Chapter 27: The Paper LESS Office: Kicking the Paper Habit in the Era of the Cloud	**213**
Chapter 28: Tomorrow in Legal Tech	**237**
Appendix	**245**
Glossary	**257**
Index	**281**

Contents

About the Authors	xv
Acknowledgments	xix
Preface to the Fifth Edition	xxi
Introduction by Ross L. Kodner, Esq.	xxiii

Chapter 1: Computers — 1

- Desktop Computers — 1
  - Personal Computers (PCs) — 1
  - Apple Computers (Macs) — 4
- Laptops — 7
  - Personal Computers (PCs) — 7
  - Apple Computers (Macs) — 9
- Netbooks — 10

Chapter 2: Computer Operating Systems — 13

- Microsoft Windows XP Operating System — 13
- Microsoft Windows Vista Operating System — 13
- Microsoft Windows 7 — 14
- Mac OS X Version 10.5 (Leopard) Operating System — 16
- Mac OS X Version 10.6 (Snow Leopard) Operating System — 16
- Mac OS X Version 10.7 (Lion) Operating System — 17

Chapter 3: Monitors — 19

- CRT Monitors — 19
- Flat-Panel LCD Monitors — 19
- Widescreen Monitors — 20
- High-Definition Monitors — 21

Chapter 4: Computer Peripherals — 23
Mouse — 23
Keyboards — 24
Wireless Keyboard Desktops — 25
External Storage Devices — 26
    External Hard Drives — 26
    Thumb Drives — 27
    FireWire Devices — 28
Speakers and Headphones — 29

Chapter 5: Printers — 31
Stand-Alone Printers — 31
Networked Printers — 33
    Low-Volume Network Printers — 33
    High-Volume Network Printers — 34
    Color Network Printer — 35
Multifunctional Printers/Copiers — 36

Chapter 6: Scanners — 39
    Low-Volume Scanner — 40
    High-Volume Scanner — 40

Chapter 7: Servers — 43
Solo—File and Printer Sharing — 43
Small Firm—File and Printer Sharing/Hosting Services — 45
Database/Applications Server — 47
Virtual Servers — 49
Peer-to-Peer — 52

Chapter 8: Server Operating Systems — 55
Microsoft Windows Server 2003 Standard Edition — 55
Microsoft Windows Small Business Server 2003 Standard and Premium Editions — 55
Microsoft Windows Server 2003 Enterprise Edition — 56
Microsoft Windows Server 2008 R2 — 57
Microsoft Windows Small Business Server 2008 Standard and Premium Editions — 58
Windows Server 2008 Standard Edition — 59
Windows Server 2008 Enterprise Edition — 59
Microsoft Small Business Server 2011 Standard and Essentials — 60
X64 Operating Systems — 60
Mac OS X Server "Leopard" — 61

Mac OS X Server "Snow Leopard"	61
Mac OS X Server "Lion"	61
Linux-Based Operating Systems	62

Chapter 9: Networking Hardware — 63

Switches	63
Entry-Level and Intermediate-Level Routers	65
Firewalls/IDS/IPS Devices	66
Racks	68
Cabling	69
Wireless Networking Devices	70

Chapter 10: Miscellaneous Hardware — 73

Fire Safe	73
Battery Backup Devices	74
Fax Machines	76
Backup Solutions	77

Chapter 11: Smartphones — 79

Chapter 12: Productivity Software — 85

Microsoft Office	85
Corel Suite	88
OpenOffice.org	89
Adobe Acrobat	91
OCR Software	94
Voice Recognition Software	95

Chapter 13: Security Software — 97

Stand-Alone	97
Enterprise Versions	98
Integrated Security Solutions	98
Antispam Protection	100

Chapter 14: Case Management — 103

Amicus Attorney	104
Time Matters	106
PracticeMaster	107
Clio	108
Rocket Matter	108
Firm Manager	109
Others	109

Chapter 15: Time and Billing Software — 111
- Manual Generation — 112
- Accounting Software — 112
- Billing Specific — 114
- Billing for a Mac — 115
- Integrated Packages — 116
- PCLaw — 116
- Tabs3 — 117
- Amicus Accounting — 118

Chapter 16: Litigation Programs — 121

Chapter 17: Document Management — 123
- DocuShare — 123
- iManage — 124
- Worldox — 124
- Acrobat — 125
- Web-Based — 125
- Plain Folders — 126
- Searching — 126

Chapter 18: Document Assembly — 127
- HotDocs — 127
- ProDoc — 128
- AIA Contract Documents — 129

Chapter 19: Cloud Computing and SaaS — 131

Chapter 20: Collaboration — 135
- Google Docs — 135
- Acrobat — 137
- Microsoft Word — 138
- SharePoint — 138
- Office 365 — 139

Chapter 21: Remote Access — 141
- Virtual Private Networking — 141
- GoToMyPC — 142
- LogMeIn — 142
- TeamViewer — 143
- Mobility Tips — 144

Chapter 22: Mobile Security — 147
Software — 147
Encryption — 148
Wireless — 148
AirCard — 149
Public Computer Usage — 151
Smartphones — 151
Final Words — 152

Chapter 23: More from Apple — 153
Hardware — 153
   Apple iPad 2 — 153
   AirPort Extreme — 155
   AirPort Express — 156
   Time Capsule — 156
   Apple Thunderbolt Display — 157
   Apple Wireless Keyboard — 157
   Apple Magic Mouse — 157
   Apple iPod — 158
Software — 159
   Microsoft Office 2008 for Macs: Business Edition — 159
   Toast 11 Titanium by Roxio — 160
   Norton Internet Security for Mac — 160
   Intuit Quicken Essentials and QuickBooks 2011 for Mac — 161
   PGP Whole Disk Encryption 10 for Mac OS X — 162
   Apple iTunes — 162

Chapter 24: Unified Messaging and Telecommunications — 165
Google Voice — 168
Voice over Internet Protocol (VoIP) — 168
High-Speed Internet — 170

Chapter 25: Utilities — 173
X1 — 173
dtSearch — 174
Credenza — 175
Outlook Send Assistant — 176
GreenPrint — 177
Winscribe for the Legal Profession — 178
Eyejot — 178
YouSendIt — 179

Copy2Contact	180
Twinbox	180
TweetDeck	181
TinyURL	181
IrfanView	181
DBAN	182
SimplyFile	183
Shred 2	183
SnagIt	184
FavBackup 2.0.2	184
QuickView Plus	185
Sam Spade	185
Karen's Power Tools	186
Metadata Assistant	186
Livescribe Pulse Smartpen	187
YouMail	188
SmartDraw VP	188
CaseSoft TimeMap 5	189
Evernote	190
WinRAR	190
Chapter 26: Navigating a Minefield: Social Media and the Law	**191**
Introduction to Social Media Tools	192
Blogs	192
Social Networking Sites	192
Social Messaging Sites	195
The "Social Media Effect"	196
Social Media's Impact on E-Discovery: The Gift and the Curse	197
An Explosion of Evidence	197
"Discovering" the Headache of Social Media	198
A Solution to the Discovery Problem?	204
A Law Enforcement Twist: Trolling Social Media for Haphazdard Tweets, Comments, or Photos	207
One Wrong Step and Ka-Boom! Social Media Mishaps	208
Lesson 1: It's Called Confidentiality, Stupid!	209
Lesson 2: Do You Know Who Your Friends Are?	210
Lesson 3: Sometimes It's Not Good to "Tweet" Your Own Horn!	211
Conclusion	212

**Chapter 27: The Paper LESS Office: Kicking the Paper Habit in the Era of the Cloud
by Ross L. Kodner, Esq.**   **213**

   I Want It NOW! Or Sooner! Life in the Age of Instancy   214
   Paper: Endless Frustration and Expense   215
   Saving the Planet, Saving Your Sanity—More Paper is NOT the Way   216
   The Cost of Being in a Paper MORE Office   216
   Fragmented Client Files Defy Common Sense   219
   Stop the Madness: Become Paper LESS in Your Practice   219
   Getting Specific About Being Paper LESS   221
   Scanning Systems—What Works?   222
   Document Management Systems:
      The Electronic Glue Holding It Together   225
   Okay, Now Let's Get to Our Documents from Anywhere, Any Time:
      The Paper LESS Cloud   228
   The Real World: Comments from the Trenches in the Paper Wars   232
   SIDENOTE: A Paper LESS Peripheral Benefit:
      Protecting Your "Paper"   234
   The Paper LESS Bottom Line . . .   235

Chapter 28: Tomorrow in Legal Tech   **237**

Appendix   **245**
Glossary   **257**
Index   **281**

About the Authors

Sharon D. Nelson, Esq.

Sharon D. Nelson is the president of Sensei Enterprises, Inc. Ms. Nelson graduated from Georgetown University Law Center in 1978 and has been in private practice ever since. She now focuses exclusively on electronic evidence law.

Ms. Nelson and Mr. Simek are the co-editors of the Internet law and technology newsletter *Bytes in Brief*. Ms. Nelson, Mr. Simek, and Mr. Maschke are the co-authors of the 2008, 2009, 2010, and 2011 editions of this book. Ms. Nelson and Mr. Simek are also co-authors of *Information Security for Lawyers and Law Firms* (ABA, 2006). Additionally, Ms. Nelson and Mr. Simek are co-authors of *The Electronic Evidence and Discovery Handbook: Forms, Checklists, and Guidelines* (ABA, 2006). Ms. Nelson is a co-author of *How Good Lawyers Survive Bad Times* (ABA, 2009). Their articles have appeared in numerous national publications, and they frequently lecture throughout the country on electronic evidence and legal technology subjects.

Ms. Nelson and Mr. Simek are the hosts of the Legal Talk Network's "Digital Detectives" podcast and Ms. Nelson is a co-host of the ABA's "The Digital Edge: Lawyers and Technology" podcast.

Ms. Nelson will become the vice president of the Virginia State Bar in June of 2012 and its 75th president in June of 2013. She is the past president of the Fairfax Bar Association, a director of the Fairfax Law Foundation, past chair of the ABA's TECHSHOW Board, and past chair of the ABA's Law Practice Management Publishing Board. She currently serves on the Governing Council of the ABA's Law Practice Management Section and as the chair of its Education Board. She is a member of the Sedona Conference and of EDRM. She is a graduate of Leadership Fairfax and serves on the Governing Council of the Virginia State Bar as well as on its Executive Committee. She is the chair of the Virginia State Bar's Unauthorized Practice of Law Committee and serves on both its Technology Committee and its Standing Committee on Finance. She also serves on the Virginia Supreme Court's Advisory Committee on Statewide E-filing. She is a member of the ABA, the Virginia Bar, the Virginia Bar Association, the Virginia Trial Lawyers Association, the Virginia Women Lawyer Association, Women's Alliance for Financial Education, and the Fairfax Bar Association.

John W. Simek

John W. Simek is the vice president of Sensei Enterprises, Inc. He is an EnCase-Certified forensic technologist (EnCE) and a nationally known testifying expert in the area of computer forensics.

Mr. Simek holds a degree in engineering from the United States Merchant Marine Academy and an MBA in finance from Saint Joseph's University. After forming Sensei, he ended his more than 20-year affiliation with Mobil Oil Corporation, where he served as a senior technologist troubleshooting and designing Mobil's networks throughout the western hemisphere.

In addition to his EnCE designation, Mr. Simek is a Certified Handheld Examiner, a Certified Novell Engineer, Microsoft Certified Professional + Internet, Microsoft Certified Systems Engineer, NT Certified Independent Professional, and a Certified Internetwork Professional. He is also a member of the High Tech Crime Network, the Sedona Conference, the Fairfax Bar Association, the International Information Systems Forensics Association, and the ABA. In addition to co-authoring the books cited in Ms. Nelson's biography, he also serves on the Magazine and Education Boards of the ABA's Law Practice Management Section. He currently provides information technology support to more than 250 area law firms, legal entities, and corporations. He lectures on legal technology and electronic evidence subjects throughout the United States and Canada.

Michael C. Maschke

Michael Maschke is the Chief Information Officer and a computer forensics examiner at Sensei Enterprises, Inc. He is a Certified Computer Examiner (CCE), an EnCase Certified forensic technologist (EnCE), and a Certified Information Systems Security Professional (CISSP).

Mr. Maschke holds a degree in telecommunications from James Madison University. He has significant experience with network troubleshooting, design and implementation, systems integration, and computer engineering. Prior to becoming the chief information officer, Mr. Maschke oversaw Sensei's information technology department, which provided support to hundreds of area law firms and corporations.

He has spoken at the American Bar Association's TECHSHOW conference on information security and is a co-author of *Information Security for Lawyers and Law Firms* as well as *The 2011 Solo and Small Firm Legal Technology Guide: Critical Decisions Made Simple*, both published by the American Bar Association.

Acknowledgments

As ALWAYS, WE ARE indebted to our good friend Ross Kodner, one of the nation's finest legal technology consultants, who has again authored the introduction to this book. Ross is the president of MicroLaw, a noted Wisconsin legal technology firm founded in 1985, with clients nationwide.

Ross's contribution to legal technology knowledge can't be overstated—his compendium of writings, his lectures, and his willingness to help one and all through the ABA's Solosez listserve have all contributed to a stellar reputation. His knowledge runs broad and deep, and we are so delighted that Ross has once again contributed an updated chapter on the Paper LESS Office. Ross originated this concept and has been a missionary on its behalf for as many years as we can remember. It was some years back that Ross was kind enough to recommend authors Sharon Nelson and John Simek as potential ABA TECHSHOW speakers. They gratefully acknowledge their debt to Ross; it is fitting that the three of us are still, after all this time, good friends and colleagues, who continue to collaborate in the ever-evolving world of legal tech. Thanks, Ross, for raising your hand once again and being such an invaluable part of this edition.

We thank Sensei's paralegal, Jason Foltin, for helping to research and draft the social media chapter in this book.

Year after year, we must thank Tim Johnson (the executive editor of LPM Publishing) for encouraging our concept of an annual publication devoted to the fast-moving world of legal technology and specifically targeting solos and small firms. For years this concept languished, but thanks to Tim, it was resurrected. We are working hard to keep it current. Tim, your hard work and professionalism have made the entire project a joy from beginning to end; we may not be able to repay our debt to you in full, but we hope there are countless dinners with you (at our expense) in the future.

Acknowledgments

Thanks to our fantastic production manager, Denise Constantine, and our editorial assistant, Kimia Shelby. We are delighted to be working with LPM's gifted new marketing director, Lindsay Dawson. As always, the Pub Board staff is a joy to work with.

We are very grateful to our good friend Dave Ries, an extraordinary litigator in Pittsburgh and a terrific self-taught technologist, who served as project manager for this book. His suggestions and thoughts enriched the final product immeasurably.

Finally, we again thank our colleagues here at Sensei, who carried the load while we were writing and were never too busy to deliberate over recommendations and offer insightful comments. We don't come to work every day; we come to play, and we really like the folks we play with. Thanks one and all!

Mike Maschke
Sharon Nelson
John Simek

Preface to the Fifth Edition

WHAT WE HOPE TO do with this book is simple: We want to help solo and small firm lawyers find the "sweet spot" of legal tech—the best value for the dollars. You don't need a yacht, and you won't be well served by a rowboat. But there is a happy medium—professional-grade hardware and software that doesn't cost an arm and a leg.

This guide is an annual one, so you can't go too far wrong with our advice. Some chapters will remain almost absolutely current. At worst, we'll only be several months behind the curve. Still, if you can't afford your own legal technology consultant and you are concerned about those who are selling snake oil, at least this book should provide you with a kind of "Consumer Reports" view of legal technology products.

As always, the parts of this book that age quickly are the hardware specifications. We are always happy to give you our latest specs—just drop us a quick line at **sensei@senseient.com**.

We do our absolute best to be vendor neutral. Readers of previous editions will be keenly aware that our advice has changed from year to year as some products excel and others, well, decline—sometimes precipitously.

This is the only book we're aware of that deals with legal technology on a collective annual basis. We are now in our fifth edition, so we must be doing something right. We seem to have a growing loyal readership that wants independent advice on legal technology and finds a yearly dose of that advice compelling. In this book we provide you with information and recommendations on computers, servers, networking equipment, legal software, cool gadgets for lawyers, and more. We take an in-depth look at the technologies that will be around in 2012 and provide information on how these technologies will shape the way solo and small firm decision makers think about their technology decisions.

Our recommendations are what we would do in a solo or small practice ourselves: Invest in quality technology that will have a good shelf life and serve you well—that means buying business-grade (not consumer-grade) technology. And don't expect more than the machines can give. A server can be expected to last four to five years and a workstation or laptop three to four. That's it, folks. As the software also evolves, it demands ever more resources, and the hardware ages both physically and in its ability to handle the new software. Remember the "Rule of Three" in upgrading: You should be upgrading one-third of your technology each year. Sometimes you can stretch it to four, but if you try to limp along patching things with spit and promises, you are likely going to be in for a "big bang" upgrade, which is acutely painful to the average solo or small law firm. Leasing may help lessen this financial burden (at least on an annual basis), but you lose the option to change course quickly without paying penalty fees.

Be mindful of the fact that this book is written exclusively for solos and small law firms. There is no attempt to include big-firm products or solutions, though many big-firm lawyers have enjoyed portions of this book. In addition, we want to stress that we have included our recommendations only, not "all available" products. If you don't see a product here, it is because that product is not among our usual recommendations. This is a "best of breed" selection to keep you from being confused by the veritable cornucopia of choices that exist. No one has time to wade through all the choices, so we've tried to give you limited but tested options that work.

We can't generally serve as your legal technology consultant unless you are in the D.C. area, although we are now providing remote backup and disaster recovery service to law firms anywhere in the country. And some firms may want an independent firm to set up new technology, then turn over support to local IT firms. Our Information Security department, which is relatively new, has been kept hopping investigating data breaches and assessing/securing law firm networks. More information about our services may be found on our website: **www.senseient.com**.

We are serious about our commitment to the legal profession and proud of our professional "giveback" through the ABA. If you have a question, we'll do our best to help. Just e-mail us at **sensei@senseient.com**. We have provided hundreds of updated specs to our readers since the first edition of this book came out. We appreciate all your comments and suggestions, as they help each subsequent edition be better than the one before. Thanks, in advance, for your continuing help!

Introduction

by Ross L. Kodner, Esq.

Independent Day(s)

We Americans have been celebrating our nation's Independence Day for 235 years as of this writing. Perhaps though, we have a new day to celebrate, one that I have started to think of as "Independent Day." What does this have to do with the 2012 edition of the *Solo & Small Firm Legal Technology Guide* written by my friends and colleagues, Sharon Nelson, John Simek, and Michael Maschke? Everything.

In the last 12 months, the world of technology has experienced revolutionary change—change that has had a profound impact on daily law practice, on all forms of business, and equally on our personal lives. The 1980s prophesy of John Gage, of the subsumed Sun Computers (now a part of Oracle Corporation), was:

> *"The network IS the computer."*

While Scott McNeely, founder and long-time CEO of Sun Computers, may have inaccurately been credited with the slogan for years, the significance of this deceptively simplistic-seeming pronouncement hit home in 2011. If we look at the technical meaning implicit in this statement, it seems, in the early '80s context in which it was first stated, to be little more than marketing hype. Networking of computing resources in the early '80s was in its infancy, at least in terms of PCs and Macs. There were networks of computers developing at the time, but foreseeing more than that was not even prescient, but rather just nonsensical.

Fast-forward 30 years to 2011 and we're experiencing what could best be termed the "Age of the Cloud." It's impossible to watch television, view websites, spend an evening Facebooking or Tweeting or Linking-In and not end up inundated in "cloud this" and "cloud that." The era of reliance on external, virtual, web-based resources, applications, meeting-places, and data repositories has roared into our business and personal lives with a vengeance, perhaps unlike any technology trend heretofore experienced.

As recently as last year, or, as it may be more appropriate to say, "way back in 2010," the legal technology world was preoccupied with the inroads that Mac systems were making into practices of all sizes. We talked of, and sparred about, operating system differences, expending not insignificant amounts of mental energy debating the relative merits of Windows 7 versus Mac OS X Snow Leopard. We obsessed over the specifications of our laptops, reveling in the horsepower advances brought by the latest Intel i7 processors, and the fact that laptops could be had with 1-terabyte hard drives and 8 GB of RAM. We fought the good fight comparing practice managers like Time Matters versus Tabs PracticeMaster. Some, admittedly on the fringes, still engaged in the perennial, time-honored legal technology fracas—once a battle royale or cause celèbre, now just an amusing side skirmish between the few remaining WordPerfect champions and the Word legion.

We also spent endless hours being tethered to our laptops and desktop computers—whether Mac or Windows—because we needed them in order to do our work, because we were beholden to all the software systems we had loaded on them and on our servers. Invisible bindings lashed us to our computers. They may have been chiseled out of sleek and even sexy blocks of burnished aluminum, but shackled to them we certainly were.

The ability to work, for most, depended on having one's computer to work on/from/with.

The ability to work, for some, depended on the physical presence of one's files.

The ability to work was dependent on one's having more than just a smartphone.

For most of us, our ability to work was dependent on having access to our own office systems, perhaps over the Internet with various remote access approaches, or via dedicated secure VPN tunnels through the otherwise wild, wooly, and insecure Internet.

And now none of it really seems to matter for many of us.

We've become independent.

Independent of what? We've become independent of almost everything that might have been some type of impediment toward getting our work done.

- We've become **location independent.** It no longer matters where we are; we can securely access our personal and business information anytime, from any place. With secure cloud-based remote access via technologies such as Citrix and Windows Remote Desktop Computing/Terminal Services, virtual network computing, and web-based services like LogMeIn.com, GoToMyPC.com, and Join.me, as well as the rapid rise in legal web-based SaaS (Software as a Service) applications, and drawing on my own Paper LESS Office processes that are updated in a subsequent chapter of this book, one can fully serve a legal client from the jungles of Borneo as effectively as in a Main Street law office, given decent Internet access.

- We've become **device independent.** It no longer really matters what kind of hardware you happen to be using. Whether a Windows or Mac desktop or laptop/netbook, the newly emerging Google Chromebooks, iPads, Android tablets, iPhones, Android phones (all work equally well, subject to some realistic efficiency limitations), it is obviously not as easy to proof a document on a 4.3" diagonal smartphone display compared to a 27" iMac's screen or a 15.6" wide-mode Windows laptop. Since our client information can be hosted somewhere and is accessible via the Internet cloud, the operating system wars that were once *de rigeur* conversation starters in comp-sci blogspaces everywhere just don't seem to matter much. Because, as John Gage and Sun Computers so futuristically projected, "The network (i.e., the Internet) *is* the computer." Fans of *Star Trek: The Next Generation* would likely opine that the Borg Collective is now more than just science fiction—it's science reality.

This Changes Everything

What this means for lawyers in all walks of practice today is that the focus of technology efforts should finally be directed to an emphasis on the only things that matter: being more profitable, better serving clients, battling malpractice, following best ethical practices, and having a better quality of life. These are a collection of overarching law practice business goals that can and should be our daily watchwords and motivators. I call them the "Five B's"—our collective *raison d'être* for being in law practice in the first place. Instead of spending valuable time and resources debating about types of computers we buy, whether we should have this Dell server or that one, we can again focus on being lawyers.

The enabling technologies are a broad range of cloud-related services, systems, resources, and concepts. Everyone's path to and through the cloud may be somewhat different. For some practices, especially the smallest ones, it may mean having no software loaded on local computers at all—using Google Chromebooks as go anywhere, access from anyplace terminals for using web-based applications for everything from document generation to legal billing to docketing and more.

For others practices, it may mean leveraging the latest iterations of virtualization to be "insource" and hosting the legal software applications they've always used—the more potent document management, legal financial, and litigation technology systems that are still more feature-rich as "terrestrial" applications that get physically installed versus accessed from web browsers. But now we will host them in an environment using cloud technologies like Citrix XenApps and XenDesktop or Windows RDC (Remote Desktop Computing, f/k/a Windows Terminal Services) to allow access to the firm's functionality and data from anywhere, any time, from virtually any device.

Cloud-based options available for lawyers today continue to multiply at a dizzying rate. Some that have moved into the mainstream are:

- Web-based document storage from services like Dropbox.com, Box.Net, SugarSync, and others.
- Web-based backup systems, while not a substitute for local backup of local systems, continue to grow in usage and capability—such as CoreVault, MozyPro, iBackup, Carbonite, and even DropBox and SugarSync, among others.
- Web-based legal software, which has continued to explode as a market segment, including practice managers such as CLIO, RocketMatter, Advologix, Houdini, Esq., and the entry from large firm player Aderant, as well as online legal billing such as TimeSolv and 59. This is the tip of the iceberg.
- Clouds you build either with your own server(s) or using a hosted server situation with Windows RDC and TS (as previously mentioned), Citrix (including the entry-level Fundamentals for

small practices), Apple's Remote Desktop Connection, and open source VNC options, as well as pure web services that include LogMeIn.com, GoToMyPC.com, and Join.Me for more simple approaches.

- Outsourcing server resources using the same methods, immediately above, using hosts such as GoDaddy.com, Rackspace, and Amazon's ECS, among a legion of smaller hosts.
- Outsourcing e-mail services, especially for Microsoft Exchange/Outlook-using firms, with Rackspace and GoDaddy being two of the largest providers.
- Web-based ancillary services covering an endless spectrum of functionality, from large file sending secure services such as Yousendit.com to a raft of fax service providers like MyFax.com, note-taking/storing such as the addictive Evernote.com, and so many more.

So "the cloud" is actually many things, in many forms, for many applications—not just a single "thing." In fact, it's not a "thing" at all, but rather a method for connecting, accessing, storing, protecting, and working.

But the bottom line is clear: The once-fanciful motto of the former Sun Computers has come to pass, in ways more complete and more all-encompassing than any might have ever imagined: the Internet *is* the computer.

And I believe that is a very good thing.

Sharon, John and Mike are once again your consummate guides to all elements of the use of technology in your law practice. While the book is again aimed at solo and small firms, the question today is, who isn't in solo and small firms? Many large firm lawyers might see themselves as solo practitioners who happen to have 500 partners—and the same guidance is just as compelling for them.

So this book is a valuable read for everyone, from the true solo to the lawyer in a 10-lawyer general practice on Main Street in a midwestern town to the partner in a global megafirm—or even denizens of corporate and government legal departments of all sizes. There's something for everyone here; we all need the same types of tools to get the job done. With cloud-leveraged technology, it may just be a matter of scaling the approach up or down to fit the case, the practice size, or the client circumstance.

There's nothing I can say about the educational abilities of Sharon, John, and Mike that I haven't stated repeatedly in my introductions to this book in three previous editions. They write succinctly, illuminating complex concepts in a way that is accessible to even the most dyed-in-the-wool techno-peasants among us. No one needs to own a pocket protector or ever don a propeller-head hat to understand their explanations of legal software, hardware, and the services needed to make it all hum.

I am privileged once again to not only craft this introduction, but to contribute an updated version of my Paper LESS Office concept—a process that seems more timely and essential than ever. You can't get to the cloud if you can't get all your information in a place where it can be electronically shared and accessed. You can't do any of this if you're still beholden to the physical presence of paper files. It's time to get over that and move on.

Read on as Sharon, John, Mike, and for one chapter yours truly guide you through this brave new world as we all begin to celebrate our first legal technology "Independent Days."

CHAPTER ONE

Computers

Desktop Computers

Personal Computers (PCs)

The Dell OptiPlex line of computers offers the perfect combination of performance and business-grade hardware, at the right price. Dell computers can be purchased with a three, four, or five-year warranty and offer a large selection of available warranty options when it comes to protecting your investment. They offer both hardware and software warranty protection, along with same-day or next-business-day response for the replacement of failed computer hardware or software. We strongly recommend the purchase of the three-year warranties. For the added premium, purchasing software technical support, in our judgment, is generally not worth the additional cost, especially when most firms have an IT provider who is familiar with their software and setup.

Dell also offers accidental damage protection for its computer systems, which covers damage caused by spilled liquids, drops, falls, or electrical surges for a period of three to five years at an additional cost ranging from $109 to $159.

Another option from Dell worth noting is its "Keep Your Hard Drive" program. Typically, if a hard drive crashes while under warranty, Dell will take the failed hard drive and replace it with a new or refurbished one. Sure, you could refuse to return the failed hard drive and be charged an astronomical fee for a new one, or service could even be refused. Citing privacy concerns—with all the recent data breaches in the news—Dell now offers its users the ability to keep their hard drives, even in the event a replacement is needed, but at an additional cost. The cost for this option ranges from $20 to $30, depending on the length of your warranty, and is a small price to pay to maintain total control over and responsibility for your sensitive and confidential data on the hard drive. Below, we provide you with our recommendations for a Dell OptiPlex business-grade system with all of the hardware components included.

Windows-Based Desktop Computer

Hardware Component	Recommendation
Computer Model:	Dell OptiPlex 990 Mini Tower
Operating System:	Microsoft Windows 7 Professional 64-Bit
Processor:	Intel Core i5 Dual Core 3.3 GHz
Memory:	4GB DDR3 Non-ECC SDRAM 1333 MHz
Video Card:	512MB AMD RADEON HD 6350 (2 DVI)
Hard Drive:	320GB SATA 6GB/s with 16MB Databurst Cache
Optical Drive:	16X DVD+/−RW
Network:	Broadcom NetXtreme 10/100/1000 PCIe Gigabit Networking Card
Warranty:	3-Year Basic Hardware Service with 3-Year Next Business Day Onsite Service After Remote Diagnosis
Other:	1394 FW Controller Card, 10 USB ports, 305-Watt Power Supply

Dell OptiPlex 990 Model Line

The Intel Core i5 Dual Core 3.3-GHz processor will provide enough power to support both current and future versions of business-grade software throughout the life of the machine. The Intel Core i5 has replaced the Intel Core 2 Duo processor and is quickly becoming the standard for business-grade systems. Dell now includes the Intel Core i7 Quad processor as an available upgrade when configuring your OptiPlex computer, but currently this upgrade isn't worth the added cost (~$100). The Intel Core i5 Dual Core processor is offered with varying levels of clock speeds, with the 3.3-GHz version currently in the upper range of processer clock speeds offered by Dell for this computer system. The faster the processor, the higher the premium you will pay for having cutting-edge technology. The amount of memory included in this system will be enough to support your business applications, handling even "memory hungry" applications with ease. Four gigabytes (GB) of memory has now become the de facto recommended standard for the minimum amount of memory in business-grade computers, given the low cost and high gain in performance for the upgrade, and is a must-have option when purchasing a 64-bit system.

The video card included in this system provides dual digital visual interface (DVI) outputs. By providing dual interfaces, this graphics adapter allows you to have dual monitors, an option we will never go without when purchasing a new computer system. (Monitors, keyboards, and other peripherals are discussed in subsequent chapters.) A hard drive plays an important role in the configuration of your computer system, because it is the hardware component that stores your data. In short, the better the hard drive, the faster your computer can read and write your data. This system comes with a 320GB Serial ATA (SATA) hard drive, which will provide enough storage space for the average lawyer user. The SATA (6GB/s) interface is the latest generation of the SATA specification (revision 3.0), allowing for more throughput and higher cache than the previous revisions of the SATA specification. In fact, Dell no longer offers earlier versions of SATA hard drives as an option when configuring an OptiPlex desktop. We wouldn't be surprised if in the near future the usage of 3.5-inch hard drives is discontinued due to the large power requirements to operate them and their propensity to fail.

When configuring an optical drive for the system, choosing the 16X DVD+/-RW drive will allow you to burn and read from both CDs and DVDs. For an additional external connection, the FireWire card adapter allows external FireWire devices to be connected to and used on the system. Although the USB 2.0 standard boasts greater data transfer rates than FireWire 400 (480 Mbps vs. 393 Mbps), it has always been our experience that FireWire devices perform faster given how the FireWire architecture works. Newer interfaces have come out on the market within the past year, such as USB 3.0 and Thunderbolt, a serial data interface currently only found on the Apple MacBook Pro, but until these technologies become standard with all new hardware purchases, use them with caution.

The Microsoft Windows Vista operating system, which all experts loathed, is now history. Now that Windows 7 is here, that's the operating system of choice. We've beaten on the operating system thoroughly, as have other experts, and Microsoft has finally gotten it right. There may be problems—there always are—but they are minimal in comparison to the disaster that was Vista, and over the past two years, most of them have been addressed. The three-year, next-business-day, onsite parts and labor warranty will cover hardware defects and failures of the computer system for three years at a relatively small cost. The cost of this warranty is built into the cost of the recommended system and should be a requirement when purchasing a new computer for your firm. To contact technical support, Dell provides the consumer with a toll-free phone number to call, and if the hardware needs to be replaced, Dell will send a support technician out to your location to replace the defective part by the next business day. The hardware replacement and labor cost is covered by the warranty, so there should be no additional out-of-pocket costs. On average, the expected life cycle of a new computer system is three years, which is covered by the three-year warranty. The recommended Dell OptiPlex 990 Mini Tower desktop computer can be configured and purchased from Dell's website starting at around $1,000.

Remember that the "sweet spot" in buying computers changes regularly. Our specs will get you close, but they will shift slightly during the lifespan of this publication. You can receive a courtesy copy of our current specs (for workstations, laptop, and servers—PC or Mac) by e-mailing **sensei@senseient.com** and simply making a request. We are generally able to get our current specs to you within 24 hours during the workweek. We are happy to report that many, many readers are taking advantage of this offer, so don't be shy. We are happy to help.

Apple Computers (Macs)

Apple Macintosh (or Mac) computers are still not as widely used in law offices as Windows-based computers, but they are starting to be chosen more frequently by solo and small firm lawyers since Apple's shift to using Intel-based processors in all of their systems. As a result of this change, Macs can now run both the Mac OS X and Windows operating systems on the same computer. In a way, it's like having two systems in one.

A Mac computer can be easily configured to connect to and function on a Windows-based network, including the ability to communicate and authenticate with a Windows Domain controller. In the past, however, Macs were used primarily by businesses with a need for multimedia functions, such as video editing and graphic design, both areas in which Apple systems have always excelled. Usually, Apple's appearance in an office environment was the result of someone having a personal preference for the Macintosh operating system over the Windows-based system.

For those concerned with computer security, Mac systems are perceived to be more secure than their Windows-based counterparts, since they are not targeted as often by malware due to the overall smaller number of Mac users. However, this isn't true. As Macs become more popular, we have seen an unwelcome attention from those who write malware. Remember, those "bad guys" who write browser exploits—pieces of malware that take advantage of vulnerabilities in Internet browsers such as Firefox—don't care what operating system the computer is running. In fact, security companies consistently warn that malware writers who attack browsers are increasingly becoming the real threat, as operating systems are less frequently targeted.

Following a busy 2010 in which Apple released a large number of security patches for its Mac OS X operating system, 2011 hasn't been any different. The continuing release of security patches, even for the latest version of its operating system, is a clear sign of just how targeted this software and its applications are by the developers of malware. For years, we have recommended that antivirus and antispyware software be installed on all computers, regardless of the operating system. Our case in point for Macs is the MAC Defender virus that targeted Mac users in 2011, described as the first major malware threat to the Mac platform. The prevalence of this malware was so great that Apple released a security update to address and remove the threat from infected computers.

While it is still not very common, we are beginning to see Apple computers make their way into smaller law offices, especially in the solo stand-alone environment. Now that Apple computers use Intel chipsets, users are taking advantage of the opportunity to better integrate with the Windows world. Some users run Windows on their Mac computers as the primary operating system. Others use Boot Camp, a free utility provided by Apple at no charge with each system, to dual-boot between Windows and the Mac OS. With Boot Camp, you can install a Microsoft Windows XP, Windows Vista, or Windows 7 operating system alongside Apple's OS X on any Intel-based Macintosh computer. To run Windows 7, you must upgrade your version of Boot Camp to version 4.0. For those users who purchased Mac OS X Lion, this updated version of Boot Camp was included. Boot Camp guides users through the processes of creating a new partition to install the Windows operating system on and using the Mac OS X Snow Leopard disc to install Windows drivers for all of the hardware.

Some users have even purchased products like Parallels Workstation or downloaded Oracle's VM VirtualBox, which allows you to run Windows, Linux, and other operating systems within the Mac OS itself. Virtual machine (VM) software is described in more detail in a later section.

The iMac desktop systems combine performance and ergonomics by putting the hardware components that make up the system in the same case as the monitor, eliminating the need for separate components. As a result, the space-saving design allows you to free up both desk and floor space without giving up performance. Below, we provide you with our recommendation for an iMac business-grade desktop system with all of the hardware components included.

Macintosh-Based Desktop Computer

Hardware Component	Recommendation
Computer Model:	21.5-inch iMac
Operating System:	Mac OS v10.7 Lion
Processor:	Intel Core i5 Quad Core 2.5 GHz
Memory:	4GB 1333MHz DDR3 SDRAM
Video Card:	AMD Radeon HD 6750 Graphics Processor
Hard Drive:	500GB SATA 7200 RPM hard drive
CD/DVD-ROM:	8X SuperDrive (DVD+R DL/DVD±RW/CD-RW)
Network:	10/100/1000 Base-T Gigabit Ethernet Port, AirPort Extreme Wi-Fi (802.11a/b/g/n), Bluetooth 2.1 + EDR
Warranty:	3-year AppleCare Protection Plan for iMacs
Other:	FaceTime HD Camera, Built-in 21.5-inch Monitor and Stereo Speakers, One FireWire 800 Port, Four USB 2.0 Ports, One Thunderbolt Port, Apple Wireless Keyboard and Magic Mouse, SDXC Card Slot

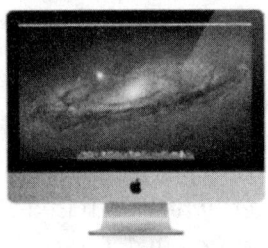

Apple 21.5-Inch iMac Computer

The 21.5-inch iMac comes with an Intel Core i5 Quad Core 2.5 GHz processor, 4GB of memory, and the Mac OS v10.7 Lion operating system. The 4GB of memory included in this system will be enough to support your legal applications, but if you are considering using an iMac strictly for multimedia purposes, you may want to consider adding more memory. Currently, you can upgrade the amount of memory when building this system online to either 8 or 16GB. The 500GB 7200 RPM SATA hard drive comes standard and will provide more than enough storage space and hard drive performance for the average lawyer. However, if you feel that you need additional storage space, the hard drive can be upgraded to 1TB or 2TB in size, or you can elect to add an additional 256GB solid-state second hard drive to the system.

The standard Ethernet adapter and AirPort wireless adapter will allow your computer to connect to the business network, whether over a wired network or wireless, even if it's Windows-based. The AirPort wireless adapter is compatible with 802.11a/b/g/n wireless networks.

The other standard hardware included with the iMac is the built-in FaceTime HD Camera, stereo speakers, 21.5-inch monitor, one FireWire 800 port, four USB 2.0 ports, one Thunderbolt port, and one SDXC memory card slot. The system also includes the standard Apple wireless keyboard and Magic Mouse. The 21.5-inch iMac computer weighs 20.5 pounds and has a depth of about 7.4 inches, making it very easy to find room on your desk for one of these systems.

Apple's standard warranty with a new iMac provides you with 90 days of telephone support and one year of service coverage. We recommend that you upgrade the warranty to the extended AppleCare Protection Plan for iMac, which provides you with telephone and service support for three years. The cost to extend the warranty plan is $169 and is well worth it. The 21.5-inch iMac computer can be purchased from Apple's online store for $1,199.

Laptops

Personal Computers (PCs)

The Dell Latitude line of laptop computers continues to combine performance and mobility in a laptop system that cannot be beat. These laptops are thin and very light, weighing less than five pounds. They are a perfect fit for the mobile lawyer and provide an ideal computing solution when on the go. Below, we provide you with our recommendations for a Dell Latitude business-grade laptop with all of the hardware components included.

Windows-Based Laptop Computer

Hardware Component	Recommendation
Computer Model:	Dell Latitude E6420
Processor:	Intel Core i5 Dual Core 2.6 GHz
Operating System:	Microsoft Windows 7 Professional 64-Bit
Memory:	4GB DDR3 1333 MHz SDRAM
Video Card:	Intel HD Graphics 3000
Hard Drive:	320GB 7200 RPM hard drive
CD/DVD-ROM:	8X DVD+/−RW drive
Network:	10/100/1000 Mbps Ethernet adapter, Intel Centrino Advanced-N 6205 802.11a/b/g/n Half-Mini Card
Warranty:	3-Year Basic Hardware Service with 3-Year Next-Business-Day Onsite Service After Remote Diagnosis
Other:	14-Inch Wide HD LED screen, 90W AC power adapter, 9-cell/90 WHr primary battery, weighs 4.56 lbs., four USB 2.0 Ports, one USB/eSATA Combo, Memory Card Reader, Digital Array Microphone and HD Video Webcam, Internal Fingerprint Reader

The Dell Latitude E6420 comes with an Intel Core i5 Dual Core 2.6 GHz processor and 4GB of memory, which should be sufficient to run all of the business applications of a mobile lawyer. The system comes preinstalled with Microsoft Windows 7 Professional.

Dell Latitude E6420 Laptop

The system's internal fingerprint reader provides the level of security needed to protect your personal files and confidential data. When enabled, you can restrict user logon access to either the biometric access or to a user name and password. A fingerprint reader keeps data on the hard drive secure through encryption, with the hardware requiring successful authentication before the data contents can be decrypted. Enabling a start-up or hard drive password in the system's BIOS is a great way to add an extra layer of protection to your system.

The Intel HD graphics card supplies crisp, clear graphics to the 14-inch-wide LED display. The 320GB hard drive will provide more than enough storage space for the mobile user, with a hard drive speed that will supply faster disc performance. The DVD+/–RW drive will allow you to burn and read both CDs and DVDs. The Ethernet adapter will allow you to connect your laptop to your network when you're in the office, and the wireless network adapter will allow you to stay connected when on the move. The Intel wireless adapter provides connectivity to 802.11a/b/g/n wireless networks, supporting dual-band operation (2.4 and 5GHz) with data rates up to 300 Mbps. The 9-cell battery is an upgrade that will supply the laptop with power longer than the standard 6-cell battery. This battery is a must-have if you plan to use the wireless network adapter when running the laptop off the battery, although this will add some slight weight to the unit. The 9-cell battery will provide you with approximately three hours' more battery life than the standard 6-cell battery, which will save you from searching for electrical outlets wherever you go. Finally, the integrated HD video webcam and digital microphone is great for videoconferences or recording audio, such as podcasts.

For frequent travelers and those who truly want to always stay connected, the Dell Latitude E6420 has a configuration option to add an internal mobile broadband card for the Verizon, Sprint, or AT&T networks for an extra $125.

The three-year, next-business-day onsite parts and labor warranty is the same warranty offered by Dell and described above in the Desktop Computers section. The Dell Latitude E6420 can be purchased from Dell's website starting at around $1,300.

If you are particularly clumsy or accident-prone, you may want to consider adding the CompleteCare Accidental Damage Protection Plan to your purchase. This plan covers any damage to the laptop, including such things as liquid spills (one client has used this plan multiple times to cover the unwelcome effects of spilling red wine) and dropping the device. Obviously, it does not cover intentional damage, theft, and normal wear and tear. For the additional $109.99 to $159, depending on the length of the warranty, you will have peace of mind when you set your coffee cup (or wine glass) on the keyboard.

Apple Computers (Macs)

The Apple MacBook Pro is perfect for the mobile lawyer who requires a powerful notebook in a compact and lightweight design. The MacBook Pro laptop comes standard with the Intel Core i5 Dual Core 2.40 GHz processor, widescreen display, built-in FaceTime HD camera, wireless network adapter, and much more. The MacBook Pro laptop is available with 13-inch, 15-inch, and 17-inch screens. The MacBook Pro is available only in the aluminum case with glass LED display. The MacBook Pro can be fully integrated into any Windows-based network without too much overhead and configuration. Below, we provide you with our recommendations for an Apple MacBook Pro business-grade laptop with all of the hardware components included.

Macintosh-Based Laptop Computer

Hardware Component	Recommendation
Computer Model:	15-Inch MacBook Pro
Operating System:	Mac OS v10.7 Lion
Processor:	Quad Core Intel Core i7 2.0 GHz
Memory:	4GB 1333MHz DDR3 SDRAM
Video Card:	AMD Radeon HD 6490M
Hard Drive:	500GB SATA 7200 RPM hard drive
CD/DVD-ROM:	8X SuperDrive (DVD+R DL/DVD±RW/CD-RW)
Network:	10/100/1000 Base-T Gigabit Ethernet Port, AirPort Extreme Wi-Fi (802.11a/b/g/n), Bluetooth 2.1 + EDR
Warranty:	3-year AppleCare Protection Plan
Other:	FaceTime HD Camera, Built-in 15-Inch LED Monitor and Stereo Speakers, one FireWire 800 Port, two USB 2.0 Ports, one Thunderbolt Port, SDXC Card Slot

Apple 15-Inch MacBook Pro Laptop

The 15-Inch MacBook Pro laptop comes with 4GB of memory and the Mac OS v10.7 Lion operating system. The AMD Radeon HD 6490M video card provides perfect high resolution to the 15.4-inch-wide LED display, with a native resolution of 1440 x 900 pixels. The 500GB SATA hard drive provides enough space to store all of your documents, pictures, and music. The 8X SuperDrive will allow you to burn and play both CDs and DVDs. The built-in AirPort Extreme Wi-Fi adapter will keep you connected on the road and supports the 802.11n standard. The AirPort Extreme Wi-Fi adapter is also backward compatible with 802.11a/b/g wireless networks. The aluminum body MacBook is also very light, weighing just 5.6 pounds.

The multi-touch scrolling trackpad gives you precise cursor control, supports two-finger scrolling, tap, double-tap, and drag capabilities. If you have been a lifelong Windows user, be forewarned: There is no right-click button on the trackpad. To right-click on a Mac, you must hold down the Control key while clicking. A tip for former Windows users: Don't want to hold down the Control key to initiate a right-click with the mouse? You can tap the trackpad with two fingers rather than holding down the Control key—you just have to enable the option within the Keyboard & Mouse settings.

Have you ever tripped over a power cord and have your laptop come flying off the desk? With the 85W MagSafe Power Adapter, you no longer have to worry. The magnetic power connector will cleanly disengage from the side of the laptop and cause no damage to the computer or the power cord. This a great gift to those of us who are occasionally less than graceful.

The sleek and elegant design of the MacBook Pro is what sets it apart from the competition. The design and celebrated ease of use makes the MacBook Pro a smart choice when purchasing a laptop for yourself or your firm. The MacBook Pro can be purchased from Apple's online store for $1,799.

Netbooks

Over the past few years, netbooks have grabbed the eye of the business consumer and have become very popular among users, including lawyers. Essentially, netbooks are highly portable mini-laptops. They are much smaller, cheaper, and lighter than a traditional laptop. As with the other computer recommendations, it is impossible to mention all of the available manufacturers and models of netbooks.

As the popularity of netbooks has increased, the number of configuration options and vendors has increased as well. Luckily, the price has decreased, and you can now purchase a well-equipped netbook for under $350.

The netbook that we recommend and frequently use is the Dell Inspiron Mini 10. For around $315, a user can get a netbook with a 10.1-inch screen, 2GB of memory, and Microsoft Windows 7 Starter Edition preinstalled.

The Dell Mini 10 is offered in six different colors and comes with a standard one-year warranty. The warranty can be extended to three years for an additional $60. We're not sure that the additional warranty is worth it, especially considering the low cost of the device. At around $300, netbooks are approaching "disposable" status. The device comes with the Intel Atom N455 1.66 GHz processor and the Intel NM10 Express graphics card, providing a 1024 x 600 resolution to the unit's 10.1-Inch TrueLife^{TM} widescreen display. The netbook can be configured with either a 160GB or 250GB SATA hard drive, both large enough for the mobile lawyer, and a 3-in-1 flash memory card reader for easy transfer of your digital pictures from your camera to your netbook. The memory included with this netbook is also configurable with a selection of either 1 or 2GBs, enough for this portable device.

The built-in Dell wireless 1397 802.11n card provides you with seamless wireless access, and the optional Bluetooth module is great for using a portable mouse. As with regular laptops, we recommend that you purchase the device with the largest battery available—in this case, the 6-cell 56WHr Li-Ion battery. The larger battery will add some extra weight to the device, but the added power will be worth it.

Dell Inspiron Mini 10 Netbook

CHAPTER TWO

Computer Operating Systems

Microsoft Windows XP Operating System

The Microsoft Windows XP operating system was released in October 2001 and was made available in three editions: Professional, Home, and the less common Media Center. Microsoft Windows XP Home was the first consumer-oriented operating system labeled as more "user friendly" than previous versions of Microsoft's operating systems. Windows XP Professional Edition was specifically designed for businesses and power users with added functionality and security. As recently as 2010, the majority of all business computers were running Windows XP Professional Edition. In the latest statistics, this has rapidly changed with the release of Windows 7—the vast majority of the business world elected to skip Vista and went straight to Windows 7. In July 2011, roughly 31 percent of all computers accessing the Internet were running the Microsoft Windows 7 operating system, according to W3Counter.

Microsoft released Service Pack 3 for Windows XP in May of 2008, which was the last service pack developed for the operating system. In April 2009, Microsoft Windows XP entered the extended support period, which will be phased out by 2014.

Microsoft Windows XP should no longer be the operating system of choice when selecting an operating system to install on your computer system. In fact, you probably won't be able to even find a valid license for this version of the operating system any more.

Microsoft Windows Vista Operating System

Microsoft Windows Vista operating system was released in January 2007 and was made available in six editions, with two editions designed for the business community. The two editions released for the business community are Windows Vista Business Edition and Windows Vista Enterprise Edition. Windows Vista Business Edition includes several new business features, such as file system encryption, a full version of Remote Desktop, system image backup and recovery, Windows ShadowCopy, and the IIS web server.

When first released, it was believed that eventually Windows Vista Business Edition would replace Microsoft XP Professional Edition as the dominant player in the business desktop operating system market, but this certainly was not the case. Many companies were hesitant to upgrade their business systems because of Vista's continuing incompatibility problems with some third-party software, licensing restrictions and costs, digital rights managements, driver issues for some peripherals, and the hardware requirements necessary to run the operating system.

Microsoft Vista turned out to be a complete failure for Microsoft. The operating system was rejected almost immediately by both consumers and businesses and ultimately was rated as the number two all-time technology flop by InfoWorld. Wow. (Trivia question: What was number 1?)

Microsoft Windows 7

Windows 7 is the latest version of Microsoft Windows, and it is the successor to Windows Vista. Microsoft fast-tracked the development of this operating system and released it on October 22, 2009. It was ready to move on from the epic failure that was Vista, and it looks like Microsoft may have finally gotten it right for the first time since releasing XP.

Windows 7 is more "XP-like," focusing on performance improvements and eliminating the compatibility issues that plagued Microsoft Vista. We have been running the various versions of Windows 7 since it was first released as a beta and absolutely love it.

Windows 7 is available in six editions, but only a few of those are worth mentioning to the solo and small firm market:

> Starter Edition—primarily for small notebooks, such as your netbook. The Starter Edition is 32-bit only, supports only a single processor, and does not support multiple monitors, such as dual displays.
>
> Home Premium Edition—comes bundled with Internet Explorer 9, allows for a connection to a home network, and is for home use only. The upgrade (from a previous operating system) retail cost for this

edition is $149.99 per license, and the full retail cost for this edition is $199.99 per license.

Professional Edition—includes all of the features located in the Home Premium Edition, plus allows connection to a company network such as a domain and includes a backup and restore utility to protect your system. The upgrade retail cost for this edition is $199.99 per license, and the full retail cost for this edition is $299.99 per license.

Ultimate Edition—includes all of the features located in the Professional Edition, plus BitLocker encryption to help secure your data. The upgrade retail cost for this edition is $219.99 per license, and the full retail cost for this edition is $319.99 per license.

All of these editions are available for purchase and download from Microsoft's website, and for an additional $14.95, you can elect to have a physical disk shipped to you as a backup.

For your business, you will need to purchase either the Professional or Ultimate Edition to install on your computer systems. Obviously, upgrading is less expensive than purchasing a full license. If you have computer systems running Windows 2000 or even Windows XP, now is the time to upgrade.

Users may also upgrade their computer systems to Windows 7 from both Windows XP and Windows Vista. However, for users upgrading from Windows XP, you must be careful when performing an upgrade. This upgrade path actually performs a "clean" installation, and the user must back up all programs and data because the upgrade will not retain any of the information. There isn't a prompt during the upgrade process to notify users to back up their data, so this step must be performed prior to beginning the upgrade process. In other words, *there is no direct upgrade path from XP to Windows 7*. You can get some advice about your hardware and software compatibility by running the free Windows Upgrade Advisor (**www.microsoft.com/downloads/details.aspx?FamilyID=1B544E90-7659-4BD9-9E51-2497C146AF15&displaylang=en**). This utility will tell you if your hardware is compatible and what software may need to be upgraded.

For users upgrading from Windows Vista, most of you will not have to worry about the process deleting all of your information. As was the case when upgrading from Windows XP to Windows Vista, you need only perform a clean install if you are going to a version that is lower on the food chain (e.g., Windows Vista Ultimate to Windows 7 Home Edition). Regardless of the upgrade path you take, we always strongly recommend that you back up your system and data prior to upgrading.

The only other installation scenario where a clean installation would be performed is upgrading from a 32-bit version to a 64-bit version operating system, regardless of the edition.

Microsoft released the first Service Pack for this operating system (SP1) to the public in February, and at the time of its release it was not a mandatory update. This Service Pack addressed a number of security issues as well as fixed a few bugs related to HDMI audio and the printing of XPS documents.

Mac OS X Version 10.5 (Leopard) Operating System

Mac OS X version 10.5 was released on October 26, 2007, and has since become a staple of the Apple movement to gain a greater market share of personal and business computers. The Mac OS X version 10.5 OS, commonly referred to as "Leopard," included a number of new features intended to make the operating system more stable and reliable than Apple's previous operating systems. Leopard supports both PowerPC and Intel x86-based Macintosh computers and in fact is the last Mac OS to support the PowerPC. The Leopard operating system includes more than three hundred changes and enhancements, including a revised desktop, an updated Finder, Time Machine, Spaces, Boot Camp preinstalled, and full support for 64-bit applications.

Mac OS X Version 10.6 (Snow Leopard) Operating System

Mac OS X version 10.6 was the successor to Leopard and was released to the public on August 28, 2009. This version, nicknamed "Snow Leopard," contained many new features and performance improvements that have allowed this operating system to be a major player in the business market.

Until now, if you wanted to integrate your Mac computer with your company's Microsoft Exchange e-mail environment, you had to purchase Microsoft Office for Macs or configure your mailbox to use the POP3 or IMAP protocols. Now, Mac users no longer have to do this. Snow Leopard included out-of-the-box support for connecting to Microsoft Exchange Server 2010 through the Mail, iCal, and address book programs. This allowed users to access their mailbox, shared calendar, public folders, and contacts just as they would if they were using Microsoft Outlook. Some of the other features and enhancements included support for more 64-bit applications, a refined user interface, more efficient performance through better utilization of multiple processor cores, QuickTime X, and an installation footprint about 7GB smaller than Leopard's. This operating system also dropped support for the AppleTalk protocol, which most IT administrators believed should have occurred much sooner.

Current Mac users of the Leopard operating system can upgrade to Snow Leopard for $29 per license. For everyone else looking to upgrade to the latest version of Mac OS X, a Mac Box Set license costs $169 and also includes licenses for iLife '09 and iWork '09. Both the upgrade and full licenses for the Mac OS X version 10.6 operating system can be purchased online from the Apple Store.

Mac OS X Version 10.7 (Lion) Operating System

Mac OS X version 10.7 is the latest operating system from Apple and was released to the public on July 20, 2011. This release was Apple's eighth major release of Mac OS X. This version, nicknamed "Lion," contains many new and changed features, such as FaceTime, AirDrop, Mac App Store, Auto Save, and Versions. As we believed, iCloud support for Mac OS X Lion is here and is included in a recent software update, v. 10.7.2.

From a security standpoint, Mac users should upgrade to Lion as soon as possible. Some of the enhanced security features include application sandboxing that restricts the way applications can interact with other parts of the operating system and full disk encryption. They also increased the security of the operating system through "addition by subtraction." Apple no longer preinstalls Adobe Flash Player and the Java Runtime Environment on newly purchased systems.

Mac users looking to upgrade can purchase the Lion operating system from the Mac App Store for $29.99. Apple originally didn't plan to distribute physical media for this operating system, offering the product as an exclusive download from the Mac App Store, but its stance has since softened. Since August 2011, Apple has provided in-store downloads to consumers who don't have broadband Internet access and now sells OS X Lion USB Thumb Drives online from the Apple Store for $69.

Unfortunately, when OS X Lion was first released, a significant security flaw was discovered relating to passwords. Apple has changed the way it stores password hashes. This change has allowed unauthorized users access to view the password hashes and crack them with ease. This huge security issue has been addressed by Apple in a recent software update, v. 10.7.2.

CHAPTER THREE

Monitors

NOW THAT YOU HAVE your brand new desktop or laptop system with a docking station, you are ready for the task of picking out that brand new monitor—and you can have all the real estate your heart desires these days. The era of 14-inch monitors is long gone. You might even be able to reclaim some territory on your desk—and actually see some wood for a change—even if you choose to have two or three monitors. We have standardized on two monitors for ourselves and our clients. Just like computers, monitors come in all varieties, shapes, and sizes, and if you don't know what you're looking for, you can be inundated with all of the technical jargon that advertisers use to get you to purchase their monitors.

Ever wondered what an HD LCD widescreen monitor with DVI, VGA, and HDMI inputs is? Purchasing a monitor can be confusing, especially if you're not familiar with all of the available options—like purchasing a computer. We will walk you through the process and explain how to weed through all of the technical jargon, providing you with solid recommendations for purchasing flat-panel LCD, widescreen, and HD monitors.

CRT Monitors

One word: No. It's time to move on.

Flat-Panel LCD Monitors

Flat-panel monitors have taken over the computer monitor marketplace, putting an end to the market for CRT monitors. The flat-panel liquid crystal display (LCD) monitors have a flat viewing screen that provides a better viewing angle than CRT monitors used to. They are also less bulky, taking up only a fraction of the desktop space and weighing next to nothing when compared to the weight of the ancient CRT dinosaurs. Flat-panel monitors have come down significantly in price over the past few years and should be seriously considered as your first choice when purchasing a monitor for your computer system.

Flat-panel monitors, like computers, come in all different sizes, resolutions, and performance. The flat-panel monitor that we recommend is the Dell Professional P1911 19-inch monitor with height-adjustable stand. This black monitor offers a maximum resolution of 1440 x 900 at 60 Hz for sharp and brilliant images, a 1000:1 contrast ratio for high color accuracy, and a 160-degree viewing angle. This monitor comes bundled with a height-adjustable stand, VGA/DVI and USB cables, weighing only 13.6 pounds.

The Dell Professional P1911 includes four built-in USB 2.0 ports, making it easier to connect your peripheral devices. The monitor also comes standard with a three-year hardware warranty, but can be upgraded to four or five years for an additional cost of $39 and $59, respectively. This monitor can be purchased online from Dell's website for $189.

Dell Professional P1911 LCD Monitor

Widescreen Monitors

A step above LCD flat-panel monitors, widescreen monitors offer higher resolutions and a better viewing platform than regular flat-panels do, for about the same price.

Widescreen monitors start at 19 inches and go upwards of 30 inches in width. Of course, the bigger the screen, the more you must be willing to pay.

The widescreen monitor that we recommend is a great compromise of both size and value—the Dell P2211H 21.5-inch widescreen LED monitor. This monitor offers an optimal resolution of 1920 x 1080 at 60 Hz, which will provide you so much desktop real estate that you won't know what to do with it all. The higher resolution will enable you to view documents, images, and videos with stunning detail, vivid colors, and seamless motion. The display can be rotated to be viewed in a horizontal or vertical orientation, depending on your preference. This monitor accepts video graphics array (VGA), digital visual interface (DVI-D), and display port (DP) inputs. This monitor also includes two built-in USB 2.0 ports to connect your peripheral devices to and weighs only 13.6 pounds. The Dell P2210 22-inch widescreen monitor can be purchased online from Dell's website for $219 and comes with a standard three-year hardware warranty.

Dell P2211H 21.5-Inch LED Monitor

High-Definition Monitors

Just like high-definition (HD) televisions, HD monitors have come down in price as the competition has increased. Currently, there are a few vendors who make HD monitors that are reasonable in price. You can find HD monitors in all shapes, sizes, and price ranges, with some designed for the avid gamer and others for the multimedia guru. All HD monitors are going to require special graphics cards to utilize the brilliant HD display.

The HD monitor that we recommend is the Dell UltraSharp U3011. This Dell 30-inch widescreen HD monitor is considered a visual wonder, sporting an optimal resolution of 2560 x 1600 at 60 Hz that offers a brilliant, clear, and bright HD display. To fully utilize the ultra-high-resolution settings, your computer must have a dual-link DVI-D graphics card that supports the 2560 x 1600 resolution.

The monitor supports EDTV (enhanced-definition TV) and HDTV resolutions of 720p, 1080i, and 1080p, which are defined standards, and has two DVI-D, two HDMI, one DisplayPort (DP) and one VGA input. The monitor has a contrast ratio of 1,000:1, a 178-degree viewing angle, four built-in USB 2.0 ports, and a 7-in-1 media card reader. This monitor is perfect for multimedia design, viewing HD movies or pictures, and for the individual who wants the best resolution for his or her business computer. This monitor weighs 33.7 pounds and can be mounted on the provided stand or on the wall.

The Dell UltraSharp U3011 can be purchased online from Dell's website for $1,499, but it is frequently discounted up to $350. At this price, not only does it cost hundreds of dollars less than its competition, but its technical specifications are as good as, if not better than, comparable models from other vendors.

Even though the cost is reasonable for a large widescreen monitor, you may want to consider using dual 19-inch or bigger monitors to get the equivalent surface area. Of course, your computer must have dual-monitor support, which most of the newer computers have by default. You will find that purchasing dual monitors will be cheaper than purchasing one large one. And anecdotally, we have found that folks who move to dual monitors never want to go back. Certainly, none of the authors would accept anything less than dual monitors—and we are all beginning to covet a third, although we would really need bigger desks, if not a special built-in shelf.

Dell UltraSharp U3011

CHAPTER FOUR

Computer Peripherals

IF YOU THOUGHT PURCHASING the right computer and monitor was tough, wait until you realize how many options there are when it comes to selecting computer peripherals. Having the right computer peripherals can make your computing experience faster, more comfortable, and a better overall experience. Wireless devices have brought peripherals into a new dimension, getting rid of that Gordian knot wire mess that we all used to struggle to untangle. Below we provide recommendations for mice, keyboards, wireless desktops, external storage devices, and speakers. As always, bear in mind that there is a universe of choices. These are our top picks.

Mouse

The optical mouse has brought the classic "rollerball" mouse to extinction. Many users can remember the days when if your mouse acted up, you would simply need to clean the dirt off the wheels. Optical technology allows you to navigate with better speed, precision, and reliability. An optical mouse uses light-emitting diode (LED) technology that bounces light off of a surface onto a sensor. It is important to note that the surface needs some texture to work properly. It won't work on glass, for instance. The sensor analyzes the patterns in the images and compares them with previous captured images to determine how far the mouse has moved and relays the coordinates to the computer. It is really quite a scientific marvel. An optical mouse contains no moving parts and therefore does not require the maintenance and cleaning that a legacy rollerball mouse does. It even works without having to use the dreaded mouse pad.

Microsoft Comfort Mouse 3000

Our recommendation for an optical mouse is the Microsoft Comfort Mouse 3000. This optical mouse provides advanced performance, ergonomic design, and three customizable buttons. As an example, one button can be programmed for "delete" and one can be defined as the "back" button for your browser. This mouse takes performance seriously, delivering extreme movement accuracy by taking measurements up to 8,000 times per second, supporting a maximum speed of 72 inches per second and a maximum acceleration of up to 28Gs. The mouse connects using USB and is compatible with both Windows and Mac computers. The Microsoft Comfort Mouse 3000 sells for $19.95 and can be purchased directly from Microsoft's website.

For portability, those users who travel with laptops and want a nifty little Bluetooth travel mouse may also want to consider the excellent Microsoft Bluetooth Notebook Mouse 5000.

Keyboards

Finding the right keyboard for your computer can be a tedious task, as you sift through all of the different keyboards and features to find one that truly suits you—and there are a world of choices and personal preferences. When selecting a keyboard, you want to choose one that is ergonomically designed so that stress placed on your wrists is minimized. Second, you shouldn't have to give up comfort to gain enhanced features, such as the My Favorites buttons or buttons that will adjust the volume level of your speakers, including the Mute button.

The keyboard we recommend for users is the Natural Ergonomic Keyboard 4000 from Microsoft. This keyboard provides a great blend of ergonomic design with functionality. The reverse slope keyboard has a cushioned palm rest that allows you to rest your wrists and hands when typing and provides greater comfort. The My Favorites keys are customizable to allow you to open your most frequently used software, pictures, videos, and music. You can even browse the Internet with the push of a button. The MultiMedia keys allow you to control your media player from your keyboard, along with the volume level of your speakers. Two of the buttons that we use most on our keyboards

Natural Ergonomic Keyboard 4000 from Microsoft

are the Mute and Calculator buttons, which are a must-have for any keyboard selection. This keyboard connects to your computer through the USB interface and comes with software to help you customize your keyboard's features. The Natural Ergonomic Keyboard 4000 from Microsoft can be purchased for around $35 from your local electronics retailer.

Wireless Keyboard Desktops

With the introduction of wireless technology, wireless keyboard desktops have become extremely popular. A wireless keyboard desktop is a keyboard and mouse desktop combination that connects to your desktop computer wirelessly using radio frequency (RF) technology. The keyboard and mouse are powered with standard or rechargeable batteries and transmit their signals to a desktop receiver that is connected to the computer. It requires very little setup to install, and it eliminates the need for cables, which have plagued computer users since the first PC came into existence.

Our recommendation for purchasing a wireless keyboard desktop is the Logitech Wireless Wave Combo MK550. This wireless keyboard desktop comes with a wave key design that provides superior comfort with full-size and full-travel keys designed for quiet operation. The slight constant curve of the keyboard features consistently sized keys, which lets you type with confidence and ease. The keyboard uses the standard QWERTY layout, so you don't have to relearn how to type, as you do with other curved keyboards. The height of the keyboard is adjustable, allowing you to choose what's most comfortable for you. The keyboard uses 128-bit AES encryption to secure data as it's transmitted from the keyboard to the receiver, and both the keyboard and mouse use the 2.4 GHz wireless spectrum to connect to the receiver.

Logitech's wireless laser mouse M510 operates up to two years before the batteries should need to be replaced. The laser mouse uses a small infrared laser instead of an LED, which increases the resolution and sensitivity of the mouse. This system is compatible with Microsoft XP, Vista, and Windows 7. The Logitech Wireless Wave Combo MK550 can be purchased for around $79.99 from your local electronics retailer or online at **www.logitech.com**.

Logitech Wireless Wave Combo MK550

External Storage Devices

External storage devices are devices that connect to your computer using USB or FireWire interfaces and are used to store electronic data. These devices come in all sizes, shapes, colors, and volumes of storage space. These devices have all but replaced the CD-ROM and DVD as the leading means to store electronic data because of their portability, low cost, and vast amount of storage space. Be sure to consider some type of secure authentication or encryption for external storage, especially if confidential client information is backed up or stored on the devices.

External Hard Drives

External hard drives are great locations to store videos, pictures, and music or to back up the data on your internal hard drive. These devices are easy to install and use. Most external hard drives are plug and play, which means you simply have to plug them in to your computer to use them. External hard drives are not as fast as internal hard drives, but they are relatively inexpensive, and for the volume of information they can store, they are a very good, inexpensive backup solution. Also, lawyers who are otherwise technically challenged seem to do well with this form of backup, which can really be reduced to the push-of-a-button or automated method that so many lawyers seem to prefer.

The Seagate FreeAgent Desk is the external hard drive that we recommend for all lawyers and users. The FreeAgent Desk comes with available capacities of 500GB, 1TB, 1.5TB, and 2TB of storage space. These capacities provide you with flexibility that allows you to select the amount of storage space that best meets your requirements. The FreeAgent Desk comes with backup software to automatically back up your data to the device and is Windows 7-compatible. All of the models should provide enough storage space to back up all of the data required by most lawyers with ease. If you're looking to back up multiple computers and/or a server, then you probably will need to purchase the larger-sized drives. These devices connect to your computer through the USB 2.0 interface and can be placed flat or on their side. The external hard drive comes pre-loaded with the backup software, along with software to encrypt your information on the external hard drive using AES 128-bit encryption.

Seagate FreeAgent Desk External Hard Drive

The drive is whisper quiet and relatively small in size, so it can sit on your desk or on top of your computer without taking away valuable space. The FreeAgent Desk external hard drive can be purchased online at **www.seagate.com** for between $50 and $100, depending on the storage capacity, and it comes with a five-year warranty.

Thumb Drives

USB thumb drives (flash drives) are small, portable storage devices that use flash memory to store electronic data. Currently, they are offered with storage volume sizes ranging from 32MB to 256GB. For the most part, USB thumb drives with capacities of 2GB and smaller have been largely discontinued. USB thumb drives offer many advantages over other portable storage devices, such as the floppy disk, CD-ROM, and DVD. In particular, they are smaller, more durable, faster, and can hold more data. Unfortunately, these devices can create a great security risk for small businesses and law firms because their small size makes them absurdly easy to lose. This risk can be minimized, however, by purchasing the SanDisk Ultra USB flash drive.

This model is available with storage capacities of 8, 16, and 32GB of storage space for your files and comes standard with AES hardware encryption to keep your data secure. Using the SanDisk SecureAccess software, a user can protect access to private files with password protection and encryption. The software will create a file vault on the USB drive, creating a secure storage location for the user to place and keep all sensitive and confidential data. This flash drive is also fast, offering data transfer speeds up to 15MB per second.

The SanDisk SecureAccess software is compatible with the Microsoft Windows XP, Microsoft Vista, Windows 7, and Mac OS X v.10.5+ operating systems. The SanDisk Ultra USB flash drive can be purchased online at **www.sandisk.com** for between $39.99 and $55, depending on the storage capacity.

SanDisk Ultra USB Flash Drive

Another excellent choice is the 4GB Personal S200 Secure Drive from IronKey, which also comes in 1, 2, 4, 8, and 16GB versions. The D200 model does come in a 32GB version, but we prefer the more robust S200 model. This USB device is designed for the needs of sensitive military, government, and enterprise networks and includes AES hardware encryption that has been validated to meet government Federal Information

Processing Standard (FIPS) requirements. The security features require no software or drivers to enforce, with all the security being handled by the device hardware, and is "always on." The device requires that a user authenticate with a password before encryption keys are enabled and data can be accessed. This device is even waterproof! As they tend to be inadvertently placed in washing machines while in the pocket of your pants, this is an excellent feature, though we've not yet put it to the test.

This device has a self-destruct mechanism (think *Mission: Impossible*) that will wipe (i.e., remove) the data contents if a user or thief tries to break into the IronKey and enters 10 incorrect passwords. The Password Manager and Password Generator applications are also included. The Password Generator application will generate very secure passwords of whatever length you desire. The Password Manager securely stores your passwords on the IronKey along with the associated Web address. Merely insert your IronKey device in your computer and go to a website that requires a user ID and password. The IronKey will prompt you to save the credentials if it is the first time the IronKey has "seen" the website. If the logon credentials are already stored on the IronKey, a dialog box will be presented to confirm if the ID and password should be retrieved from the secure Password Manager application. Make sure you back up your password "vault" to the IronKey site in case the IronKey is lost or damaged. The password information is backed up to IronKey in a secure encrypted fashion. If you ever lose your IronKey device, just retrieve your password information from the IronKey website. The device even comes preloaded with a portable version of Firefox, which, when launched and used with the provided Secure Sessions Service, encrypts and keeps all of your Internet traffic private and secure. The IronKey Personal S200 Secure Drive can be purchased online from IronKey's website (**www.ironkey.com**) for from $79 to $299, depending on capacity.

IronKey USB Thumb Drive

FireWire Devices
FireWire devices are similar to USB devices, except that they take advantage of the FireWire standard and offer transfer rates of up to 786 Mbps, often referred to as FireWire 800 devices. You may see some devices still supporting FireWire 400, a previous version of the FireWire standard, which offered data transfer speeds up to 393 Mbps, but they are currently being phased out. FireWire devices are great for professional applications, digital audio/video, graphic design, and system backups. These devices

are identical to other external hard drives except for the additional FireWire interface that they support.

The external LaCie d2 Quadra Hard Disk is an ultra-quiet hard drive in a sleek design that comes with enough storage capacity to meet your storage requirements. This model comes with four different interfaces—USB 2.0, FireWire 400 and 800, and eSATA—to connect the device to your computer and is available with storage capacities of 1, 2, and 3 TB.

When taking advantage of the eSATA connection, you can transfer data at rates up to 115 MB/s when used with a SATA-II hard drive, which is screaming fast. This device is both Mac and Windows compatible and requires very little setup. Setup is nearly effortless (just plug and play) and offers automatic formatting with LaCie Setup Assistant software. The LaCie Genie Backup Assistant software for both PCs is included as well as Intego Backup Assistant software with data restore for Macs. The LaCie d2 Quadra Hard Disk can be purchased online at **www.lacie.com** for between $159.99 and $289, depending on storage capacity, or from your local electronics retailer.

LaCie d2 Quadra Hard Disk

When selecting an external hard drive or USB flash drive, be careful of vendors' dubious marketing claims. Currently, many vendors are rebranding their devices as USB 3.0-compliant, offering faster data transfer rates. Please note that although the USB 3.0 standard has been approved, it's still not readily available in most computer hardware and may not be for a while. Until then, be cautious.

Speakers and Headphones

Lawyers (and their staff) often tell us that the most important peripheral device they need for their computer is a pair of speakers. They like to be able to listen to their music while they work and are adamant about fidelity. Without breaking the bank, reasonable-quality desktop speakers can be purchased to provide the user with a clear, true sound. Logitech, a leading provider of speaker systems for computers, makes the LS21 speakers. The LS21 speakers offer 2.1 stereo sound with a subwoofer, providing enhanced bass, and the speakers come in a slim, stylish profile. These speakers offer quality audio at a reasonable price. The speakers have a stereo headphone jack, an auxiliary input where you can connect your iPod or MP3 player, and integrated controls located on a wired remote. They even include a cable-management system to help reduce the clutter of wires. The Logitech LS21 speakers can be purchased online for around $30 from **www.logitech.com**.

Logitech LS21 Speakers

Be careful of speaker "wars" in the office as people battle for the loudest music. Headphones may be a consideration in providing a quieter office environment.

If you purchase one of the recommended Dell flat-panel monitors, consider adding a sound bar. The sound bar clips onto the bottom edge of the Dell flat panel and gets its power from the monitor itself. It provides a clean installation and doesn't take up any additional desk space.

If you use a laptop or desktop computer system that supports Bluetooth and wish to keep your music to yourself, there are a number of wireless headphone options available. Sony makes the DR-BT101 Bluetooth wireless stereo headphones, a lightweight headset featuring a built-in microphone with echo cancellation for crystal-clear audio and voice reception. The device includes a rechargeable battery that lasts up to 11 hours on a single charge, provides up to 110 hours of standby time, and weighs only 4.4 ounces. The wireless device supports Bluetooth 2.1 EDR, including Hands Free Profile (HFP), Headset Profile (HSP), Advanced Audio Distribution Profile (A2DP), and Audio/Video Remote Control Profile (AVRCP). This headset can be purchased online or from your local electronics retailer starting at just $38.

CHAPTER FIVE

Printers

EVEN IN THE ERA of the "paperless office," most law firms still print a lot of documents on a daily basis, probably more than any other business. To say that the practice of law tends to be "less than green" is a massive understatement; at least most have implemented a recycling program. Nonetheless, it is certainly critical to have a good, reliable printer to ensure that your firm is printing quality documents in the shortest amount of time. Below, we discuss and recommend printers for stand-alone systems, network systems, and multifunctional printers/copiers.

Stand-Alone Printers

Your most basic type of printer is the stand-alone printer. This printer connects directly to a computer and is not placed on the network. It only has to be capable of handling one user's print jobs at a time. Even when networked printers are used, there can be reasons to also have stand-alone printers—perhaps so the bookkeeper can keep financial records from inadvertently being picked up by someone else. Senior partners may feel their information is so confidential that they want a printer in their office (though their staff often mutters that they are just too lazy to walk down the hall). There are many makes and models to choose from when selecting a stand-alone printer, and each has different performance specifications, features, and available fonts.

The questions about going with an ink-jet printer are gradually declining. We highly recommend going with a laser printer. Ink-jet printers typically result in a higher cost of ownership over the long haul, with ink cartridges printing at a higher cost per page than the average laser printer. There are even studies that show a cost of $3,000–$5,000 per gallon for name-brand ink cartridges. Human blood is cheaper. Laser is better quality and more economical—case closed.

A stand-alone printer can be shared through enabling File and Print Sharing on your local computer, but we strongly counsel against this practice. It creates a host of security vulnerabilities that could compromise not only your system but your entire network, and causes a lot of headaches for the administrator to manage and configure the device.

When discussing printers with our clients, we are frequently asked, "Should I purchase a color or a black-and-white laser printer?" You will pay a premium for a color laser printer, and in most instances it is not worth the cost when purchasing a stand-alone printer. It is usually more cost-effective to purchase a color laser printer to be placed on the computer network so that more than one user can print to it.

The Hewlett Packard (HP) LaserJet Pro P1606dn printer is the perfect solution for the stand-alone or network (up to five users) printer. The printer has a built-in Ethernet connection for network connectivity and prints in duplex (two-sided) mode by default. This printer prints as many as 26 pages per minute, comes standard with a paper input capacity of 250 sheets, and has a recommended monthly volume of up to 2,000 pages. The printer has a first-page-out speed of 7 seconds and supports all the common page types, such as letter, legal, executive, and envelopes. This printer comes standard with 32MB of memory and connects to your computer using the USB interface. It should be noted that the printer doesn't come with a USB cable, which will have to be purchased separately. For those mobile users, this printer is compatible with Apple's Airprint service, which allows users to print to the device from their iPad, iPhone, or iPod touch.

This black-and-white printer was designed for quick business printing and offers a cost-effective solution to personal printing. The printer is both Mac and Windows compatible, including Vista and Windows 7, and comes standard with a one-year limited warranty. The HP LaserJet Pro P1606dn printer can be purchased online for around $199.99 (before discounts) from **www.hp.com**.

HP LaserJet P1606dn Printer

Networked Printers

Networked printers are used to provide a printing resource to multiple users. Networked printers are generally installed in a central location and then shared throughout the local network. The administration and security of these printers can be integrated into your network's security infrastructure, such as through Windows Active Directory for a Windows-based network, and is much more secure than sharing a printer through the File and Print Sharing service. Installation in a central location simplifies both the management and security of these devices. The networked printers can be shared out to the various computers and users that make up your network with very little overhead. There are many types of networked printers, and depending on your need—low volume, high volume, color—your options will vary. A popular request from many law offices is to have multiple trays for the printer. This capability to have multiple paper types loaded is usually available in the mid-range to higher-end printer models.

Low-Volume Network Printers

Low-volume network printers are designed for workgroups of users having a small to moderate print volume as high as 5,000 pages per month. These printers are moderately priced and are primarily used to segment printing within offices based on user group or physical location. Network printers have more robust hardware than stand-alone printers to handle multiple jobs from different users at the same time.

The HP LaserJet P2055dn black-and-white network-based laser printer is great for a small law firm because it provides users with a highly reliable, cost-effective printer that is capable of handling the expected volume produced by an average small firm. The HP LaserJet P2055dn prints as many as 35 pages per minute and has a monthly recommended volume of up to 3,000 pages. It comes standard with an input capacity of 300 sheets and 128MB of memory and handles all sizes of paper. As an added feature, the printer allows for automatic duplexing for printing double-sided documents. The printer has an embedded gigabit Ethernet network adapter to attach the printer to your local network. For additional security, this printer can prevent unauthorized access with management features including 802.1x authentication and password protection. It

HP LaserJet
P2055dn Printer

should be noted that the printer doesn't come with a USB or network cable, which will have to be purchased separately.

The memory of this printer can be upgraded if desired, and the printer's drivers are compatible with both Mac- and Windows-based systems, including Vista and Windows 7. The printer comes with a standard one-year warranty and includes a CD-ROM with the drivers and software necessary to configure the device. The HP LaserJet P2055dn black-and-white laser printer can be purchased online for around $400 (prior to any discounts) from **www.hp.com**.

High-Volume Network Printers

High-volume network printers are designed for businesses that need the capacity to print a large volume of pages on a monthly basis and are usually considered when your firm needs a printer that can produce more than 5,000 pages per month. These devices contain hardware that can handle the volume load and are built to be constantly printing.

The HP LaserJet M4345x Multifunction Printer is ideal for firms that print large volumes of documents on a monthly basis. This printer has a recommended monthly printing volume of 5,000–20,000 pages and prints up to 45 pages per minute. The printer comes with a standard input capacity of 1,100 sheets, three paper trays, 256MB of memory, and an embedded gigabit Ethernet network adapter to attach the printer to your local network. This printer handles all sizes of paper and can easily be upgraded with more memory, an optional hard drive, paper trays, or envelope feeders. The network connectivity can be upgraded to support wireless networks, a must-have option for those firms that use a wireless infrastructure for their local network. It should be noted that the printer doesn't come with a USB or network cable, which will have to be purchased separately.

For future compatibility, this printer is IPv6-ready. For added security, this printer supports network authentication (LDAP, SMTP) that lets administrators control device access.

The printer comes with a one-year, next-business-day onsite warranty. The printer is compatible with both Mac- and Windows-based networks, including Vista and Windows 7. A CD-ROM that contains both printer driver files and software necessary to manage and configure the device is included. The HP LaserJet M4345x Multifunction Printer can be purchased online

HP LaserJet M4345x Printer

for around $3,699.99 from **www.hp.com**. At this cost, you may want to investigate using your digital copier as a printer depending on your anticipated monthly print volume and cost per page.

Color Network Printer

Color network printers are essential for any law firm or small business that wants to print a significant volume of documents in color. If the color printer is networked, multiple users can have access to the shared resource, which is far more cost-effective than giving everyone their own color printer. HP is still the leading manufacturer of color printers in terms of value, selection, overall reliability, and performance. Their color LaserJet printers are reasonably priced and produce high-quality color documents.

For a small business or law firm, the HP Color LaserJet CP3525x printer is perfect for everyday color printing. This printer prints as many as 30 pages per minute for both black and color, has a recommended monthly volume of 1,500–5,000 pages, and a first-page-out speed of less than 17 seconds, so that the color print job starts almost as soon as it has been sent to the printer. The standard input capacity is 850 sheets, and the printer supports all sizes of paper and can be upgraded with an envelope feeder.

The printer comes standard with 512MB of memory and an embedded gigabit Ethernet network adapter that enables the printer to connect to your local network. The printer's drivers support both Mac- and Windows-based systems, including Vista and Windows 7, and can be networked for easy accessibility. The printer comes with a one-year, next-day, onsite limited warranty.

The HP Color LaserJet CP3525x printer can be purchased online for around $1,300 from **www.hp.com**. It should be noted that the printer doesn't come with a USB or network cable, which will have to be purchased separately.

The largest operational cost for a color laser printer is the consumables. Color cartridges are not cheap, and color prints can be very expensive. One configuration point to make on all computers networked to your color printers: Change the default color setting to black. This will save on the printing and subsequent waste of color cartridges for unnecessary color copies.

HP Color LaserJet CP3525x Printer

Digital copier manufacturers are beginning to take over the task of color printing. Investigate using a color copier for your color print needs versus a stand-alone color printer. You might be surprised at the amount of money you could save.

Multifunctional Printers/Copiers

Don't you wish there was a single device that you could install on your local network that could do everything your office needs—printing, faxing, scanning, and copying? Happily for lawyers, today such devices are becoming a standard fixture. Multifunctional printers (MFPs) offer the capability to print, scan, copy, and fax from the same device, combining the functions of multiple devices into just one and eliminating the need to purchase them separately. In the long run, purchasing or leasing an MFP can save you the time and money often expended to upgrade and service multiple devices.

MFPs are very expensive and are generally leased because of the high cost to purchase. When looking at whether to buy or lease MFPs, keep some functionality questions in mind:

- Do you want the ability to print in color and in black-and-white?
- Do you need duplex printing?
- Do you want to scan documents to your hard drive, user box, or e-mail?
- Do you want incoming faxes to be sent to e-mail as an image file or just printed?
- Do you want to be able to link the use of the MFP to the firm's billing program?
- What does your printing capacity need to be?
- Do you need any finishing capabilities (e.g., stapling, folding)?
- Do you need to implement any security on the unit, and if so, what?

By answering these questions, you will be able to provide your vendors with enough detail to provide you with the MFP device that best meets the firm's needs. Your digital copier may already have some of these features installed but not configured. Check with your vendor to see what capabilities your current copier has. In our office, we have a Konica Minolta Bizhub C220 MFP device. It allows us to print both in color and in black-and-white at speeds up to 22 pages per minute; scan to hard drive, user box, e-mail, or FTP; and fax documents, although we do not use that feature. We are able to download our scanned documents from a built-in secure internal website as JPG, PDF, XPS, or TIFF files, as well as scan to an internal e-mail address. The Bizhub has advanced security features such as job erase, hard drive sanitizing and lock, user authentication, IP address filtering, and secure print and scan encryption. Needless to say, the Bizhub provides us with a secure MFP option. We are huge fans.

Konica Minolta Bizhub C220

As you work with your copier supplier, make sure you negotiate a low cost per color copy and only pay for the number of pages that you print. Don't pay for the consumables (e.g., toner cartridges), as these should be included as part of the per-page cost.

CHAPTER SIX

Scanners

ALMOST AS COMMON AS printers, scanners have become a necessary piece of equipment in most offices as more paper documents are being scanned and stored electronically. The drive to a paperless office is still very much under way (see Ross Kodner's chapter, "The Paper LESS Office: Kicking the Paper Habit in the Era of the Cloud," which covers this topic), but certainly there is steady progress in that direction. The setup and operation of scanners have become simple to the point where even the most novice computer user can do it. Many of the tasks that once had to be performed manually are now automated, and the hookup entails connecting a single wire and inserting a CD to install software. Network scanners may be a little more complex to set up and would require the assistance of the IT staff to configure.

Most desktop scanners communicate with the computer via the USB or FireWire interface and come with a variety of software to assist in the scanning and file-conversion process. Some models come standard with optical character recognition (OCR) software that will read the scanned image and produce a document that is editable. Fujitsu, a manufacturer of home- and business-grade scanners, produces scanners that have been constantly rated the best models for businesses. Below, we make recommendations for both low-volume and high-volume scanners from Fujitsu.

Some law firms may already have scanning capability in their digital copier. As we previously stated, check with your vendor to see if scanning with your copier is a more cost-effective solution than purchasing a stand-alone unit.

Low-Volume Scanner

The Fujitsu ScanSnap S1500 scanner is a great value for a solid auto-document feeder (ADF) scanner. This desktop scanner scans up to 20 pages color per minute, has an ADF capacity of 50 sheets, and can handle both legal- and letter-sized paper. The scanner has a maximum scanning resolution of 600 x 600 dpi and connects to the computer via the USB interface. This scanner is compatible with Microsoft Windows 2000 (SP4)/XP (SP2)/Vista and Windows 7 (32-bit and 64-bit). For Mac compatibility, you will need to purchase the Fujitsu ScanSnap S1500M scanner. This scanner comes with bundled software that includes Adobe Acrobat 9.0 Standard Edition, ScanSnap Organizer v4.1, ABBYY FineReader for ScanSnap 4.0, and CardMinder v4.1.

Adobe Acrobat 9.0 Standard software allows you to automatically convert scanned data into searchable PDF files. Some of the automatic features of this device include auto paper-size detection, auto de-skew, and auto blank-page removal. The auto blank-page removal eliminates the need to edit scanned documents because the scanner has the ability to recognize the deleted blank pages. The ABBYY FineReader software allows you to scan documents directly to applications such as Microsoft Word, Excel, and PowerPoint. The scanner comes with a standard one-year limited warranty that can be upgraded to the Advanced Exchange service program. The Fujitsu ScanSnap S1500 scanner can be purchased online from Fujitsu's website (**www.fujitsu.com**) for $495 and comes with a one-year limited warranty. The inclusion of Acrobat Standard makes this a very worthwhile purchase.

Fujitsu ScanSnap S1500 Scanner

High-Volume Scanner

The Fujitsu fi-5530C2 is perfect for legal professionals who need a high-speed scanner on a modest budget and are serious about scanning documents. The built-in automatic document feeder (ADF) holds 100 pages and scans up to 50 pages per minute (100 images) in 200 dpi black-and-white mode. Everything needed for creating a paperless office is included free with the fi-5530C2, including Adobe Acrobat 9.0 Standard Edition, ScandAll Pro, and Kofax VRS Professional.

Using the Fujitsu fi-5530C2 scanner, you can convert any document to Adobe PDF using the Adobe Acrobat Standard software that is included with the scanner. The scanner can handle a vigorous duty cycle of up to

4,000 documents per day and can handle documents ranging in size from a business card to a legal document. The Ultra SCSI and USB 2.0 interface allows for simplified connectivity to your computer. The scanner is compatible with Microsoft Windows 2000/XP/Vista and Windows 7 systems. The Fujitsu fi-5530C2 scanner can be purchased online from Fujitsu's website (**www.fujitsu.com**) for around $2,700 and comes with a three-month, on-site limited warranty.

Fujitsu fi-5530C2 Scanner

This is a lot of money for a solo or small firm operation, especially to spend on a scanner. We're sure that your digital copier could provide a less expensive solution for your scanning needs, especially if you have a newer unit. Consider that before you make a purchasing decision and you might be able to save yourself some money.

CHAPTER SEVEN

Servers

ONE OF THE BIGGEST, most important, and most expensive decisions that you will have to make regarding technology for your firm is purchasing a server. This is the mother ship of the network, and the purchase decision should be made very carefully. This is absolutely not the time to be pennywise and pound foolish.

Like workstations, servers come in every make, model, and flavor. Unlike workstations, however, servers can be very expensive and can consume a large chunk of your technology budget rather quickly. Your firm will need to engage in careful planning when selecting a server so that future needs can be discussed and addressed, including the desirable hardware and software components the server must have in order to meet your future goals. Plan carefully, because you don't want to have to buy a new server every other year. Generally, the average life span of a server is four to five years—so start planning!

Solo—File and Printer Sharing

The most simple and basic reason for getting a server is for file and printer sharing. By centralizing the storage of electronic files, administration, and installation of printers, you will save time, money, and headaches when it comes to maintaining and managing your network. There are servers designed specifically for the purpose of sharing files, documents and printers. These servers come with the most basic hardware and software and are relatively inexpensive when compared to the mid-range to higher-end servers.

Dell PowerEdge
T310 Server

The Dell PowerEdge T310 server was designed for the small business to provide the most basic file and printer sharing capabilities. A listing of the server's hardware and software components, along with some technical specifications, are provided below.

File and Printer Sharing Server

Hardware Component	**Recommendation**
Chassis:	Tower
Operating System:	Microsoft Windows Server 2008 R2 SP1, Standard Edition with 5 CALs
Processors:	Intel Xeon X3470, 2.93 GHz, 8MB Cache
Memory:	8GB Memory, 1333 MHz Single-Ranked RDIMM
Primary Controller Card:	Perc 6/I SAS internal RAID adapter, PCI-Express card
Hard Drive Configuration:	RAID-5—Add-in PERC6i/H700 (SAS/SATA Controller)
Hard Drives:	Three 146GB SAS, 3.5-inch 15K RPM hard drives
CD/DVD Drive:	DVD-RW drive, SATA
Network Adapter:	Onboard Dual Gigabit Network Adapters
Warranty:	3-Year ProSupport 4HR 7x24 Onsite
Other:	Redundant Power Supply

This Dell PowerEdge T310 was customized through Dell's website (**www.dell.com**) and contains an Intel Xeon 2.93 GHz processor with 8GB of RAM. This server comes with the Microsoft Windows Server 2008 R2 SP1 64-bit Standard Edition operating system with five Client Access Licenses (CALs). CALs are needed for each computer or user that accesses the server.

The three SAS (serial-attached SCSI) 146GB hard drives are configured in a RAID-5 (redundant array of inexpensive disks) hard drive configuration for increased performance and fault tolerance. In a RAID-5 hard drive configuration, if one of the hard drives were to fail, the server would continue to operate until the failed hard drive could be replaced. In most other hard drive configurations, if a server's hard drive were to fail, the server would be inoperable until the disk was repaired or replaced. The RAID-5 configuration offers both fault tolerance with the parity hard drive and better performance than most other RAID or mirrored disk configurations. RAID-5 hard drive configurations are strongly recommended for all law firm servers.

In total, there is about 292GB of hard drive space available for the storage of electronic data, programs, and other applications. You used to be able to save a little bit of money by reducing the number of hard drives purchased and setting up a RAID-1 hard drive configuration, but since hard drives have come so far down in price, we no longer recommend this as an option.

The onboard dual gigabit network adapters will allow clients to connect to the server at gigabit speeds, assuming the rest of your network components are gigabit as well. The DVD-RW drive will allow you to both burn and read CD-ROMs and DVDs from the server console.

One of the most important features to consider when purchasing a server is the warranty. In most cases, you will not need both the hardware and software support. At a minimum, you must include a hardware warranty that will cover the hardware and labor cost to replace any of the server components that fail during its life cycle. This Dell PowerEdge server comes with a three-year, four-hour/same-day, onsite parts and labor warranty. Having a hardware warranty for your server is critical to protecting your equipment, data, and business. This is no time to be miserly. The included warranty covers seven days a week, 24 hours a day, with a four-hour onsite response time. This means that a repair person will be at your site with replacement parts within four hours of the problem being diagnosed. This Dell PowerEdge T310 server was quoted on Dell's website for approximately $3,900 at the time of this writing.

Small Firm—File and Printer Sharing/Hosting Services

When purchasing a server for your network, you must decide what function the server will have in your day-to-day operations. In addition to file and printer sharing, it's common for small firms to host their company's e-mail. Although you can also host a website, we recommend that you outsource that to a website hosting provider because of potential security and administration issues. The added hosting services (e-mail and/or web) will require a server

Dell PowerEdge T710 Server

with upgraded hardware to be able to provide the necessary resources for the services to operate reliably.

The Dell PowerEdge T710 was designed for small firms or businesses that are looking for a cost-effective solution to hosting their own e-mail or website. The server's hardware and software components, along with some technical specifications, are provided below.

File and Printer Sharing/Hosting Services

Hardware Component	Recommendation
Chassis:	Tower
Operating System:	Microsoft Small Business Server 2011, Standard Edition With 5 CALs
Processors:	Dual Intel Xeon X5670 2.93 GHz Processors
Memory:	16 GB Memory, 1333 MHz Dual Ranked LV RDIMMs
Primary Controller Card:	PERC H200 Integrated RAID Controller
Hard Drive Configuration:	RAID-5 for PERC 6/I or H700 Controller
Hard Drives:	Three 146GB SAS, 3.5-inch 15K RPM hard drives
CD/DVD Drive:	DVD-RW drive, SATA
Network Adapter:	Two Dual Port Embedded Broadcom NetXtreme II 5709 Gigabit Ethernet NIC
Warranty:	3-Year ProSupport 4HR 7x24 Onsite
Other:	Redundant Power Supply

The Dell PowerEdge T710 listed here was customized through Dell's website. It contains Dual Intel Xeon 2.93 GHz processors with 16GB of memory. The server specified above was customized in a tower chassis; however, the same model is available in a rack mount chassis at no additional cost. The rack mount chassis is for those firms and small businesses that maintain their servers and networking equipment in a rack. The processors will supply more than enough horsepower to configure the server as an e-mail or Web server, and the 16GB of memory will allow these services to run smoothly and will prevent the server from lagging or becoming bogged down.

The server comes with Microsoft Small Business Server (SBS) 2011 Standard Edition preinstalled, which includes the Microsoft Exchange Server 2010 software for e-mail hosting and the Internet Information Server for website hosting. Five CALs are also included, so you may have to budget for more if more than five devices or users in your firm are accessing the server.

The three 146 SAS 15K RPM hard drives are configured in a RAID-5 hard drive configuration and provide about 292GB of storage space for applications and data. Again, this PowerEdge server comes with the three-year ProSupport 4HR 7x24 Onsite hardware warranty, which provides three years of four-hour, same-day parts and labor warranty. The Dell PowerEdge T710 server was quoted on Dell's website for approximately $8,700 at the time of this writing.

Don't forget to consider backup software and any additional (e.g., antivirus, antispyware, antispam, etc.) applications when configuring the server because you might get a better discount from the vendor when bundled and purchased with the server hardware.

Database/Applications Server

Your firm's software requirements, current and future, will play a big role in determining what hardware and software components your server will need to contain in order to adequately support your firm in the coming years. So far, we have discussed the hardware and software specifications for a server used primarily for file and printer sharing and one capable of handling basic hosting services, such as e-mail and a website. When planning to use a server to host a database application, case management software, or e-discovery software, you must look at the minimum requirements for each piece of software and then go above and beyond the specifications that vendors provide. What vendors list should be regarded cautiously as a "bare minimum." To run well and reliably, the software almost always requires more horsepower.

The recommended Dell PowerEdge T710 server is capable of handling most database and software applications, as long as it's configured with advanced hardware to handle the powerful and robust database applications. The server's hardware and software components are provided on the next page.

Database/Applications Server

Hardware Component	Recommendation
Chassis:	Tower
Operating System:	Microsoft Windows Server 2008 R2 SP1 Enterprise Edition
Processors:	Dual Intel X5687 3.60 GHz 12M Cache Processors
Memory:	64GB Memory, 1333MHz 2R LV RDIMMs
Primary Controller Card:	PERC H700 Integrated RAID Controller
Hard Drive Configuration:	RAID-5 For PERC 6/I or H700 Controller
Hard Drives:	Three 146GB SAS, 3.5-inch 15K RPM hard drives
CD/DVD Drive:	DVD-RW drive, SATA
Network Adapter:	Two Dual-Port Embedded Broadcom NetXtreme II 5709 Gigabit Ethernet NIC
Warranty:	3-Year ProSupport 4HR 7x24 Onsite
Other:	Redundant Power Supply

The PowerEdge T710 server described above was customized through Dell's website and contains Dual Intel Xeon 3.60 GHz processors and 64GB of memory. The processor is faster than the processor included with the server discussed in the previous section, "Hosting Services."

Dell PowerEdge T710 Server

This server comes with the Windows Server 2008 R2 SP1 Enterprise Edition operating system with Hyper-V capability for virtualized environments. The Windows Server 2008 operating system does not come bundled with Microsoft Exchange Server or Microsoft SQL Server. However, Microsoft's SBS Premium does. So, if you want a single server to do "everything," such as file and print sharing, e-mail, and database hosting, SBS Premium may be a good alternative, but that's a lot of functionality to run on a single server and is not a recommended solution. For most databases, case management software, and e-discovery applications, vendors recommend a dedicated server.

The three 146GB hard drives are configured in a RAID-5 hard disk configuration and provide about 292GB of storage space for applications and data. If more storage space is needed, this upgrade can be made during the configuration of the server to meet your needs, especially if you plan to use virtualization.

The redundant power supply allows the server to stay powered on in the event that one of the power supplies were to fail. The server comes with dual embedded Broadcom Ethernet adapters and a DVD-RW drive. The PowerEdge server comes with a three-year ProSupport 4HR 7x24 Onsite hardware warranty, which provides three years of a four-hour, same-day parts and labor warranty. The Dell PowerEdge T710 server was quoted on Dell's website for approximately $13,500 at the time of this writing.

Virtual Servers

The large push within the IT industry to move toward virtualization seems to be working, as Microsoft sold as many licenses for virtual machines as it did physical hardware last year. Expect the trend to continue.

Simply put, virtualization means that a single piece of hardware contains and hosts multiple server or desktop images, otherwise known as machines. Virtualization enables the consolidation of data and applications onto a single physical hardware server. The reduction in hardware saves energy, management, and administration effort and reduces overall hardware and software costs, especially if your firm needs multiple servers. Virtualization is used for the separation of hosting services and applications, allowing for one virtual server to be down for maintenance without affecting the others. For example, if Windows updates were downloaded on a virtual server hosting File and Print Sharing services, the virtual server could be rebooted without having to bring down the entire host system, keeping other virtual servers online and available to users.

Virtualization is commonly used by larger firms and is not typically found in a small firm environment; however, we are recommending that more small firms begin to consider virtualization technologies when making server hardware and software purchasing decisions, especially in scenarios where the client is hosting services internally.

Is server virtualization the best choice for your network environment? A number of questions will need to be answered before making this determination.

First, what services and applications are running on your network? If your network is running Microsoft Exchange Server, SQL Server, and a case management application, most likely you will need multiple servers to host all of these services and software. Most case management applications now require a separate server to run on. By using virtualization, the purchase of another physical hardware server can be avoided by installing the case management software on its own virtual server.

When purchasing a host system (the server hosting the virtual servers), the most critical hardware options that need to be considered are the amount of memory, number, and type of processors, and the amount of storage space. For each virtual server, 2 to 4GB of memory or more will need to be allocated for the virtual server to operate. A larger amount of memory will be needed if the virtual server is hosting a database or memory-hungry service. This does not account for the 1 to 2GB of memory that the host system will require as well. For example, if you have a host server running three virtual servers, you will need a minimum of 8GB of memory installed in the host server to supply the host and all of the virtual servers with enough memory resources to operate. To accommodate the necessary hardware, the host system will have to be running the Windows Server 2008 Enterprise Edition.

When running virtual servers, you will need to ensure that the host system has enough processing capability to handle the processing load. At a minimum, you will want the system to contain Intel Xeon processors with a processing speed of 2.53 to 3.6 GHz. The optimum solution is to use Intel Xeon processors with the same speed range, and in virtualization solutions, you will need to have multiple processors. The multicore processors combine two or more cores onto a single integrated circuit, providing multiprocessing capabilities to the chip. Multiprocessing allows the execution of multiple concurrent software processes in a system, which is vital in a virtualization solution.

The amount of storage space that will be required to run all of the virtual servers and the host system will vary from solution to solution. When determining the amount of storage space the systems will require, you will need to consider the services and applications that will be hosted. For example, a virtual server hosting Microsoft Exchange Server will require enough disk space to account for the size of the Exchange Database stores, along with the program files and operating system. The amount of storage space allocated to each virtual server can be independently configured and can be modified at a later time if more space is needed. For ease of configuration and setup, bearing the cost of additional hard drive storage up front makes more sense than waiting to add more hard drives later on. Plus, it's always recommended that more than enough hard drive space is available to the host system and virtual servers so that problems with low disk space can be avoided. We have clients who have terabytes of disk space available just for their File and Printer Sharing virtual server.

Microsoft offers two free server virtualization solutions for Windows Server 2003 and Server 2008. Microsoft Virtual Server 2005 R2 SP2 is offered as a free download from Microsoft's website and provides support for guest and host operating systems running Windows Vista SP1 (Business, Enterprise, Ultimate), Windows XP SP3, and Windows Server 2008 (Standard, Enterprise, Datacenter, Web). The software provides centralized management and administration of virtual servers, allowing for quick deployment of virtual servers that are reliable, secure, and scalable. For host systems running Windows Server 2008, Microsoft has included the Hyper-V virtualization system with the Server 2008 operating system. Like the former, Hyper-V enables the consolidating of multiple server roles as separate virtual servers running on a single host system, allowing for different operating systems such as Linux, Windows, and others to run in parallel. For a complete list of the Guest operating systems supported by Hyper-V, you can visit Microsoft's website at **http://technet.microsoft.com/en-us/library/cc794868(WS.10).aspx**.

Hyper-V was designed with enhanced security features in mind, providing an architecture that is less vulnerable to attack. This software includes a set of management and administration tools that can be used to manage the host and virtual system's hardware from the same interface. Depending on the operating system of the host system, these are two Microsoft-based software options available for server virtualization, and they are fully supported. We have observed that the free Hyper-V implementations may have some issues with sharing of peripheral devices across the virtual machines. As an example, you may not be able to share the USB ports of the hardware with a virtual machine, which means that you can't copy files from a USB flash drive from the host system to the virtual system.

Software licensing will also play a role in determining your firm's ability to move to a virtualization environment. When using the Microsoft Server 2003/2008 Enterprise Edition, licensing allows up to four virtual instances of the software on the same hardware system. This is one of the reasons the cost to purchase a single license of Enterprise Edition is much higher than the Standard Edition. For every other operating system, both servers and desktops, an additional license will need to be purchased for each virtual server or machine desired. However, we strongly recommend, if you are planning on implementing a virtualization environment, that the host system run Microsoft Server 2008 Enterprise Edition, as Windows Server 2003 Enterprise Edition is no longer available from Microsoft and has moved into Extended Support.

There are other alternatives to Microsoft's virtualization solutions, such as VMware's vSphere Hypervisor (ESXi). If you are investigating alternative virtualization solutions, you will need to work with your IT vendor to see what other options might be available. We recommend and use the VMware solution over Microsoft's Hyper-V solution. VMware has been in the virtualization game a lot longer than Microsoft, and you can share those USB ports with the virtual machines, as well as some other useful and time-saving administration capabilities with VMware Tools.

The cost to purchase the hardware and software necessary to implement a virtualization environment for your network will be significantly less than the cost of purchasing multiple servers to fill the necessary roles your applications and services require.

Peer-to-Peer

Many small firms use the built-in peer-to-peer network capabilities of their computer systems as an alternative to purchasing a server. A peer-to-peer network, in its simplest form, is two or more computers that are able to communicate with one another to share files and folders, printers, and applications without using a server to accomplish these tasks. Peer-to-peer networks are commonly used in solo or small firm offices with only two or three computers. The computers, located on the same local network and belonging to the same Workgroup, can access shared resources in the Workgroups to which they are joined. "Workgroup" is Microsoft's name for a peer-to-peer network. Unless a computer is joined to a domain, it belongs to a Workgroup. By default, on Windows XP computers the Workgroup name is "MSHOME," and in older versions of Windows the default Workgroup is "WORKGROUP." Just to complicate matters, Microsoft has changed the default Workgroup name in Windows 7 back to the original "WORKGROUP."

Peer-to-peer networks may sound like a good solution for small firms that have only a few computers, but there are some significant disadvantages when choosing to set up this type of network when compared to purchasing a server. First, when networking computers together, you are going to experience a slowdown and inconsistency in your system's performance. Workstations are not capable of handling concurrent access of their files by other computers. When this occurs, the system's resources are severely taxed, causing disruption to the users. Think of this as a tug-of-war for data. Your computer is trying to use data at the same time someone else needs it. Because of the inconsistency and unreliability of the peer-to-peer network, corruption of shared files, such as case management and billing systems, occurs frequently. Since computers in a peer-to-peer network can be running different operating systems, software incompatibilities between the systems can occur. The decentralization of critical firm data can lead to unnecessarily complex data backup scenarios, often resulting in important data not being backed up and protected. On top of all the issues above, the need to manage and administer multiple copies of the same software, such as antivirus protection on each individual computer, becomes needlessly tiresome. Software that is centrally managed is much more cost-effective to purchase and maintain, as opposed to managing each computer's software suites independently.

There is an inaccurate perception that peer-to-peer networks save money and cost less than client/server networks. Yes, purchasing a server might seem expensive at first, even the lower-end units. However, in the end this is never the case. The costs of managing and maintaining a peer-to-peer network will always be higher than the costs that would have been incurred if you had implemented a server/client network in the first place. Peer-to-peer networks can have higher licensing costs for software, because you are purchasing single licenses at a time. Software that is administered and maintained on independent computers will take more time to complete than if it were centrally managed from a server. Technical support and consulting costs will be much higher in a peer-to-peer environment, which is usually not taken into consideration when making the initial decision to purchase and use a peer-to-peer network. For most small network environments, even with those involving as few as two computers, purchasing a server to centralize applications and data can save time and money in the long run.

CHAPTER EIGHT

Server Operating Systems

CHOOSING THE HARDWARE COMPONENTS is just one step in selecting the right server. The next step is determining what operating system and software will be necessary to best meet both the current and future needs of the firm. There are many variations of server operating systems currently available, and they are described in detail below.

Microsoft Windows Server 2003 Standard Edition
The Windows Server 2003 operating system was produced by Microsoft as the successor to Windows Server 2000 operating systems. The Windows Server 2003 operating system delivers better performance, is more scalable, and offers more enhanced security features than its predecessor. The Microsoft Windows Server 2003 Standard Edition was released to target small to medium-sized businesses. The Standard Edition supports file and printer sharing, centralized desktop application deployment, and enhanced security and access management through upgrades to Active Directory. Microsoft Windows Server 2003 Standard Edition supports up to four processors and 4GB of memory. This version of Microsoft Windows Server should no longer be used.

As of July 13, 2010, Microsoft Windows 2003 Server went into Extended Support and will continue to offer security updates until July 2015.

Microsoft Windows Small Business Server 2003 Standard and Premium Editions
Microsoft Small Business Server (SBS) 2003 was developed and designed to provide small businesses with an operating system that would provide a complete technology solution. The technologies integrated with

Microsoft SBS include remote access, Remote Web Workplace, Terminal Services, enhanced security features, Fax Server, unified messaging console, and enhanced monitoring and logging. The Standard Edition of SBS includes Windows SharePoint Services used for work collaboration, Microsoft Exchange Server 2003 for e-mail, Active Directory, and other features. The Premium Edition of Microsoft SBS 2003 includes Microsoft SQL Server 2000, Microsoft Internet Security, Acceleration Server 2004, and also everything included with the SBS 2003 Standard Edition.

SBS Client Access Licenses (CALs) are more expensive than CALs for other editions of Windows. The reason for the increased cost is because the license for bundled software—e.g., Microsoft Exchange and Microsoft SQL Server—is included and is less expensive than buying licenses for all of the different products individually. The CALs can be purchased either per device or per user.

The SBS operating system bundle provides small businesses with a cost-effective, complete solution, but it does have some disadvantages or limitations:

- Only one computer in a domain can be running Windows SBS 2003.
- Windows SBS 2003 is limited to 75 CALs (user or device).
- Windows SBS 2003 cannot be set up to trust any other domains.
- Windows SBS 2003 is limited to a maximum of 4GB of memory.
- Terminal Services can operate only in Remote Administration mode for a maximum of two concurrent connections at once.

While you may still be able to find licenses for Small Business Server 2003, we don't recommend deploying it on any new systems. This is an aged version of the server operating system. Small Business Server 2011 is the version you should consider for current needs.

Microsoft Windows Server 2003 Enterprise Edition

Microsoft Windows Server 2003 Enterprise Edition is aimed toward medium- to large-sized businesses that need a server that can provide enterprise-level features and service. Such cases would be when a client has applications that require more than 4GB to run.

Microsoft Server 2003 Enterprise Edition supports up to eight processors and up to 32GB of memory. Remember, Microsoft Windows Server 2003 Standard Edition and SBS support only up to four processors and 4GB of memory. The Enterprise operating system also provides Enterprise-class features, such as clustering using Microsoft Cluster Server (MSCS). This operating system is recommended for servers that will be hosting database applications, case management applications, or other software that requires large amounts of processing power and memory addressing—more than the Standard and SBS operating systems can support.

As with Small Business Server 2003, you may be able to find licenses for this version. However, we would not recommend utilizing this version of the server operating system at this time on any new system. Server 2008 is the current operating system of choice.

Microsoft Windows Server 2008 R2

Microsoft Windows Server 2008 R2 is the successor to Windows Server 2003 and was officially launched in late February 2008 and built from the same code base as Windows Vista. However, it is not the nightmare that Vista is.

This operating system includes a lot of new features and enhancements, such as native support for IPv6, new security features such as BitLocker, and an improved Windows Firewall with a more secure default configuration. Also, the manner in which this operating system handles processors and memory is different from previous versions. Processors and memory are now treated as plug-and-play devices, meaning they are "hot-swappable." They can now be removed and replaced without shutting down the server, although sticking your hands into a hot, running server is probably not a very bright idea.

Windows Server 2008 includes expanded Active Directory functionality and a major upgrade to Terminal Services. Terminal Services now supports Remote Desktop Protocol 7.0, which provides the ability to share a single application over a Remote Desktop connection rather than the entire desktop, as was the case in previous versions. It also provides additional support for stronger encryption algorithms for keeping data traffic secure as well as for multiple monitors.

In previous versions of the Windows operating system, if corruption or errors were found on a new technology file system (NTFS) volume, the volume would have to be dismounted and taken offline for the errors to be corrected. Windows Server 2008 supports a "self-healing" NTFS format that can detect and fix errors while online without having to bring down the entire system. Microsoft Windows Server 2008 is offered in both 32- and 64-bit versions.

Windows Server 2008, like previous versions, is offered in the following editions:

- Standard Edition
- Enterprise Edition
- Datacenter Edition
- HPC Server
- Web Server
- Storage Server
- Small Business Server
- Essential Business Server

Most of the editions listed above would not be considered when purchasing a server solution for a small business or law firm and will not be discussed in more detail in this book. However, the Standard, Enterprise, and Small Business Server editions are described below.

In February 2011, Microsoft released Service Pack 1 for Windows Server 2008 R2, which introduced two new features as well as addressing a number of security issues present in this version of the operating system. The two new features, RemoteFX and Dynamic Memory, add support for 3D graphics within a Hyper-V-based virtual machine, as well as dynamic memory allocation based on the resources required at the current time by the virtual machine. It is recommended that if you're running Windows Server 2008, you download and install Service Pack 1 as soon as possible.

Microsoft Windows Small Business Server 2008 Standard and Premium Editions

Windows Small Business Server (SBS) 2008 is based on Windows Server 2008 and includes Microsoft Exchange Server 2007 Standard Edition, Windows SharePoint Services 3.0, and trial subscriptions for Microsoft's new security products, such as Forefront Security for Exchange.

The SBS 2008 operating system was officially launched on November 12, 2008. Like previous editions of SBS, the 2008 version is offered in both Standard and Premium editions. The Standard Edition is regarded as a single server solution for small businesses, your all-in-one operating system. In one server, you get file and printer sharing, e-mail, and web hosting, and the ability to set up a domain for up to 75 users and/or devices. The Premium Edition contains all of the features and software that Standard Edition has, plus a license for the Microsoft SQL Server 2008 Standard

Edition. The Premium Edition requires two separate servers, one for Windows Server 2008 with Exchange and the other solely for SQL Server. This is going to be a problem for small firms on a tight budget, but it may be more affordable if used in a virtualized environment.

Windows SBS 2008 is offered only in a 64-bit version due to the requirements of Microsoft Exchange Server 2007, whose production version is 64-bit. This is an important distinction when considering your hardware purchase. Make sure you have 64-bit hardware if you are considering using these new server operating systems.

On a more positive note, Microsoft has finally changed the way CALs are purchased for SBS. In earlier editions, CALs could be purchased only in groups of 5, 10, or 20 licenses, but not anymore. CALs for SBS 2008 can now be purchased individually.

We still hold to our previous recommendation that Small Business Server 2011 be the current version that should be deployed in your firm. While you may find that licensing is slightly cheaper for the 2008 version, its life will be much shorter, and some of the current features will not exist.

Windows Server 2008 Standard Edition

The Windows Server 2008 Standard Edition was designed to increase the reliability of your server infrastructure, while simultaneously saving time and reducing costs when it comes to server maintenance.

Standard Edition comes with enhanced security features to help protect your data and network and includes powerful tools that give you greater network control. Windows Server 2008 Standard Edition comes with IIS 7.5, a powerful Web hosting and services platform. The operating system also includes Windows Server Hyper-V, virtualization software designed to support machine virtualization, and an upgraded version of Terminal Services that supports Remote Desktop Protocol 7.0.

In terms of security, Standard Edition includes tools to improve auditing, secure startup, and enable disk encryption using BitLocker. Standard Edition supports up to 32GB of memory, four multicore processors, and up to 250 concurrent Terminal Service connections.

Windows Server 2008 Enterprise Edition

Microsoft Windows Server 2008 Enterprise Edition, like its predecessor, is an operating system that is aimed toward medium-sized to large businesses looking for a server capable of handling enterprise-level services. Microsoft Server 2008 Enterprise Edition provides mission-critical applications through such features as failover clustering, fault-tolerant memory synchronization, and cross-file replication. This edition also features the latest advancements in security and is extremely scalable to support mission-critical applications.

This operating system is recommended for servers that will be hosting database applications, case management applications, or other software that requires more processing power and memory addressing than the Standard and SBS operating systems can support.

Microsoft Small Business Server 2011 Standard and Essentials

Microsoft Small Business Server 2011 (SBS 2011) is the successor to SBS 2008 and is offered in two versions: Standard and Essentials. A separate SBS Premium Add-on is available for small firms that require SQL Server.

The Standard edition is designed for small businesses and supports up to 75 users and/or devices. Like the previous versions, this edition provides a single server solution for small businesses that includes e-mail, remote access, and file and printer sharing. This edition includes both Microsoft Exchange Server 2010 and SharePoint Foundation Server 2010.

The Essentials edition is designed for small businesses and supports up to 25 users and/or devices. This edition is integrated with Microsoft's cloud services and doesn't require the end-user to purchase any CALs. This edition, unlike the Standard edition, doesn't include Microsoft Exchange Server or SharePoint Foundation Server 2010.

For those small businesses that need to deploy additional servers on their network to run SQL Server 2008 R2 Standard, the Premium Add-on license is the component that you'll need to purchase. Additional server and SQL CALs are required with this component and will add cost to the purchase depending on the number of users and computers needing to access this system.

X64 Operating Systems

Until recently, 32-bit processors dominated the commercial marketplace, and 64-bit processors were found only in supercomputers or very-high-end and expensive servers. Now, however, 64-bit processors are becoming more the standard rather than an option when configuring a server or a desktop computer to purchase. The 64-bit operating systems have been developed to run on these processors and offer many advantages over their 32-bit counterparts. In fact, some of the newer versions of Microsoft's server operating systems are offered only in 64-bit versions.

First, these systems process more data per clock cycle, and second, they offer direct access to more virtual and physical memory than 32-bit systems. These advantages provide for more scalable, higher performing computing solutions, which is a requirement when running a virtualized environment. There are far less device driver issues with X64 operating systems than previously, when 64-bit systems first appeared on the market; however, it's always important to make sure everything is compatible before migrating from a 32-bit environment to a 64-bit environment.

Microsoft Windows 2003/2008 Standard Edition and Enterprise Edition operating systems are both offered in 64-bit versions, as well as Windows Small Business Server 2008 and 2011.

Mac OS X Server "Leopard"

The Mac OS X Server 10.5 release, code-named Leopard, was released for Mac servers on October 26, 2007. OS X version 10.5 includes applications that allow administrators to more easily manage their users and computers, host websites and e-mail, and provides services such as file and printer sharing. The Mac OS X Server combines proprietary Apple applications and open-source technologies to provide administrators with a powerful tool set that rivals the features and functionality provided by Windows-based operating systems. The Mac OS X Server allows for groups of employees to collaborate and communicate through an internal Wiki website that comes complete with calendar, blog, and mailing list functionality. Users can create and edit their own Wiki pages, tag and upload files and materials, and have the ability to search.

Mac OS X Server "Snow Leopard"

The Mac OS X Server 10.6 replaced the Leopard version of the Mac OS X server operating system and included new features and software, such as iCal Server 2, Podcast Producer 2, and new Address Book server capabilities. The Snow Leopard operating system uses a 64-bit kernel, allowing for the support of greater amounts of memory and number of multicore processors. Also included is Mail for e-mail hosting services, Apache for hosting websites, and the Mobile Access Server to provide remote accessibility to clients.

Mac OS X Server "Lion"

In keeping with the tradition of releasing a new version of its server operating system in conjunction with its latest desktop operating system, Apple has released Mac OS X Server 10.7, code-named "Lion."

This new version includes an application called the Server app, which is a simplified configuration process for setting up and administering the most critical functions of the server, including file sharing, e-mail, contacts, backups, and remote access, to name a few. The new software also includes Apple's equivalent of Microsoft's Active Directory and a new feature that provides wireless file sharing for iPad devices that allows access to documents on the server.

Lion Server also includes updated versions of the iCal Server 3, Wiki Server 3, Mail Server 3, and Xsan software. This software requires a base purchase of OS X Lion from the Mac App Store and is actually purchased as an add-on or a bundled group of apps packaged and sold as Mac OS X Lion Server. The Lion Server is available from the Mac App Store for $49.99.

Linux-Based Operating Systems

Linux-based operating systems are similar to Unix-based operating systems and are built on an open-source kernel packaged with system utilities, software, and libraries. The underlying source code of the operating system can be freely modified, used, and redistributed and is supported by a community of programmers and volunteers.

Linux is now packaged for different uses, primarily servers, which contain modified kernels along with a variety of software packages tailored to different requirements. Some of the commercially available distributions that are backed by corporations are Fedora (Red Hat), SUSE Linux (Novell), Ubuntu (Canonical Ltd.), and Mandriva Linux. Each of these distributions has versions specifically designed and programmed to run on server-based hardware to provide management, web and e-mail hosting services, and file and printer sharing, along with other services and functionality that are available in both Mac- and Windows-based server operating systems. There are also desktop versions for each of these versions of Linux, which only hold a microscopic fraction of the desktop operating system market share.

Unless you're a serious technologist, you don't want to go anywhere near Linux-based operating systems.

CHAPTER NINE

Networking Hardware

NETWORKING HARDWARE TYPICALLY REFERS to equipment that allows network devices to communicate with one another, but not always. Some other types of networking hardware can include server racks, cabling, and other devices that help make up the computer network. Below, we provide descriptions and recommendations for the most common types of networking hardware that you will find and require in a solo or small firm computer network.

Switches

A switch is a piece of networking hardware that connects network segments (discrete sections of the network), allowing multiple devices to communicate with one another. For example, if two or more computers are connected into the same switch and are located within the same defined network, the switch will allow these devices to communicate. Switches inspect data packets as they are received and, based on the source and destination hardware addresses, will forward the data packet appropriately. By delivering the packet of information only to the device it was intended for, network bandwidth is preserved as well as confidentiality, and the information is delivered in a much quicker manner. In comparison, network hubs send the traffic to all ports, irrespective of the destination device, and are rarely seen in a production environment anymore. Unlike network hubs, switches are "intelligent" devices and can operate on more than one layer of the Open Systems Interconnection (OSI) model, such as a multilayer switch. Switches allow traffic to pass through them at speeds of 10 Mbps, 100 Mbps, 1 Gbps, or 10 Gbps, depending on the speeds of the ports.

The OSI model was created by the International Organization for Standardization as a way of subdividing a communications system into seven layers: Physical, Data Link, Network, Transport, Session, Presentation, and Application. We could write a whole book on the OSI model, but others already have.

Most solo and small law firms will not need expensive, high-end network switches for their computer infrastructure. In the majority of situations, a switch is needed only to connect computer workstations to the server and the Internet. NETGEAR offers reasonably priced switches in a variety of configurations to meet almost any solo or small firm need. The ProSafe Unmanaged Desktop series is a good choice for the solo or small law firm because of the low cost, ease of setup, and reliability. Setup of these devices requires no configuration—just plug in your network cables and you're off.

When purchasing a switch for your business, you will need to determine the number of connections or ports the switch will need. Next, you will have to determine the speeds of the ports that you will require. Will all of your computers need the ability to connect to the server at gigabyte speeds, or just a handful of devices? Remember, you certainly will pay more for a 48-port switch with 48 gigabit ports than if you bought a 48-port switch with only two gigabit ports and 46 10/100MB ports. The ProSafe Unmanaged Desktop Switches from NETGEAR can be found on its website at **www.netgear.com**.

NETGEAR
ProSafe Unmanaged
Desktop Switch

For those law firms that require or desire tighter security controls over their computer systems and users, a managed switch may be the solution. A managed switch, unlike an unmanaged switch, is a device that can be administered or controlled. Such advanced features include the ability to limit what computer systems can "talk" with one another at the physical level (private virtual LANs), advanced performance monitoring, and increased bandwidth control. These switches also support Quality of Service (QoS), which can be used to prioritize certain network traffic over other functions, such as if your firm is using VoIP phones. A good, cost-effective managed switch for small to medium-sized law firms is the ProSafe Gigabit Smart Switch from NETGEAR. This managed switch can be found on NETGEAR's website (**www.netgear.com**) starting at around $225.

NETGEAR ProSafe 24-Port
Gigabit Smart Switch

Entry-Level and Intermediate-Level Routers

A router is a computer-networking device that connects two or more independent networks together—e.g., your firm's local network to your Internet Service Provider's (ISP) network. A router's job is to determine the proper path for data to travel between the networks and to forward data packets to the next device along the path. Routers come in all shapes and sizes and with different features. For a solo or small firm, a basic router will be sufficient to connect the local network to the Internet, as well as to protect computers and other hardware devices on the local network from outside attacks. A basic router will require some configuration from the default values to get it configured and communicating with the ISP's network, as well as to strengthen the security and protection it provides to your information systems. Most basic routers are capable of handling only broadband Internet connections, such as cable or DSL. If your firm has a T-1 or any variant of this Internet connection, you will probably be provided with a router by your ISP.

There has been a lot of discussion recently, with the increasing number of data breaches, about what router a solo or small firm should use. Regardless of the router your firm chooses, it must have a built-in firewall and logging capabilities. There can be no exceptions.

Previously, for a basic routing solution for solo and small firms, we recommended a Linksys router. When configured correctly, this device can provide adequate protection for your firm's data and information systems. However, our recommendation has changed.

Today, the "bad guys" have gotten so good at breaking into law firms that it's becoming increasingly hard to keep them out. When they do get in, most law firms don't realize that they've been compromised until it's too late. Because of this, there is no entry-level routing solution that we can recommend with confidence anymore. You firm's data is just too valuable.

Given the types of information that your firm stores, such as Social Security numbers, credit cards, and possibly patient records, the only way to combat hackers and have a chance of keeping them out is through the implementation of a defense-in-depth security strategy. This type of information protection strategy provides security at all levels of your computer network, including at the point at which your local network interfaces with the public Internet. For this reason, even for a solo lawyer, we recommend the Cisco Secure Series line of routers.

The Cisco 500 Series Secure Routers provide high-performance connectivity for small businesses and include built-in threat defense, including a firewall and available Intrusion Prevention System (IPS), as well as content filtering to restrict a user's access to undesirable websites that may contain malware and phishing attacks. The Cisco 520W Secure Router offers a wireless option for those firms that require it. The Cisco 500 Series Secure Routers start at around $200. If you're considering purchasing the license for the IPS integration, then it might be worthwhile looking at an IPS/IDS device, described in the next section.

Cisco 500 Series Secure Routers

A Cisco device is a little more complicated to configure from the command line, although a graphic user interface (GUI) is available to assist those less familiar with the Cisco configuration syntax. Unless you are comfortable with the syntax of Cisco's IOS (yes, Apple used iOS after Cisco), we recommend that you not attempt to configure the device. Seek out the expertise of your IT professional or another resource that "speaks" Cisco's IOS language.

It's becoming harder to find a router for a small to medium-sized business that doesn't include wireless 802.11 capabilities. Be careful when purchasing these devices for your firm's computer network, as you may unintentionally open up your network to unwanted guests if your system is not configured properly. The majority of these devices come preconfigured with open, unsecured wireless networks. Make sure you consult with your IT vendor on best practices when implementing a wireless network for your law firm. And for heaven's sake, make sure all the default settings are changed. Even "script-kiddies" know all the default settings.

Firewalls/IDS/IPS Devices

An Intrusion Detection System (IDS) is used to detect many types of malicious network traffic and computer usage that can't be detected by a conventional firewall or router. These attacks include network attacks against vulnerable services (web hosting, e-mail, databases); data-driven attacks on applications; host-based attacks, such as privilege escalation; unauthorized logins; and access to sensitive files. Privilege escalation is the act of exploiting a known vulnerability in an application to gain access to resources that would have otherwise been protected. When used in combination with an Intrusion Prevention System (IPS), they also can detect and prevent malware such as viruses, Trojan horses, and worms from entering the network.

An IDS/IPS device is commonly placed at the gateway of the computer network so that all incoming and outgoing network traffic passes through it. This allows the device to scan all incoming traffic before it is passed on to the destination located on the local computer network, denying any malicious traffic the ability to enter. A firewall has the ability to permit or deny data traffic based on port number, originating or receiving Internet Protocol (IP) address, and protocol type, to name just a few capabilities, and it is usually based on rules that are set up and configured by an administrator. An IP address is a unique address or identifier assigned to a networked device, such as a computer, that allows the device to communicate with other networked devices. Just think of an IP address as being the same as a home address, which is a unique way to identify your home's physical location.

A firewall device with these described capabilities is critical for the protection and security of your firm's computer equipment and information systems. For those users that have a broadband Internet connection at home, a firewall should also be used to protect your home computer network from outside attacks. This is especially important for those lawyers who work from home, because you do not want your client's data to become compromised while working offsite. According to the Internet Storm Center, which is part of the SANS Institute, it takes only 20 minutes or less for an unprotected and unpatched computer connected to the Internet to become compromised. Imagine if that computer were yours and it contained confidential client data. This is the stuff of which nightmares are made.

For this reason, we recommend the Cisco ASA 5500 Series Adaptive-Security Appliance, which provides a good solution for solo and small firms looking to secure their local computer network from outside attacks. This appliance integrates a world-class firewall, unified communications (voice/video) security, SSL (Secure Socket Layer) and IPSec (Internet protocol security) VPN, intrusion prevention, and content security services into a single piece of hardware. By combining all of the functionality into one piece of network hardware, it eliminates the need to purchase a single device for each function. This saves time in both setup and configuration, eliminates complexity, and tremendously reduces the cost to adequately secure your business computer network.

The Cisco ASA 5500 Series provides intelligent threat defense and secure communications services that stop attacks before they affect your firm's business continuity. The firewall technology is built on the proven capabilities of the Cisco PIX family of security appliances, allowing valid traffic to flow in and out of the local network while keeping out unwelcome visitors. The URL and content-filtering technologies implemented by the device protect the business as well as the employees from the theft of confidential and proprietary information and help the business comply with federal regulations, such as HIPAA and Gramm-Leach-Bliley. The application control capabilities can limit peer-to-peer and instant-messaging traffic, which often lead to security vulnerabilities and the introduction of viruses and threats to the network. The implementation of a Cisco ASA 5000 Series device will deliver comprehensive, multilayer security to your computer network and will help you to sleep better at night knowing your electronic data and equipment are protected. The Cisco ASA 5500 Series Adaptive-Security Appliance can be purchased from Cisco Systems online at its website (**www.cisco.com**) or through a distributor.

The cost of the Cisco ASA 5500 Series device can range in the thousands of dollars, depending on the number of licenses, features, warranty, and support purchased with the product. When purchasing this device, we absolutely recommend that you get SmartNet maintenance. SmartNet allows you access to the excellent technical support personnel of Cisco, hardware replacement for failures, and upgrades to the device operating system. Make no mistake about it—this is an excellent, high-end firewall well worth the investment to protect your network and confidential information.

Cisco ASA 500 Series Adaptive Security Appliance Devices

Racks

A rack unit or enclosure is a piece of hardware that is used to store, organize, and secure your networking and computing equipment. Most often, rack units are used to hold rack-mount servers and network communication equipment such as firewalls and switches. There are many types of computer and networking hardware that are offered in rack-mount sizes due to the need to place and secure equipment within a single physical location. Rack units can be portable units mounted on caster wheels, bolted to the floor, or, if small enough, mounted on the wall. The amount of space that is available for the servers and networking equipment will greatly affect which type of rack to purchase. The leading manufacturers of rack units and enclosures are American Power Conversion (APC) and Chatsworth.

APC NetShelter SX enclosures are rack enclosures with advanced cooling, power distribution, and cable management for server and networking devices. The 19-inch rack is vendor neutral and is guaranteed to be compatible with all EIA-310 compliant 19-inch equipment, which covers nearly all rack-mountable equipment. The 19 inches refers to the horizontal distance between the mounting screws for the equipment. These enclosures offer large cable access slots in the roof to provide overhead cable egress, which is useful when cable runs come down through the ceiling. The bottom design allows for unobstructed cable access through a raised panel floor, which is common in network datacenters. The enclosures are well ventilated with perforated front and rear doors to provide ample ventilation for servers and other networking hardware that require unobstructed air flow to keep systems cool. The front and rear doors can be arranged to open in either direction, depending on the layout of the room.

The enclosure contains rear cable-management channels to assist in managing the plethora of cables the servers and network equipment require. The frame design of the NetShelter SX enclosures is made with heavy-gauge mounting rails and casters to provide support for up to 3,000 pounds of equipment. APC's NetShelter SX enclosures are offered in four different sizes and can be purchased with accessories, such as UPS battery backups, retractable keyboard, mouse pad, flip-down monitor, cable-management arms, additional fans, and power distribution centers. The APC NetShelter SX rack enclosures can be purchased online at its website (**www.apc.com**), and the basic enclosures start at around $1,500.

APC NetShelter SX Enclosure

Cabling

Now that you have all of your computer equipment selected and purchased, you will need to decide how to wire your data and voice network and what network patch cables should be purchased to connect your computers to the network drops (cables from the wall outlet to the hub/switch location). These patch cables come in various lengths and are primarily offered in two different types.

First, you have the category 5e cable, which is not the same as the generically termed Cat5 specification. Second, you have the category 6 cable, more commonly referred to as Cat6, along with category 7 cables used for networks requiring data transfer speeds of up to 10GB/s. Each type of cable has a different maximum throughput speed that it is capable of handling. As with computers, as time progresses, newer cable standards are developed that are capable of handling greater data transfer speeds.

The Cat6 standard cable is starting to become increasingly popular as more and more networking and computer devices operate and communicate at gigabit speeds. Current data transfer rates and applications operating at speeds of 1GB per second are starting to push the limits of category 5 cabling, although category 5e cable is rated for gigabit speeds but should be used with caution. The trends of the past and predictions for the future indicate that data rates have been doubling every 18 months. The category 6 cables offer double the amount of bandwidth capacity over category 5 cables and a better transmission performance. The category 6 cable provides a higher signal-to-noise ratio, allowing for higher reliability for current applications and higher data rates for the future. Analysts have indicated that the majority of all new wiring installations are using Cat6 cabling. This is a fairly easy decision, because all Cat6 cabling is backward compatible with Cat5e cabling.

Category 7 cabling is only commonly seen in data centers and is not yet widely used in local networks. If your firm is planning on wiring the office for data and voice, from a future perspective, it makes all the sense in the world to wire with Cat6 cabling. Remember, once the dust has settled from the construction, it would be extremely costly to have any type of cabling pulled out and replaced. The approximately 10 percent premium that you currently will pay for Cat6 cabling over Cat5e cabling is worth the added cost. As time goes on, the premium is getting smaller and smaller.

Wireless Networking Devices

A wireless networking device allows for communication between devices without being physically connected by wires or network cables. In a solo or small firm, if the investment cost to wire an office space with data cables is too expensive, a wireless solution may be the answer. Plus, who wants networking cables all over the place? This is particularly true in older properties—and may be aesthetically desirable in historic premises. A wireless network is extremely convenient for lawyers who use laptops, smartphones, or tablets because they can move from their office to the conference room with these devices and still stay connected to the local network and Internet. The cost to purchase a wireless networking device is extremely low, and the benefits gained are worth the small investment. However, do not implement a wireless network without taking the proper security precautions. By default, most wireless routers and access points are preconfigured not to enable encryption. This means that by default, all communications between computers and the wireless device are unencrypted and are not secure. How many people have connected their laptop to an unencrypted wireless network so that they could check their e-mail or perform online banking? We see this all the time—even at legal technology conferences!

Wireless networks should be set up with the proper security. First and foremost, encryption should be enabled on the wireless device. Most wireless devices come preconfigured with either an unencrypted network or a network encrypted using the wired equivalent privacy (WEP) 64- or 128-bit algorithm. Ultimately, neither of these solutions is adequate.

WEP is a weak encryption algorithm and can be cracked in a matter of minutes using open-source software. Do not use WEP.

Frankly, the Federal Trade Commission and the Canadian Privacy Commissioner have both found WEP encryption insufficient to secure credit card information, so we suggest it not be used at all. Some time ago, WPA using the TKIP (temporal key integrity protocol) algorithm was cracked by a group of Japanese scientists in about a minute. This means that you should be encrypting using WPA2 only.

If the wireless network is for the firm only, enable MAC (media access control) filtering on the wireless device. MAC filtering essentially limits the devices that may communicate with the wireless device. If the MAC address of a computer's wireless network card does not match an authorized MAC address, then the wireless device will not communicate with the unauthorized computer. This is an added layer of security. Most commonly, wireless routers and access points ship with default network names such as LINKSYS or NETGEAR. While in operation, these devices will broadcast their names so that wireless clients can locate the wireless networks. It is strongly recommended, for security reasons, that the default name of the wireless network be changed and that SSID (service set identifier, which is essentially the network name) broadcasting be disabled.

If your router doesn't come equipped with built-in wireless support, there are other wireless solutions available for the solo and small firm that provide reliable and secure network connections.

Linksys is a popular manufacturer of wireless networking devices for residential and small- to medium-sized businesses. Its products have only gotten better since the company was purchased by Cisco. The Linksys E3200 High-Performance Dual-Band N Router is an all-in-one Internet sharing router with a four-port switch. Although this router can be used to connect your local computer network to the Internet, it should be implemented as a wireless access point only in coordination with another firewall/IDS/IPS device. The 802.11n wireless standard protocol is used by this device and offers data transmission speeds up to 300 Mbps. This standard is about six times as fast as the 802.11g standard, which offered data transmission speeds up to 54 Mbps. One of the benefits of the 802.11n standard is that it is backward compatible with 802.11b/g devices. This router supports the latest wireless security encryption standards, such as WPA2, to keep your data communications secure. The Linksys E3200 High-Performance Dual-Band N Router can be purchased online from the Linksys website (**www.linksys.com**) or from your local electronics retailer for around $59.99.

Linksys E3200 High-Performance Dual-Band N Router

Wireless device manufacturers continue their push to get consumers to purchase their 802.11n wireless products. The 802.11n standard has finally been approved, so it's fine to purchase 802.11n products. Wireless networks that utilize the 802.11n standard will see an improvement in connection speeds and range beyond previous 802.11 standard connections. To utilize the new standard, all wireless devices will have to be 802.11n compatible; otherwise, the wireless network will only operate using the same standard as the "oldest" wireless device on your network. Further, to get transmission speeds as fast as advertised, you'll have to be relatively close to the access point, and only a limited amount of devices can be connected and using the wireless network at the same time.

CHAPTER TEN

Miscellaneous Hardware

ASIDE FROM ALL OF the computer hardware, software, and networking equipment, many other pieces of hardware deserve to be discussed. These can provide mobility, security, or functionality that would benefit a solo or small firm.

Fire Safe

A fire safe is an important and often overlooked piece of hardware to have in your office to protect your backup media, software licenses, and other valuables from destruction during a fire or other natural disaster. And don't put them in and leave the door open; it is astonishing how often we see this. Let the safe serve its purpose, and don't succumb to the temptation of convenience by leaving it open. Most come with a locking mechanism, so take advantage of the added security to protect your firm's information.

It is strongly recommended that you store backups, software licenses, copies of technical contracts with third parties, and other important documents in a fire safe. Purchasing a fire safe is a relatively inexpensive investment; they can be purchased from your local office supply store for a couple of hundred dollars. There are many sizes and shapes of fire safes, so you shouldn't have a problem finding one that suits your needs. The key specification is the rated internal temperature. The safe may be rated to keep the contents from burning, but it also needs to not damage the contents, such as melting the tape casing, which is why the internal rated temperature is important. If you keep important business records offsite

Miscellaneous Hardware

for redundancy, make sure that this information is stored in a fire safe as well. Your ability to recover from a disaster is only as good as the weakest point in the plan.

Battery Backup Devices

A battery backup device is an electronic device that supplies secondary power in the absence of main power, such as during a power outage. Battery backup devices can also protect electronic hardware from power spikes and dirty electricity. Battery backup devices come in all sizes and power capacities, and, depending on what devices you are looking to protect, this will affect the size and capacities you choose. APC is the leading manufacturer of battery backup devices used for protecting computers, servers, and other networking hardware.

It is strongly recommended that every computer within the local network be placed on a battery backup device, such as the APC Back-UPS 350. At our office, we have all of our computers, printers, routers, switches, phones, and voicemail system on battery backup devices to protect our hardware investment. This battery backup device will supply your computer with power for up to five minutes after an outage has occurred. During this time, the battery backup device will communicate with the APC software that comes bundled with the purchase of the device and will instruct the computer to shut down properly. The Back-UPS 350 supports up to 210 watts and has three NEMA 5-15R battery backup outlets and three NEMA 5-15R surge protection outlets.

Many computers and servers will experience software or hardware errors after a power outage because they did not have the opportunity to shut down properly—often referred to as a hard shutdown—which is a quick way to lose or corrupt your data. When computers and (horror of horrors) servers go down hard, the result is often not pretty. There is a great chance for data loss or system failure in the event of an outage. By purchasing battery backup devices for your computers and other electronic equipment, you are protecting your hardware and software investment and avoiding possible IT costs to correct all the problems that might ensue from a hard power-down. The APC Back-UPS 350 can be purchased from APC's website (**www.apc.com**) for $79.99.

APC Back-UPS 350

That takes care of battery backup devices for workstations and laptops, but what about servers? Servers require much more power to operate than a desktop or laptop computer. Therefore, they will require more battery capacity to allow them to operate during a power outage and/or the time necessary to properly shut down. On top of that, they take much longer to shut down properly than a workstation due to the greater number of services and processes constantly running on a server. The average server will take upward of 15 minutes to properly shut down, or more if the server is hosting multiple virtual machines, so supplying the server with enough power to accomplish this task is important. Certainly, you do not want your server to experience a hard shutdown, because the risk is great for data loss or hardware failure. Battery backup devices for servers can be purchased as a tower unit or rack mountable, depending on what your firm needs to support its server configuration.

The APC Smart-UPS 1500VA is an ideal battery backup solution to protect a single server from power outages, power spikes, or dirty electricity that can damage the server's internal hardware components. The Smart-UPS 1500VA is offered in both tower and rack-mountable forms and can supply the server with enough power to allow the server to shut down properly. Note that this unit has only enough capacity to supply power to one server and its peripheral devices. If there is a need to purchase a battery backup device for multiple servers, there are models with greater capacities that will be able to handle the load.

As with all batteries, someday they will need to be replaced. Happily, the batteries in these devices are hot-swappable, which means they can be replaced without the need to shut down the battery backup device or the devices connected to the unit. It is important to replace batteries as soon as they fail so that the systems connected to the battery backup device continue to be protected in the event of a power failure, and—trust us—you'll know when the battery needs to be replaced, because the beeping alarm is really loud. Replacement batteries for these devices can be purchased online from APC's website. Because the batteries in these units are replaceable, this is one hardware investment that you will not be replacing every one to two years. In our experience, these devices will always outlast the life of the computers, servers, or equipment connected to them.

The APC Smart-UPS 1500VA comes bundled with software that can be installed on the server itself to enable the battery backup device to communicate with the server. This is necessary so that, in the event of a power outage, the battery backup can alert the software installed on the server of the need to begin the shutdown process. The battery backup device connects to the server through a USB or serial cable. The APC Smart-UPS 1500VA can be purchased from APC's website for $579.

APC Smart-UPS Models

You can also purchase an optional network card for many of the larger UPS devices. The network card allows you to connect the communication over your data network and can support multiple servers. You configure the network card with an IP address, and the servers use the APC network shutdown software to "talk" to the UPS for status.

Fax Machines

Even though the need for fax machines has dwindled, they are still a staple in a law office and do get some use from time to time. Sometimes there just isn't enough time to scan a document and then e-mail it to a recipient, and instead the document will be faxed. We still see plenty of solos and small firms where there is no interest in learning how to scan. The fax machine is the devil they know, and they don't want to change. So even with all of the advancements in technology, the fax machine has a continued role. As previously stated, many digital copiers have fax transmission/receipt capabilities. Check with your vendor representative to see if using the copier is more cost-effective than purchasing a separate device.

If your firm is in the market for a fax machine, the device we recommend is the Brother IntelliFax-2920, which is a high-speed laser fax, phone, and copier. This model was designed for multiple users in a small business to easily share the benefits. Its design incorporates a high-capacity, front-loading paper tray that makes replenishing the paper an easy task that doesn't require a degree in engineering to accomplish.

The IntelliFax-2920 is equipped with 16MB of memory, allowing multiple faxes to be stored in memory for transmission when it senses the line is free. The 33.6 Kbps SuperG3 fax modem optimizes throughput transmitting as fast as two seconds per page. The front-loading paper tray has a 250-sheet capacity that is easily accessible and reduces time spent reloading paper. The paper tray can adjust to hold either letter- or legal-size paper. This fax machine also comes with a 30-page auto document feeder. Access to incoming faxes can be protected through the use of a password, ensuring that only the appropriate parties see confidential faxes. Finally, if your needs exceed or grow beyond just faxing and copying, this device comes with a USB interface and can serve as a laser printer capable of printing up to 15 pages per minute. This device comes with a standard one-year limited warranty. The Brother IntelliFax-2920 can be purchased online at Brother's website (**www.brother-usa.com**) for around $300.

Brother IntelliFax-2920

Backup Solutions

As hard drive sizes get larger and the volume of electronic data created increases, larger media is required to store the daily, weekly, and monthly backup files. Luckily, the days of having to purchase expensive tape drives, autoloaders, and media have long passed. The options for media to store backups have increased, while the cost for many of these viable options has decreased. Solo and small firms no longer need to purchase or implement an expensive backup system. Usually, a set of inexpensive external hard drives will do the trick. They offer more capacity than most tape media, are portable, have faster transfer rates, and are relatively inexpensive. And don't forget that you should keep at least one complete backup set offsite in the event that your entire office is lost—or inaccessible—during a disaster.

Depending on the backup solution that has been implemented, a lot of storage space may be necessary, especially if your firm has implemented a system where a full backup is run on a nightly basis. The Iomega Ultra-Max Plus adds secure, high-capacity storage to your computer system and is compatible with both PCs and Mac computers. It comes pre-formatted with the HFS+ file system, so if you're planning on using this device on a Microsoft Windows-based network, you will have to format the external hard drive NTFS or FAT32, depending on your requirements. The quad interface (eSATA, FireWire 800 and 400, and USB 2.0) allows the hard drive to deliver transfer rates up to 800 Mbps and can be connected to any computer or server that supports these types of connections.

The high-performance drive comes preconfigured in a RAID-0 hard disk configuration for higher data throughput, but it also can be configured in a RAID-1 hard disk configuration if you prefer. The RAID-1 hard disk configuration provides better fault tolerance, but you will lose half of the storage space for disk mirroring. Nevertheless, we recommend using a RAID-1 hard disk configuration when configuring the device to store your backup files so that there is some level of hardware redundancy.

The Iomega UltraMax Plus has a storage capacity of 2 or 4TBs, providing enough storage space for the average small to medium-sized firm backups. The hard drives are hot-swappable, allowing for business continuity and easy replacement should one of the drives fail. The unit also comes with a power adapter and connection cables to connect the device to a computer or server. If you have not yet purchased backup software, the device comes bundled with MozyHome Online backup software that can be installed and used on both a computer and a server to back up your system and data files. The device comes with a three-year limited warranty. The Iomega UltraMax Plus can be purchased online from Iomega's website (**www.iomega.com**) starting around $239.99 for the 2TB model and $349.99 for the 4TB version.

Iomega UltraMax Plus External Hard Drive

CHAPTER ELEVEN

Smartphones

SMARTPHONES HAVE BECOME THE number one tech accessory among lawyers. According to the most recent ABA Technology Survey, across the country, 88 percent of all lawyers now carry a smartphone, but only 78 percent of solo practitioners. It wasn't too long ago when a lawyer would carry two separate devices, a cell phone and a PDA. The cell phone was used to make phone calls and the PDA was used to keep your notes and calendar. Some even allowed you to view your e-mail, captured during your last synchronization with your work computer. Since that time, everything has changed. Smartphones are becoming more and more like laptops—able to perform almost every function a laptop can but at a fraction of the size. Because they have so many capabilities, lawyers in large firms regard them as a necessity—and that trend is moving downward to solos and small firms as well. Smartphones have become computers in and of themselves, with increasing functionality.

The smartphone debate has evolved into major warfare. Since its introduction and with its growing popularity, the Apple iPhone has grabbed huge market share, although things appear to be slowing down. There are now five major players for your smartphone business. The BlackBerry is no longer "the king of the hill." That honor now goes to Google's Android, with the iPhone now ahead of the BlackBerry. To show you how fast this world moves, we are now predicting the death of the BlackBerry. RIM (Research in Motion), BlackBerry's manufacturer, may have been lulled into inaction by its success, but the hot new technology clearly belongs to the Androids and the iPhones. The Windows Phone 7 phones are still around, but certainly not as popular. Finally, Symbian-based phones round out the fifth position. Those stats are for U.S. smartphone users.

In a 2011 ABA survey, RIM is still number one, followed by the iPhone, Android, Microsoft and then Symbian. We think the ABA results will line up with the U.S. statistics in the next year or two. The WebOS-based Palm Pre is also in there, but we haven't seen one of those in actual use for a very long time.

A key functional requirement for any smartphone is the ability to synchronize data with your computer or server. E-mail synchronization is at the top of all lawyers' lists, followed closely by calendar synchronization. The BlackBerry accomplishes this in one of two ways. The first way is to use a BlackBerry Enterprise Server (BES), which connects your mail server to the BlackBerry device. The requirement to purchase a BES made the overall implementation of a BlackBerry phone very expensive due to licensing cost and the installation of a specialized BES. RIM (Research in Motion, the maker of BlackBerry devices) has addressed this cost issue and now provides a BES Express for free. The BES Express can easily handle 75 phones (sometimes more) for no cost. BES Express doesn't have all of the hundreds of security and management options that the full-blown version contains, but the core functions are more than adequate for a solo or small firm environment. We currently run BES Express in our shop and have it configured for such items as requiring a password on the BlackBerry phone, encrypting the SD memory expansion card, wiping the phone after seven invalid password attempts, pushing our Public Folder contacts to each phone, autolocking the phone after a period of inactivity, etc. Data transmitted between the BES and the handheld is encrypted, protecting your confidential communications while in transit. Because of our disenchantment with the BlackBerry, you may find us on Androids in the next edition.

The Windows Phone 7 (previously known as Windows Mobile), iPhone and some Android phones synchronize with Microsoft Exchange servers via ActiveSync. This doesn't require any special hardware or software as the function is built natively into Exchange. However, there are limitations, such as no ability to synchronize with Public Folders over the air. You may have to purchase third-party products to get all of the features you need for over-the-air synchronization.

Not all small firms, especially solo practitioners, host their own e-mail. In this scenario, users retrieve e-mail directly from their ISP. BlackBerry users in this type of configuration typically install a desktop application to their computer to synchronize with their phone. This does require that the computer be left on and connected to the Internet, which can pose a potential security problem. The debate over which smartphone is better, more feature-rich, and compatible has been going on and probably will continue for years to come.

In 2010, Apple released its new version of the iPhone (iPhone 4), replacing the third-generation iPhone with a phone that contains a greater amount of memory, increased features and functionality, and encryption. Overall, this version of the iPhone was more business friendly. In October, 2011, Apple released the latest iPhone 4S and iOS 5. They include new functionality, including a new Voice Assistant, but do not include any announced security enhancements. Building on a strong consumer following from the earlier generation iPhone and looking to solidify its place in the smartphone marketplace, Apple continues to support Microsoft Exchange e-mail by licensing ActiveSync from Microsoft. The latest generations of the iPhone (3GS, 4, and 4S) are now "enterprise ready" and support over-the-air synchronization of e-mail, calendar, and contacts with a Microsoft Exchange Server; however, the phone natively lacks support for rich-document editing and creation, requiring users to purchase or download freely available third-party software to complete these tasks.

Apple iPhone 4S

Our continuing recommendation for any lawyer (or anybody wanting to keep his or her data secure) is not to use an iPhone. Apple has made all kinds of marketing claims, yet there are many examples of why an iPhone should not be trusted. On iPhones running certain versions of the Apple iOS firmware, the PIN keylock code is easily replaced by a "blank" code. The iPhone also claims to store its data in encrypted form. That is true, but with some versions of the iOS firmware you can place the phone in recovery mode and transfer the data to your computer. Apple conveniently decrypts the data as it sends it over the SSH connection, thereby negating the encryption scheme. You can remotely wipe the iPhone, but it needs to be connected to the cellular network to do it, unlike the BlackBerry and Windows Mobile phones. This only applies to iPhones on AT&T's network and not to the Verizon and Sprint iPhones. Not much has changed in the security model, or lack thereof, of Apple's iPhone devices. There still are security problems with the current generation of the devices. Within days of each new firmware version released, a new jailbreak method has been discovered, although it looks like iOS 4 held up better than its predecessors and iOS 5 is too new to tell. With all the security problems that have continued to plague the iPhone, we are still strongly against using the device for business purposes. We may change our recommendation if the PIN stays secured on the new generation iPhone without being hacked for a year or more since the iPhone 4 only lasted about six months before the PIN was cracked.

During 2011, Motorola Mobility released a series of Droid phones designed for business use. They include enhanced security and enterprise management capabilities, like encryption, support for virtual private networks, support for more ActiveSynch controls, and remote locking and wiping. In October 2011, shortly after Apple's release of the iPhone 4S and iOS 5, Google announced the release of version 4 of Android, called Ice Cream Sandwich. It includes on-device encryption, which required third party apps on earlier Android phones. The new Motorola phones and the release of version 4 make Android a strong contender for business and law firm use. As Android matures and continues to increase in popularity, it's very possible that it may become the smartphone of choice, even surpassing the iPhone among attorneys.

Motorola Droid Bionic

For those users looking for a smartphone recommendation, we strongly recommend migrating away from BlackBerry devices and investigating Android phones. A few years ago we converted the smartphones used at our office from Palm Treos running Windows Mobile to BlackBerrys. Aside from some minor problems we continue to have with the BlackBerry Enterprise Server (BES), we are happy that we made the switch. Our handheld smartphones, the BlackBerry Tours, are easy to use and manage. We've had no problems receiving our e-mails in a timely manner on the device from the BES server, and we love the convenience of having our Public Contacts readily available, although Public Folder Calendar entries must be manually synchronized as they will not sync over the air. As we move forward, we are going to keep a close eye on the progression of Android phones and the software required to centrally control and manage the devices, with an eye toward moving to the Android phones.

BlackBerry Torch 9850

The key message is that any Windows Phone 7–based phone or iPhone will provide immediate integration with your Exchange messaging server.

Some Androids provide immediate integration, while others require third party apps, like Nitro Desk's Touchdown. We recommend that you choose your wireless carrier first and then see what smartphones it provides and supports.

Over-the-air synchronization with Exchange Public Folders is a requested feature by many solo and small firm lawyers. You may require a third-party server implementation such as Goodlink to perform these functions. Good Technologies, Inc., makers of Good Mobile Messaging products, provides enterprise-level messaging and control for iPhone, Android, Windows Phone 7, Symbian, and PalmOS phones. Hosted versions of Good for Enterprise are available through the major cell carriers. Another alternative may be to install special software on your computer to synchronize with the Public Folders. Your computer must be powered up and logged into Outlook for the over-the-air synchronization to occur. As you can imagine, this is a potential security vulnerability and must be carefully considered and engineered, requiring a lot of administration by your IT provider.

On a side note, everyone is familiar with getting spam in their inboxes, but how about on your phone? Spam text messages can be costly, since most carriers will charge for both text messages sent and received. There is no anti-SMS-spam software available to install on cell phones to prevent receiving these messages, but there is a way to block cellular spam, and it's quite simple. The vast majority of spam text messages originate on the Internet and do not come from other cell phones. Why? Because spammers don't have to pay anything when using the Internet to send the text messages. Most carriers, led by AT&T and Verizon Wireless, offer spam-SMS-blocking features. To enable this feature, just log into your online account manager and the options should be available within your account profile. Sprint and T-Mobil currently only allow you to block SMS messages from certain phone numbers and addresses. What are you waiting for? We've signed up.

> AT&T (**mymessages.wireless.att.com**)
>
> Verizon Wireless (**vtext.com**)
>
> Sprint (**www.sprint.com**)
>
> T-Mobile (**www.t-mobile.com**)

Make sure you pay attention to smartphone updates and security notices, as the number of malware threats targeting smartphones have skyrocketed over the past year. Currently, Android devices are the most frequently targeted by malware due to their popularity, open-source operating system, the relatively lawless Android Market, and the availability of apps from multiple sources.

Even with the rising threat of malware, there are some basic steps you can take to protect yourself. First, make sure that when you're downloading an application, you do so only from the Android Market or App Store. Be sure when choosing an application to try or to purchase, you carefully read through the reviews. Also, pay attention to the access permissions that an app requests when you install it, especially on an Android device. Finally, vendors of security software are now offering antivirus and antimalware products for smartphones. This is software that you should seriously consider purchasing to protect your mobile devices, especially if they contain confidential information.

Basic security measures for any smartphone should include strong passwords or PINs, automatic logoff after a set time, encryption of the phone and storage cards, and remote wiping capability.

CHAPTER TWELVE

Productivity Software

HAVING WORKED WITH SO many solos and small law firms through the years, we know that lawyers are constantly striving to be more productive. We see that some lawyers still prefer to use Corel WordPerfect over Microsoft Word, but that number is continuing to drop.

Microsoft Word is what the business world uses and will continue to use for the foreseeable future. There are alternatives, but they all come with some degree of pain and a large learning curve. There are adherents of WordPerfect who are religious in their fervor and others who are evangelical in their admiration for open-source solutions. Whether you are a fan of Microsoft or not, the reality is that Word is the preferred application of the business world, and your clients will expect you to use it. They will not appreciate any conversion problems that may occur if you are using something else. In this section we detail the latest and greatest releases of productivity software that can help lawyers be more productive.

Microsoft Office

Microsoft Office 2010 is the most recent version of Microsoft's productivity suite and is the successor to Microsoft Office 2007. Microsoft Office 2010 contains an updated user interface and additional support for extended file formats, and is offered in a 64-bit version for some operating systems. One of the newest features included in Microsoft Outlook 2010 is the support for e-mail message threading. As technology advocates, we subscribe to a number of mailing and support lists. In prior versions of Microsoft Office, following a conversation thread was hard, and in most instances, nearly impossible. In the latest version, Microsoft Outlook will actually group all e-mail messages belonging to the message thread, regardless of where they exist within your mailbox. This setting can be customized on a per-folder basis.

Also new to the latest release is the debut of free online versions of Microsoft Word, Excel, PowerPoint, and OneNote, called Office Web Apps. The online versions work in all of the popular Internet browsers, including Internet Explorer, Mozilla Firefox, and Google Chrome. The ribbon interface is continued from the 2007 version and now exists in Outlook, too.

Microsoft appears to be listening to its customers and seems to be reducing the confusion about which Office suite to buy. Office 2010 is available in six versions, three of which are retail packages. The retail suites are Office Home and Student, Office Home and Business, and Office Professional. The costs are $149.99, $279.99, and $499.99, respectively, and Microsoft dropped upgrade licensing with the introduction of Office 2010. Volume license and qualified organization pricing is available for Office Standard, Office Professional Academic, and Office Professional Plus.

Also, still available and used less frequently is Microsoft Office 2007. The retail release of this product coincided with the release of Microsoft Vista back in late January of 2007. Microsoft Office 2007 is offered in eight different versions, with each of the different version suites described in the chart on the next page.

The majority of solo and small firms will require only the Small Business or Professional editions.

Microsoft Office 2007 contains many features, the most notable of which is the graphical user interface called Ribbon (except in Outlook 2007 Explorer), which replaced the standard menus and toolbars that we all grew accustomed to over the years. With the Ribbon, to get to the File menu, you click on an Office 2007 button. This has changed in Office 2010, where the File menu option has been restored. The Ribbon was designed to make features of the application more discoverable and accessible with fewer mouse clicks. Live Preview allows the user to temporarily apply formatting to an object and preview the appearance of the changes before actually applying them. The new Mini Toolbar is a menu that is displayed when text is selected. This toolbar provides access to the most commonly used formatting tools, thereby eliminating the need to right-click.

Microsoft Office

	Microsoft Office Basic 2007	Microsoft Office Home & Student 2007	Microsoft Office Standard 2007	Microsoft Office Small Business 2007	Microsoft Office Professional 2007	Microsoft Office Ultimate 2007 NEW!	Microsoft Office Professional Plus 2007	Microsoft Office Enterprise 2007 NEW!
Microsoft Office Word 2007	●	●	●	●	●	●	●	●
Microsoft Office Excel 2007	●	●	●	●	●	●	●	●
Microsoft Office PowerPoint 2007		●	●	●	●	●	●	●
Microsoft Office Outlook 2007	●	●					●	●
Microsoft Office Outlook 2007 with Business Contact Manager[1]				●	●	●		
Microsoft Office Accounting Express 2007[2]				●	●	●		
Microsoft Office Publisher 2007				●	●	●	●	●
Microsoft Office Access 2007					●	●	●	●
Microsoft Office InfoPath 2007						●	●	●
Microsoft Office Groove 2007						●		●
Microsoft Office OneNote 2007		●				●		●
Microsoft Office Communicator 2007[3]							●	●
Integrated Enterprise Content Management[4]						●	●	●
Integrated Electronic Forms[5]						●	●	●
Advanced Information Rights Management and Policy Capabilities[6]						●	●	●

One of the most important changes with Microsoft Office 2007 is the file format change. Microsoft Office 2007 uses a new file format called Office Open XML as the default file format. It is based on the XML and ZIP file formats and allows for documents created in this format to be 50 to 75 percent smaller in size than they would be if saved in the previous file formats used in older versions of Microsoft Office. Microsoft Office applications can be set up to save in formats previously used in older versions. For example, Microsoft Word 2007 can be configured to save document files using the .doc file extension rather than the new .docx extension. This allows users with older versions of the software to open and view documents created with Microsoft Word 2007. The same can be done for all of the Office programs.

If the default file format is not changed, users who have older versions of Microsoft Office will have to download a compatibility pack from Microsoft's website to open and view files created with Microsoft Office 2007 programs. This is the number-one complaint we hear from our non-Office 2007 clients. You may run into this problem if you receive an e-mail attachment that was created using Microsoft Word 2007 and you are currently using Microsoft Word 2000 or 2003. You can just Google "Office 2007 File Converters," or, to make things easier, you may download the compatibility pack at the following URL:

http://www.microsoft.com/downloads/details.aspx?FamilyId=941B3470-3AE9-4AEE-8F43-C6BB74CD1466&displaylang=en

If you're using Microsoft Office, be sure to check for software updates, which include bug fixes and security updates. To do this in Microsoft Office 2010, you can click on File, then Help, followed by Check For Updates. In Office 2007, you can click on the Office button, then select Word Options, open the Resources section, and click Check For Updates.

For those users looking for an automatic solution, you can use Microsoft's Update Center to automatically check for and install Office updates.

Corel Suite

WordPerfect Office X5 is the latest version of Corel's Office Suite and is available in both Standard and Professional editions for the business user. WordPerfect Office X5 was released in March 2010 and is the successor to WordPerfect Office X4. The components of WordPerfect Office X5 Standard Edition include:

- WordPerfect X5—word processor
- Quattro Pro X5—spreadsheet application
- Presentations X5—presentation/slideshow creator
- Lightning—digital notebook
- Mozilla Thunderbird—e-mail client
- Nuance PaperPort 12 SE—document manager

The Professional Edition also includes the Paradox database management program and the WordPerfect Office Software Development Kit, neither of which are included in the Standard Edition.

The Standard Edition would be the edition best suited for serving solo or small firm needs. Unless you are going to need to use a database application, there is no reason for a solo or small firm to invest in the Professional Edition. Some of the new features of Corel WordPerfect Office X5 include support for Microsoft Office OOXML and SharePoint. It also provides suite-wide PDF capabilities that will allow you to create documents, spreadsheets, and presentations in PDF format without spending hundreds of dollars on a license for Adobe Acrobat, although we highly recommend Acrobat 8, 9, or 10 Professional for a law office. An enhanced metadata-removal feature is included, which will allow you to remove hidden confidential information from your documents, as is a new redaction tool that allows you to replace sensitive and confidential information.

One of the touted advantages of WordPerfect over Microsoft Word is the Reveal Codes option, which allows users to manage documents formatting with a fine-tooth comb. We are constantly amazed when lawyers mention the reveal code "excuse." Perhaps they are unaware that Word 2007 and 2010 actually have a reveal code type display, where the user can see formatting codes. Service and support for Corel WordPerfect X5 is a bargain when compared to the costs of support for Microsoft Office 2007 or 2010. Users can request help via e-mail for free, and a toll-free support number is also provided, costing users only $20 per incident. For those who want to look for help themselves, Corel has a thorough online knowledge base that can be searched and reviewed for free.

Even with the new features included with WordPerfect Office X5, we still prefer the more seamless, although imperfect, Microsoft Office 2010. Corel has priced the software suite at a much-reduced cost when compared to Microsoft Office, particularly for business-friendly packages. Users who don't need all of the extensive features, however, might opt instead to use a product such as OpenOffice, which is free.

Corel WordPerfect Office X5 Standard Edition costs $179.99 for the full license and $129.99 for the upgrade license. Professional Edition costs $279.99 for the full license and $179.99 for the upgrade license.

Corel, like Microsoft, has released bug fixes and security patches for its WordPerfect Office suite. If you're using this product, you should download and install the latest update, which is Service Pack 2, from Corel's support website or from within the Office suite.

OpenOffice.org

OpenOffice.org (formally just OpenOffice) is a free, open-source software office suite that is available for many different operating systems, including Linux, Windows, and Mac OS X. The latest release of OpenOffice.org (version 3.3.0) was released in January 2011 and contains many features and functionality that are present in Microsoft Office and Corel WordPerfect Office. This suite was developed to reduce Microsoft Office's dominating market share by providing a free, open, and high-quality alternative.

OpenOffice.org can read and write most of the file formats found in Microsoft Office, including Office 2007/2010 file formats, which is important if you are going to choose to use a free utility for your productivity software. It also natively supports the standard OpenDocument file formats (ODF) and has the capability to read WordPerfect Office, Rich Text Format, Lotus, and other common productivity file types. The goal of OpenOffice version 3 was to provide the public with an office productivity suite that had improved performance, speed, less memory consumption, greater scripting capabilities, better interoperability with Microsoft Office, and improved overall usability.

The components of OpenOffice.org work closely together to provide the features expected from a modern office suite and include:

> Writer—word processor
>
> Calc—spreadsheet application
>
> Impress—presentation program
>
> Base—database program
>
> Draw—an editor used for drawing
>
> Math—allows for creating and editing mathematical formulas

All of the components of the OpenOffice.org suite look and feel like the corresponding components in Microsoft Office and Corel WordPerfect Office. Microsoft, seeing the need for and popularity of the open-source movement, has sponsored the development of a converter from Office Open XML to OpenDocument format and vice-versa. Microsoft and Corel have included add-in support for the ODF file format into their office suite products to allow reading and writing to the format.

However much we all grimace at Microsoft's domination, we do not recommend that you use OpenOffice.org as your primary productivity suite. Because it is developed and maintained by freelance programmers and other companies that make contributions to the project, such as IBM and Oracle, the software is not very well supported and may not contain all of the features provided by other productivity suites. In addition, most law office staff have never seen OpenOffice.org, so the learning curve would be pretty steep.

Some of the additional features supported in version 3 include:

- Personal Information Manager
- PDF import into Draw
- OOXML support for opening documents created in Microsoft Office 2007
- Extensions, to add third-party functionality
- Support for multiscreen presentations

The current release of OpenOffice.org can be downloaded from the website free of charge at **www.openoffice.org**.

Adobe Acrobat

Adobe Acrobat is a family of application software developed by Adobe Systems that uses portable document format (PDF) as its native file format. The PDF specification was originally a proprietary format but is now a published and approved ISO standard. The latest version of Adobe Acrobat (Acrobat X) was released in October 2010. Like its predecessor, Acrobat X continues to provide the ability to store and share files online by using the Adobe SendNow service. There is a free seven-day trial that has a maximum file size of 100MB, total storage of 500MB, and 100 downloads per file. There are two other subscription plans that start at $9.99 per month. Users can sign up at **acrobat.com**.

Acrobat X is packaged differently from the prior versions. There are three offerings for Acrobat X: Acrobat X Standard, Acrobat X Pro, and Acrobat X Suite. The Acrobat X family builds upon the features of the previous versions. The feature comparisons can be viewed at **http://www.adobe.com/products/acrobat/matrix.html**. We would still recommend that you purchase the Pro version for the redaction, metadata removal, and Bates numbering capabilities.

The redaction and metadata removal tools can help mitigate the risk of unintended disclosure of information while submitting legal documents to clients, opposing counsel, or the courts. Bates numbering is a method of applying identifying labels to a set of related documents, where each page is assigned a sequential Bates number that uniquely identifies it while also establishing its relationship to other Bates-numbered pages.

Acrobat X Pro contains some cool features that we're sure you'll take advantage of:

- PDF to Word
- PDF Portfolios
- Rich Media
- Action Wizard
- Version Comparison
- Extending Reader Functionality
- Streamlined Document Reviews
- Interactive PDF Forms
- Permanent Information Removal
- Standards Support (PDF/A, PDF/E & PDF/X)
- Online File Sharing

Adobe Acrobat X allows you to combine multiple documents to create an Adobe PDF package while retaining the properties of the individual documents. Using an Adobe PDF package, legal professionals can associate related project or client files, while individual files in the package can be encrypted, digitally signed, rearranged, removed, or added so that each recipient of the package can read or access only the relevant files that he or she has permission to view.

Security has been a big concern for Adobe for the past year. In an effort to minimize the impact to a user's system, Adobe has concentrated on reducing future vulnerability. A quote from Adobe:

The Acrobat X Family of products delivers better application security on all platforms as a result of continuing code hardening work, additional administration capabilities that provide more granular control over the execution of JavaScript, tighter integration with the Microsoft® Windows® security architecture, and other best practices in secure software development, following the Adobe Secure Product Lifecycle (SPLC) methodology.

The Adobe Reader X PDF viewer has a Protected Mode to limit the level of access to a user's system. Effectively, this is a "sandbox" type of environment, reducing the potential security threats on a client system via persistent malware.

We've assembled what we would call the top 15 highlights of the new Acrobat X release.

1. SharePoint integration
2. Office 2010 compatible (single click PDF)
3. New user interface
4. Improved enterprise deployment
5. New PDF Portfolio Wizard
6. Customizable PDF Portfolios
7. Export to Word, Excel, PowerPoint and Access
8. Automation of common tasks
9. Improved OCR
10. Adobe Reader Protected Mode Security
11. Quick Tools for frequently used commands
12. New PDF reading mode
13. Unified tool for markup and comments
14. New Acrobat X Suite for dealing with multimedia
15. Improved browser integration

Even with some of the new features, Acrobat X doesn't excite us as much as version 8 did. Here is our recommendation: If you currently are using Adobe Acrobat 7.0 or earlier, then the upgrade to Acrobat X Pro is a must. The software contains added features for legal professionals that were not available in earlier versions of Acrobat, and those features alone are worth the purchase. If you are a user of Acrobat 8 or 9 Professional, stay with your current version unless you want to take advantage of some of the highlighted features mentioned above.

Adobe Acrobat X Pro can be purchased online from Adobe's website (**www.adobe.com**) or from your local electronics store for $449 for the full version, which is the same price as the 9 Professional version. The upgrade price is $199, which is a $40 increase from the previous upgrade pricing.

We have discovered a little "trick" for obtaining Adobe Acrobat X Pro for a much lower price if you don't own any version of Acrobat (or one prior to version 7). Search the Internet and purchase a copy of Adobe Acrobat 7 Standard (eBay is a great resource). The last time we checked, you should be able to get a copy for between $30 and $70. Then go to Adobe's site and buy the upgrade to Acrobat X Pro for $199. This means that you will pay no more than $269 for a $450 product. What a deal!

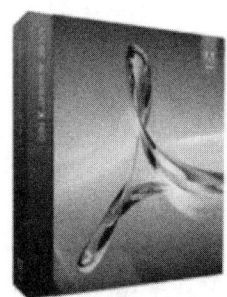

Adobe Acrobat X Professional Edition

Adobe, like other vendors, frequently releases security patches and updates for its products. By default, Adobe Acrobat X products check for updates automatically. If you'd like to check for updates manually, you may do so from within the Help menu listing of your Adobe product.

OCR Software

Optical character recognition (OCR) software translates graphical images into editable text. This capability is used most commonly to edit a scanned document or image. It's widely used in law firms to convert scanned paper documents in a case file to searchable electronic files. OCR software will translate the image to editable text, such as a Microsoft Word document.

OmniPage Professional 18, by Nuance Communications, Inc., is an OCR software product enabling the conversion of paper documents and TIFF files to a text-based format for amending as needed with prominent business communications software. OmniPage Professional 18 can convert scanned images to Microsoft Word, Excel, Corel WordPerfect, Lotus 123, e-mail, and HTML. The program generates a formatted text document that preserves the layout format, character, font, and style of the scanned image. This software boasts a 50 percent greater accuracy rate than its competitors when converting, and the updated recognition dictionaries for financial, legal, and medical specialties allow for legal-specific word recognition, which means that you will spend less time editing your legal documents.

OmniPage supports data capture from a digital camera. The software can "read" a digital photograph, which may come in handy for lawyers who use photographs as exhibits. This software is the first OCR application designed for the multicore-processor computer, taking advantage of hyperthreading to increase the conversion speed of documents. It also is the first OCR software to support Microsoft Office 2007/2010 native formats. When converting legal documents, OmniPage now has a greater ability to recognize formatting such as line numbers, Bates stamps, signatures, and more.

Some of the other new features included in OmniPage Professional 8 worth mentioning include the ability to convert a scanned document into a readable format and send it to an Amazon Kindle electronic book reader and a "one click" toolbar in the Microsoft Office Suite that allows for document conversion with a simple click and a faster load time than previous versions.

Also new in the latest version of OmniPage is the eDiscovery Assistant for searchable PDFs. eDiscovery Assistant provides the ability to safely convert a single PDF or batches of PDFs of all types into searchable documents without having to open PDF files one by one, giving the user greater flexibility when applying an OCR process to an entire group of documents.

As more and more firms look to utilize the features the Internet cloud provides, so do vendors. OmniPage includes the Nuance Cloud Connector application, which integrates with Evernote and Dropbox. The Cloud Connector also provides access to a number of cloud services, including Microsoft Live SkyDrive, GoogleDocs, Box.net, and more, allowing for users to scan and/or save their documents to the cloud.

OmniPage Professional 18 can be purchased online from Nuance's website (**www.nuance.com**) for $499.99 for the full version and $199.99 for the upgrade version.

Adobe Acrobat includes an OCR engine, too. We recommend purchasing Adobe Acrobat first to see if it meets your OCR needs before expending funds on another product like OmniPage.

Nuance OmniPage Professional 18

Voice Recognition Software

Arguably one of the biggest recent advances in productivity software is the continuing refinement of voice recognition software. Dragon Naturally Speaking 11.5 by Nuance (**www.nuance.com**) has finally made voice recognition software a respectable addition to your productivity arsenal. Many solos and small firm lawyers are now using Dragon as their primary composition tool. This is especially valuable for those who are not very accurate or fast typists. It takes only a short period of time to train Dragon to your voice, and its accuracy is astonishing. Nuance claims that version 11 is 35 percent more accurate than version 9, which is still a darn good product.

A key component to the success of voice recognition is the use of a good quality USB microphone headset. We have had great success using a Plantronics 510 headset/microphone system, but they are no longer manufactured. The Plantronics Audio 626 DSP is available for $40 from the Plantronics website (**www.plantronics.com**) and should be an excellent replacement for the older 510 model. The lightweight headphones with noise-canceling microphone connect to your computer using a standard USB connection.

Dragon can be used to compose e-mail messages, draft documents in your word processor, and even launch software applications without touching the keyboard or mouse. The software now allows users to search the Web and their computers through the use of voice shortcuts.

The latest version also provides users the ability to post to Facebook and Twitter by voice along with new formatting and editing commands, and even allows users to use their iPhone or iPad as a wireless microphone, untethering them from their computer.

This is a great tool for handicapped individuals and is used by many with disabilities. But make no mistake—this is a mainstream product, and the able-bodied are moving to this technology in hordes!

Dragon Naturally Speaking comes in several versions. We recommend using the Legal or Professional versions if you can afford it (it carries a $799.99 price tag). The Legal version contains vocabulary specific to the legal profession. The Professional version is a higher-end package that allows for roaming user profiles and allows multiple custom dictionaries. The Professional version costs $599.99 and may be purchased from many online stores. The Premium package costs around $200 for physical shipment of media, $179.99 for digital download, and may be a good alternative for some lawyers, as it also supports digital recording devices, smart formatting, and text-to-speech. Dragon Naturally Speaking 11.5 is licensed on a per-user basis. You can install and run it on multiple computers, but you need a license for each user's voice file.

The most important tip about using voice recognition software is to proof any output from Dragon. The speech-to-text is very good, and it "learns" and improves with time, but it's not perfect, either. Make sure you proofread your documents, especially those that may be submitted to a court.

If you use Dragon on multiple computers, make sure you know how to move your voice files among machines. This will save on the "retraining" time when you use several computers. The process is most appropriate for those lawyers who use a computer at home and one at the office. Moving the voice files between the machines allows you to take advantage of the aggregate training time instead of each machine being seen as a stand-alone operation.

Dragon Naturally Speaking 11.5 Legal Edition

CHAPTER THIRTEEN

Security Software

COMBINED WITH NETWORK FIREWALLS or IDS devices, security software provides another line of protection in the defense-in-depth information security strategy against malware, including viruses, Trojan horses, and worms. The defense-in-depth approach to securing your network is the best practice to keeping your systems safe from both internal and external threats. These threats can be extremely harmful to a corporate network and very costly to remove once an infection has occurred, assuming you've been able to identify that a breach or infection has occurred. Even in a solo or small firm network, your client data is of the utmost importance, and securing your computers, servers, smartphones, and information should be taken very seriously. Below, the top security protection suites providing antivirus, antispyware, and antispam protection for stand-alone computers and networks are discussed with recommendations regarding the setup and configuration of the software.

Stand-Alone

The software selections described in the stand-alone section are primarily for the computers and laptops of solo practitioners.

We are no longer recommending stand-alone products for targeted protection, such as antivirus. The Internet security suites are the way to go, where you get much more functionality and protection for your computer at a much more affordable price.

Solos and small firms should definitely consider acquiring a single integrated product to deal with spam, viruses, and malware. Norton's security suite is a top seller for the single computer market, but we highly recommend avoiding the Symantec Norton Internet Security 2011 software. We continue to find it to be a heavy load on computer processing, and it causes stability problems with many programs. It is also hard to remove once installed without causing further damage to your system. The same holds true for McAfee. We continue to remove McAfee from our clients' computers because of performance issues. Maybe it's our bad luck, but Symantec and McAfee seem to cause our clients the biggest headaches.

For those users who want avoid all of the problems caused by Norton and McAfee, we recommend using Kaspersky Internet Security 2012. This product contains firewall, antivirus, antispyware, rootkit detection, antispam protection, and much more. The included firewall with this software provides two-way protection, scanning both incoming and outgoing network traffic. Kaspersky is available directly from **www.kaspersky.com** and costs $79.95 for one-year protection on up to three computers. This is an excellent choice for the small firm environment.

Kaspersky Internet Security 2012

Enterprise Versions

Enterprise versions of integrated security solutions are designed for small, medium, and large computer networks, and the software administration is performed from the server. The client software is installed or pushed from the server to the local workstations. The server supplies the clients with program and definition updates and will provide an interface to centrally manage all clients from a single location. Of course, enterprise licenses are a little bit more costly than purchasing a single license, but not by much. Even with the slight increase in cost for an Enterprise license, you'll more than make up for it on the money you will not have to pay your IT consultant to manage and support the product.

Integrated Security Solutions
Kaspersky Business Space Security protects both Windows, Novell NetWare, and Linux-based servers (including 64-bit versions) from all types of mali-

cious programs and threats. The product provides protection from threats such as viruses, Trojans, worms, keyloggers, malware, rootkits, bots, etc. This is a new direction that we are seeing in the security product market. Former providers of antivirus software are beginning to provide protection from spyware and other malware, offering a more complete security solution to their business customers and all but eliminating the need for multiple applications to protect your systems from viruses and malware. This software provides real-time protection by scanning all files that are opened and quarantining infected files. The application can scan specified areas of the file system based on preconfigured scheduled scans or upon demand from the administrator. The scanning of critical system areas such as running processes and startup objects helps prevent malicious code from launching.

Kaspersky Business Space Security software is a scalable security solution, allowing administrators to define the number of instances of the program they would like to run simultaneously to accelerate the processing of server requests. The software offers flexible administration through centralized installation and control. The administration tool can be used to centrally install and manage client applications and to push updates to the clients once they are downloaded and installed for rapid deployment of critical security updates.

Kaspersky Business Space Security, similar to other integrated security solutions, scans not only for viruses but also for other threats and malicious programs, such as spyware and key loggers. In most instances, this solution can serve multiple functions. We use this security solution on our network systems to provide us with antivirus and antispyware protection. By using an integrated solution that is capable of handling both antivirus and antispyware protection, that is one less product we have to purchase and renew on a yearly basis. The product also allows for different configuration settings depending on the type of network your computer system is currently connected to, similar to the way Microsoft Windows 7 handles the different firewall settings.

As the security of smartphones is brought to the public's attention, more vendors are integrating smartphone security with their products. Kaspersky is no different. Kaspersky Business Space Security offers to protect smartphones from data leaks, malware, and viruses, and also allows an administrator to remotely lock and wipe the device should it be misplaced, stolen, or lost. Currently, Symbian, BlackBerry, Android, and Windows Mobile smartphones are supported.

There is a 10-license minimum purchase for Kaspersky Business Space Security software. Cost for the product begins at $39 per license and includes technical support and upgrades for a year. Kaspersky is priced much lower per license than its competition and is an affordable, complete security solution that is rapidly taking over the market. This software product is offered for purchase with one-, two-, and three-year subscriptions. Licenses can be obtained directly from Kaspersky's website (**www.kaspersky.com**) or from an authorized reseller.

Besides Kaspersky, we also recommend using the enterprise product from Trend Micro. Symantec has fallen from favor, especially since the introduction of their Symantec Endpoint Protection product. We have been diverting clients away from Symantec because of significant performance and stability problems. Worst-case situations include servers going into deadlock conditions for absolutely no reason. Miraculously, the servers function properly after Symantec is uninstalled. We have had so many bad experiences with Symantec over the last several years and such a pleasant experience using Kaspersky that it will be several more years before we even attempt to use Symantec's product again.

Trend Micro Worry-Free Business Security is a highly regarded product that is available in three editions: Advanced, Standard, and Services. We don't recommend the Services solution, as the entire configuration is set up and maintained by Trend Micro as a hosted solution.

All of the editions include antivirus and antispyware capabilities. The software will protect both servers and computers from malicious threats and will automatically change settings on laptops to set for protection of employees when they are out of the office. The software will monitor active processes and applications to prevent unauthorized and harmful changes to your computer. Unlike the Standard Edition, the Advanced Edition includes antispam filtering for Microsoft Exchange Servers as well as multilayered spam protection. Cost for the product starts at around $33 per license for the Standard Edition and $60 per license for the Advanced Edition, which includes technical support and upgrades for a year. This software product is offered in one-, two-, and three-year subscriptions, and licenses can be purchased directly from Trend Micro's website (**www.trendmicro.com**).

Antispam Protection

We have come to use and love a better product for antispam protection as opposed to a product that is locally installed. Postini is a lower-cost alternative service for e-mail antispam and antivirus without any of the headaches that come along with other products. Note that your e-mail flow will be rerouted so that it goes through the Postini servers before being delivered to your mail server or e-mail client. You can purchase the Postini service directly or through a reseller. When you purchase directly, the costs are lower, but you have to configure and set up the installation yourself and do not receive any support. Purchasing through a reseller costs slightly more, but you obtain 24/7 support and assistance with the complete operation. Postini provides a Web-based interface to manage the quarantine, where spam messages are held. Users receive a quarantine message once a day, in which they are provided with a summary of the e-mail messages quarantined throughout the day. From this message, a user can choose to release a quarantined message with just a simple click of the mouse. That's all you need to do to release a captured "false-positive."

Postini has a very good reputation for quality service, and clients seem to be very happy with it. Since we started using Postini a few years ago, most of our clients have switched as well, and the feedback continues to be excellent.

CHAPTER FOURTEEN

Case Management

IF YOU STILL LIVE in the paper world, you may not know that a case management application would provide all of the functions that you are probably currently performing. You use a Rolodex or some other type of method to aggregate your contact information. You have a calendar to schedule events. You have a file for each client or each client matter. We hope you use a word processor—or at least your secretary does—to generate documents. You track what you do for each client matter. You probably even generate some sort of status concerning each matter. These are all functions of a case management system.

Even in a world full of smartphones and wireless devices, it just amazes us that most solo and small firm lawyers still don't use a computerized case management software application. Case management is a must-have for today's modern law office. You may have heard other terms that describe the same type of software. Vendors attempt to differentiate themselves by describing their products with different names. You may hear descriptions such as practice management, contact management, litigation management, and so forth. Bottom line: They are all case management products, though they vary greatly in functionality. Arguably, the term "practice management" is more inclusive and encompasses what is termed "front office" (case/client information) and "back office" (accounting and billing).

There are several choices for case management, some of which we will cover here. The features vary by manufacturer, so make sure you understand what you're buying. Probably the feature we are asked about most is the integration of e-mail and contacts with case management. Make sure that the product will work with your e-mail system and that you understand how it needs to be configured. The synchronization is getting better, but most of our clients are less than impressed with many of the implementations of synchronization support. For example, how does the software deal with a common firmwide Public Folder Calendar? Will the product synchronize with your PDA or smartphone? What if you don't have an Exchange server and use hosted Exchange services? Can you still synchronize with a hosted Exchange environment? What e-mail clients are supported?

There are two mistakes that we consistently see when firms decide to implement a case management system. The first mistake is the failure to require everyone in the firm to use the system. You will not realize the full return on your investment if only a few employees use it. In fact, it tends to cause a whole new set of problems, because sometimes there is crossover between lawyers and cases, and some operate within the case management system and some don't. The second most common mistake is the failure to invest in training. Training will allow all employees to fully utilize the features of the case management system, thereby becoming more efficient and properly organizing all data for a client matter. Simply dumping a case management system into a firm is worse than useless. When you price the software, price the training as well.

As with other sections of this book, we cannot mention or address every case management package or every feature of every product. We mention the most popular and widely used case management packages that we see being used among solos and small firms. If you need more detailed information and advice on which product to purchase, get a copy of *The Lawyer's Guide to Practice Management Systems Software,* by Andy Adkins, which is available at the ABA Web store. This is an excellent and comprehensive guide to case/practice management programs.

Amicus Attorney

Amicus Attorney (**www.amicusattorney.com**) is a good small firm package that provides a fairly simple approach to case management. The technical requirements are very reasonable and don't require a huge and expensive computer to run. There are essentially two versions available. The 2011 Small Firm Edition should work for most solo and small law firms. It is limited to a maximum of 10 users. The pricing has not changed in the last three years and remains at $499 for the first user license and $399 for each additional license.

The 2011 Premium Edition uses SQL Server 2008 to achieve unlimited user and unlimited data access. The good news is that the Premium Edition includes the required SQL Client Access Licenses (CALs) for SQL Server 2008 Standard Edition Runtime for use with Amicus Attorney, so you don't have to make a separate purchase. However, these CALs are only for Amicus Attorney and can't be used with other products.

For very large-scale installations, a separate SQL server is recommended. Certainly a consideration is the cost for the SQL Server software and the hardware to run it on, which can add a hefty price to the implementation costs. Another improvement over prior years' versions is the support for 64-bit versions of the operating system and SQL server. The big price hike took place last year and remains unchanged for now. The first user license for the premium edition costs $999 and each additional user is $599, which is the same as last year's pricing.

If you are a true road warrior, then consider getting Amicus Mobile 2011, which works on your Windows Mobile (version 5, 6, or 6.5—Note: No support for Windows Phone 7) or BlackBerry (Style 9670, Torch 9800, Tour 9630, Storm2 9500 series, Bold 9700/9000 series/9650, Curve 8300/8500/8900/9300, Pearl 9100/8200/8100 series, 8800 series, 8700r/8703e model) smartphones. You'll need to purchase the Mobile server for $499, which is the same cost as last year. The Mobile server is a web server and must be accessible from outside your network via a public IP address. This means you'll have to open up your firewall to all the remote connections. Each device will also need a $149 license to run Amicus Mobile. This is also the same cost as last year. Amicus Mobile uses ActiveSync (Windows Mobile) or the BlackBerry connection services (e.g., BlackBerry Enterprise Server or BlackBerry Internet Service) to achieve real-time, over-the-air synchronization between your phone and the Amicus Attorney Premium Edition. The Amicus Mobile add-on is not available for the 2011 Small Firm Edition. If you need to access Amicus via your smartphone, you'll have to pony up the additional bucks and hardware to run the Premium Edition. As you can see, running this add-on can get really pricey.

A trial version of Amicus Attorney is available and highly recommended if you are considering purchase. Try the product first to make sure that it meets your needs and will work in your computing environment. Amicus Attorney is often mentioned in reviews as being the most "user-friendly" product, probably because of the graphic representation it uses as the interface.

Time Matters

LexisNexis has a couple of offerings suitable for the solo and small firm market. Time Matters (**www.timematters.com**) used to be the most popular case management package for solo and small firms, but we are continuing to see lawyers jumping ship at a rapid rate just as in prior years. Over the last several years, we have replaced Time Matters for our clients and have yet to do a single new installation. Time Matters is a very powerful case management application, but it can also be fairly complicated for many small firm lawyers. It is an absolute necessity to purchase training if you are considering implementing Time Matters in your firm. The learning curve is steep but well worth it, because Time Matters is truly a feature-rich program.

The current version is Time Matters 11, which now includes a Mobility service to keep you connected via your smartphone. A dedicated server is recommended for the installation of Time Matters. This significantly increases implementation costs for the solo and small firm lawyer, but does provide for a larger and more robust case management application. Licensing for Time Matters is based on concurrent users. Time Matters 11 starts at $950 for the first user and includes a maintenance plan for the first year. Additional new users are priced at $550 each, including maintenance. Other pricing options depend on the number of users, add-on features, custom training, or support needed for your firm.

Perhaps this new pricing model is why we haven't seen any solo or small firm lawyers implement Time Matters over the last several years. In our geographic area, it appears that more users are choosing PracticeMaster as their case management environment. In fact, they are actually abandoning Time Matters altogether. Perhaps the pressure to purchase maintenance contracts, poor technical support, and the rapidly rising costs of licensing are reasons to choose other products. The steady erosion of the Time Matters client base has caused a lot of concern, as have heavy-handed tactics from LexisNexis in selling support for the product. Some consultants are predicting the eventual demise of Time Matters, feeling that LexisNexis has really mishandled what was an excellent product.

PracticeMaster

A highly rated case management application (and our personal favorite) is PracticeMaster by STI (**www.practicemaster.com**), which is the choice among most solo and small firms in our area. Version 16 was newly released in early 2011 and contains some significant new features. PracticeMaster comes in three versions: Basic Edition, Premier Edition, and the newly named Platinum Version, which was previously known as the Client Server Version (CSV). The first license for PracticeMaster Basic Edition is already included if you have the Tabs3 billing software. The Basic Edition is just that—basic. The Premier Edition contains a number of useful features that most lawyers would desire. You can view the comparison chart at **www.tabs3.com/products/practicemaster/pm_comparison.html**.

PracticeMaster introduced workflows with version 16. Workflows are essentially triggers that automate tasks within the software. In addition, PracticeMaster has one of the best e-mail integration schemes that we've seen. Smartphone support is excellent as well.

PracticeMaster Basic costs $150 for the first user license. Each additional user license is $95. PracticeMaster Premier costs $395 for the first user license, and each additional license will set you back another $195. Pricing has gone up for this version, which is certainly justified given the value of the additional new features.

In addition to the two versions mentioned, STI offers PracticeMaster in a client server version, which scales to larger implementations. The Premier Platinum edition costs $890 for the first user license and $250 for each additional user. Don't forget to add the cost of the client server environment when calculating the total cost of the project. As an example, the Platinum Server Software is required for any client server implementation of Tabs3 or PracticeMaster. This Server Software could cost from $745 for eight connections up to $5,795 for 1,024 server connections. This product is consistently well reviewed and making tremendous inroads.

Finally, it is highly recommended that you obtain the trial version of PracticeMaster. This will help you determine whether the product is right for your practice and your installed infrastructure. We don't think you can go wrong with this product, especially since it has won the top honor for the eighth consecutive year in the 2011 *Law Technology News* Awards.

Clio

Clio (**www.goclio.com**) is another SaaS solution that is targeted to the solo and small firm market. Themis Solutions, the makers of Clio, is based in Vancouver, BC and has a very loyal Canadian following and has many US users as well. Themis Solutions listens to their customers and is constantly enhancing Clio based on suggestions from the users. A key capability is the option to choose where your data will be hosted. Early users of Clio needed an option to store their data in the United States and not have to potentially deal with cross border issues. Users can now select to have their data stored in Canada or the United States.

Clio is a full featured practice management platform. Features such as document management, time tracking, calendaring, tasks, billing, etc. provide a complete solution for the solo and small firm lawyer. The billing component works well for hourly billing. Flat fee billing is possible with a little creative configuration. Clio can also be configured to synchronize with Outlook to provide bidirectional sync of calendar, contact and task entries. Clio also integrates with several e-mail clients.

Another key feature is the ability to export your data and back it up to your own device. This means that you have complete control over your data.

Be sure to take advantage of the free 30-day trial to make sure it will work for you. The cost is $49 per month for each attorney that uses Clio and $25 per month for each support staff user. Clio is our favorite SaaS practice management system and highly recommend it. Several of our clients have converted to Clio and never looked back.

Rocket Matter

Rocket Matter is the "new kid on the block" when it comes to case management systems, although they have been around since 2007. Rocket Matter is a web-based practice management system designed specifically for the legal industry. It also contains a time and billing function, which provides almost all you need for your law practice. Rocket Matter is very popular among Macintosh users, as it is web-based. There really isn't any case management application that is geared toward the Apple user community, so Rocket Matter meets that need through web browser access. You can still use Rocket Matter if you are a Windows shop, too, since all you need is an Internet connection and a web browser.

Rocket Matter will cost you $59.99 per month for the first user, $49.99 per month for the second through sixth users, and $39.99 per month for users seven through twenty. If you have 21 or more users, you can now utilize Rocket Matter for $19.99 per user per month. These dollars can add up quickly. As an example, your annual costs will be over $3,000 if you have five users. The good news is that these are the same prices as last year. There is a 30-day money-back guarantee, so you can try it out before making the financial commitment.

Rocket Matter is an SaaS (Software as a Service) implementation and carries the same issues as other providers. The data is being held by a third party even though it is transmitted on an encrypted channel. Rocket Matter is addressing the issue of connectivity and is working to provide some level of offline access to your data should the Internet connection go down. Those who have used Rocket Matter generally give it favorable reviews.

Firm Manager

Lexis has just introduced its version of a hosted case management system, which is called Firm Manager. It appears that Lexis has Rocket Matter and Clio squarely in its cross-hairs as it enters the SaaS market. Firm Manager is priced at $49.99 per month per user following the 30-day trial period. This puts it in a similar price band as the more established Clio and Rocket Matter, but it still has a long way to go. Frankly, we don't think Firm Manager is going to get much traction, especially since there is no billing component.

Others

There are additional products available, but the vendors aren't public with the cost or system requirements. We are less than impressed with companies that aren't public with their pricing or technical requirements. Products like ProLaw (Thomson Elite) and AbacusLaw (Abacus Data System Incorporated) require you to fill out a contact form so that a representative can contact you about pricing. We're not fond of this practice and recommend a relationship with more open vendors, especially when you are entering this arena and want to make an apples-to-apples comparison.

CHAPTER FIFTEEN

Time and Billing Software

PROBABLY THE SECOND MOST important function of your law practice is billing your clients for services rendered. Practicing law is clearly the most important, but getting paid is second, thereby ensuring the continued success and sustainability of your practice. Lawyers tend to hate the billing process and are not much fonder of the software that helps them generate invoices. There are still a lot of solos and small firms generating invoices manually. We'll look at both options and try to give you some guidance.

There are a lot of options for generating your bills, from a completely manual system to the fully automatic capture and assembly of invoices. There are two components that comprise items in your bills. One is the time component. This component is calculated by taking the hourly rate and applying it to the amount of time spent on a task. You can capture this time manually or automatically while the task is being accomplished. Flat fees are also considered time components, where the dollar amount is applied irrespective of the time spent. The second component is the fixed-cost items of the invoice. This would include such expenses as postage, copier costs, filing fees, courier charges, and any other fixed fees. As with the hourly components, you can track these expenses manually or automatically (to some level or another) through the use of technology.

We are beginning to see more and more firms adopting some sort of AFAs (Alternative Fee Arrangements) for their practice. Essentially, this can be viewed as a hybrid type of billing, where there may be a flat fee portion and an hourly portion. AFAs are more complicated to automate because of the various customized rules that may apply. The good news is that many of the software packages are sophisticated enough to handle customized rules, and they are getting better and better as time goes by. You may have to deal with some manual override techniques if the billing software can't accommodate a particular AFA scenario.

Manual Generation

Pencil and paper are the simplest way to capture time and expense. With manual generation, however, you must remember to log your time, number of copies, or whatever other chargeable component needs to be tracked. Make no mistake about it, studies have shown over and over again that this manual tracking results in a lot of lost time and expense. Because a lawyer's time equals money, many lawyers are shortchanging themselves by not moving to a technology-based solution.

Nevertheless, if this is what you do, on a periodic basis (daily, monthly, the end of the case, and so forth) you total the charges and generate the bill. Many solo practitioners start by using a word processing package or perhaps a typewriter to generate their bills to save some money. They are professional enough in appearance but still require manually adding up numbers and multiplying other numbers. There also has to be another method to keep track of payments made by the client and/or transfers of funds from other sources, such as the trust account. As the practice becomes more complicated, the billing process becomes more subject to mistakes.

If you must start with a manual method for generating your invoices, invest in billing software as soon as possible to improve your accuracy, maximize your billable hours, and minimize your losses.

Accounting Software

Some lawyers are actually using a financial accounting package to generate their bills. Probably one of the most popular software applications is QuickBooks by Intuit (**http://quickbooks.intuit.com**). Using QuickBooks to generate invoices allows the firm to have a total financial package, where all sorts of financial reports are available. Another advantage of using QuickBooks is the ability to generate payroll. This may not be a compelling reason for many lawyers, especially given the added cost, complexity, and reporting requirements. In general, it is more cost-effective to use a third-party service provider, such as ADP or Paychex, to handle solo and small firm payrolls. QuickBooks also handles processing of credit card payments, thereby integrating another piece of the financials into a single product. We hear that most lawyers began using QuickBooks because their accountant told them to. Make sure your accountant sets up your chart of accounts in QuickBooks so that you know where certain charges and fees should go. Your CPA should be familiar with financials for a law firm. If not, it's probably time to look for a new accountant.

QuickBooks comes in several different versions, and there is even an online version that allows access from any computer and does not require any software to be installed. We don't recommend using the online version, as it requires that your data be stored at Intuit. Your financial data is highly sensitive, and we recommend that you control your own data and not risk compromise by holding it at a third-party site. Consider, too, the possibly severe consequences if the third party is "down" and you can't manage the financial part of your law practice. In the last quarter of 2010, Intuit announced that it was shutting down the Quicken Online service and you could only export your data in CSV (comma separated values) format. While Quicken is a consumer-based product, we certainly wouldn't want to be stuck in the same situation if Intuit decided to shut down QuickBooks Online.

Since QuickBooks is an accounting package, some knowledge of financial principles is helpful. You will need to set up a chart of accounts for your practice. We recommend consulting with your accountant prior to configuring QuickBooks so that your financial categories are consistent with the accountant's needs. If you are new to QuickBooks, you may want to consider purchasing a support plan to help you learn the features of the software and get technical help. Many local community colleges also offer evening classes for QuickBooks, which would be a relatively inexpensive way to get some training in how to use the product.

The QuickBooks versions vary in cost from $229.95 to $600 per user for the Enterprise versions. The cost variance is due to the capabilities of the software and the number of concurrent user licenses that are needed. Most solo and small firms will find that QuickBooks Pro is more than sufficient for their needs. The cost is $229.95 for a single user or $649.95 for three users. There is a version for Macintosh computers too. Accountants love it when lawyers use QuickBooks as their billing software. They can take the QuickBooks data file at the end of the year and generate tax returns with relative ease.

Billing Specific

Arguably the most popular and widely used billing software in use among solo and small firm lawyers is Timeslips by Sage (**www.timeslips.com**). Timeslips is a billing specific software package that generates bills, tracks receivables, and manages trust accounting. We see more Timeslips installations in solo and small firm offices, especially those that have no case management system. Even at that, we are beginning to see firms going more and more with the integrated solutions that we describe later on.

Probably one of the reasons for the popularity of Timeslips is that it can be configured specifically for the legal industry. When you first install Timeslips, you select the type of business. This configures Timeslips to use the types of tasks and expenses that are specific to the industry. As an example, when you select the legal profession, default tasks are automatically created that deal with those tasks that are performed in the law office. There will be tasks for consultations, document review, depositions, and so forth. The expenses are also automatically created and would include such costs as copier usage, courier fees, postage, and the like. Trust accounting is also built into Timeslips, which is another reason that the software is very popular in solo and small firm offices.

Timeslips is licensed on a per-machine basis. Each computer that needs to access Timeslips will require the purchase of a license. In a small office, it is often the case that only one computer is used to process billing. The time keepers (typically lawyers) may elect to manually track their time on paper and give the time sheets to the office manager for entry into Timeslips. This arrangement keeps licensing costs down and allows for growth in the law firm. As the firm grows, additional licenses may be purchased and network access configured for the Timeslips database. Those larger firms that may use a terminal server need licenses only for the number of concurrent users. With the expanded interest and implementation of virtual computers, this concurrent license model may be a way to control costs.

The current version is Timeslips 2012. Timeslips costs $499.99 for a single station, which is the same price as last year. Additional network stations may be added for $249.99 each (an increase of $50 per license over last year) up to a total of 10 stations. Bundled pricing is available if you need 11 or more licenses. Support options are also available for Timeslips. If you have never used Timeslips, we recommended that you purchase a support plan at least for the first year of operation. After the first year, we do not recommend that you prebuy any support unless you intend to use and implement features of the newer versions. Access to the free online knowledge base is usually sufficient to work through most issues that you are likely to experience.

There are two support plans available. The Billing Assurance Essential Plan is the recommended one if you are going to purchase support. It covers most incidents that you will encounter. The Billing Assurance Premium Plan is more inclusive and includes database repair services. We don't feel that the Premium Plan is worth the additional cost. You should be backing up your database on a daily basis anyway. Timeslips was notorious for data corruption issues with past versions of the software. The recent versions of Timeslips databases seem to be much more stable. Currently, we use Timeslips for billing and haven't experienced a data corruption issue for over three years, but we do have our daily backups as well.

Timeslips can also link with QuickBooks. Setting up this integration is a manual process and can be complicated. You have to make sure that the Timeslips tasks and expenses have a corresponding QuickBooks account. Permissions (Timeslips and QuickBooks) also need to be considered. If you run a networked version of QuickBooks, multi-user versus single user could also cause some complications with the integration. A reader of a previous edition of this book advised us that Timeslips technical support will not help with any of the accounting aspects dealing with the QuickBooks link, as they feel it is giving financial advice and do not want the liability. Perhaps this is one of the reasons why our clients who use Timeslips and QuickBooks don't bother with the integration and manually input data to QuickBooks.

Billing for a Mac

SaaS offerings are very popular in the Mac community. All you need is an Internet connection and a web browser. Bill4Time is one billing package we see used in law offices with Macs. It is a secure hosted environment that is available from any computer at any time. A free 30-day trial will allow you to see if it fits your needs. You will want to get the Professional version, since it can handle unlimited clients. The Lite version can deal with a maximum of only 20 clients, which is far too few for most firms. The Professional version is $39.99 per month for the first user (an increase of $20 per month from last year) and $19.99 for each additional user (an increase of $10 per month from last year). At those prices, you may want to consider a fully integrated practice management solution like Clio.

Many of the practice management implementations also include some sort of billing mechanism, so you may not need a separate software application. We'll mention a few of the billing packages that are available for the Mac but will not mention them all. One such stand-alone package for the Mac is EasyTime. EasyTime, by BrightLight Software, runs natively on Mac OS X (10.4 or higher) and does not require any third-party database packages. The cost is $135 for a single user and $215 for a network version, which is the same price as last year.

Another popular package is Billings (**www.billingsapp.com**) by marketcircle. It is a very affordable piece of software at $39.99 per user. They also offer a "pay as you go" plan, which is $5.95 per month per device.

Integrated Packages

Many of the case management products now support integration with billing packages. This means that you enter your information into the case management system, and the time or expense is automatically captured for the billing process. There are advantages to using the same vendor for your case management and billing needs. The products are designed to work together and share information in a very efficient manner. However, selecting these "all-in-one" packages may not give you the best features of each package. If you really want a "best of breed" implementation, then make sure you investigate how the case management and billing packages share the data. Many case management applications provide links to billing packages by other vendors. Be careful to understand how to configure these links, especially if it is a manual process. We've seen clients who added tasks to their case management software and forgot to define the linkage to their billing software. This means that you may not bill for the effort when you use these newly defined tasks.

PCLaw

LexisNexis has several billing options to address the needs of solo and small firm law offices. A very popular package is PCLaw Version 11 (**http://www.lexisnexis.com/law-firms/practice-management/specialized-law/pclaw.aspx**), which includes the new mobility function. PCLaw includes some features that you would expect from a case management system. You can keep track of contacts, calendar entries, phone calls, notes, etc. This may be a good alternative for a solo practitioner to keep start-up costs down.

Perhaps Lexis has been getting pushback from customers about its pricing model. Last year you had to contact Lexis if you had more than one user, and they required a maintenance plan. This year you have an option of buying PCLaw without maintenance if you so desire, although you may not want to. The Annual Maintenance Plan (AMP) gives you the following:

- Major and Minor Software Upgrades
- Service Packs
- HotFixes
- 24/7 on-demand training
- Telephonic Technical Support
- Online Documentation

This new policy took effect on May 1, 2010. Even though you have the option of not purchasing AMP, you really don't have a choice, especially if there are bugs in the product. Without AMP you won't get any software updates (except for HotFixes), even if the update fixes known problems with the product. That means no service packs or minor upgrades. Seems pretty silly, doesn't it? We're sure glad other software vendors don't have this policy.

The cost for the first user is $950 with a maintenance plan. Each additional user is $480, which also includes the first year of maintenance. For those who don't want maintenance, the first user is $600, and each additional user is $400.

Juris is another billing software offered by Lexis. It is typically used by larger law firms or in integrating with Time Matters. We have never seen Juris used in a solo or small firm setting. Like some of the other products mentioned, you have to contact Lexis just to get pricing information.

Tabs3

Another popular billing package is Tabs3 by STI. Tabs3 is the companion product to PracticeMaster, which is the case management software from STI. Tabs3 pricing is based on the number of billable entities. Single-user prices start at $295 for two timekeepers and go to $795 for up to nine timekeepers. You'll need to purchase the multiuser version if you need more than nine billable entities. Multiuser network versions start at $495 for two timekeepers up to $3,995 for 39 timekeepers. STI defines a timekeeper as someone whose time is tracked in the software.

Unlike other billing packages, Tabs3 has separated out various financial functions and priced them as individual components. As an example, there are additional components, such as trust accounting, general ledger, and accounts payable. This means that you can expand Tabs3 from a pure billing package into a complete accounting package. You can find more information about Tabs3 at **www.tabs3.com**. Tabs3 is as highly regarded by us as its case management counterpart, PracticeMaster. It is also consistently rated highly by legal software experts.

Amicus Accounting

A less widely used billing option is provided by Amicus Attorney. A lot of solo and small firms use Amicus Attorney as a practice management package, but few use the billing option. There are two billing packages available, depending on which version of Amicus you are running. The Amicus Premium Billing application would be used if you are running Amicus Attorney Premium Edition. If you are running Amicus Attorney Small Firm Edition, then the Amicus Small Firm Accounting software is for you.

Amicus Premium Billing 2011 adds billing, collections, and trust to your Amicus Attorney installation. Like most billing packages, you can capture time and expenses for hourly, flat fee, and contingent billing. Each license is priced at $199, which makes it one of the lowest-cost billing packages. This product will not run by itself and is an add-on to the Amicus Attorney case management software. Maintenance and technical support plans are also available. You can purchase a maintenance plan that includes unlimited technical support and product updates. The first license will set you back $420 a year but also covers Amicus Attorney software maintenance. Each additional license is $320, so the dollars will add up quickly if you have more than a couple of users. You also have the option of purchasing a technical support plan only, without product updates. Unlimited technical support for a year is $395 for the first license and $145 for each additional license.

Amicus Small Firm Accounting 2011 integrates with the Amicus Attorney Small Firm product. Unlike the Premium version, the Small Firm version can be used as a stand-alone package. The initial license cost is $399, and each additional license is $299, which is the same price as last year's Accounting package. Like the Premium package, you can purchase maintenance or technical support only plans for the Small Firm version. There are a couple of more options, since the Small Firm Accounting software can run all by itself and not with a base Amicus Attorney installation. The maintenance plan, which includes product updates and unlimited technical support, is $230 per year just for Small Firm Accounting for the first license and $350 per year if you have Amicus Attorney Small Firm Edition too. Each additional license is $130 per year for just the accounting package and $250 per year if you have both the accounting and case management software. Unlimited technical support only is $295 per year for the first license for just the accounting software and $395 per year for the Small Firm Edition and Accounting combo. Each additional license would be $95 per year for the Accounting only package and $145 per year if you have both. There have been some issues with billing software for Amicus, but that was some years ago.

One of the higher-level (expensive) billing alternatives is provided by ProLaw, which is a Thomson Elite product. ProLaw is an integrated package, and the billing component is not available as a separate function. Very few solos and small law firms have chosen this route, in our experience.

Most of our clients have chosen QuickBooks or Timeslips for billing, and they are generally quite happy with what they have chosen—though everything has a learning curve. All of these vendors are happy to let you sample their product in one manner or another, so don't hesitate to try before you buy. Also, if you aren't keen on accounting, talk to your friends who are equally numbers challenged and see what has worked for them. In many cases, the choice has been made by someone at the firm who is going to perform the accounting/bookkeeping functions, and that's fine—as long as you stay with one of the "majors," you won't be left scrambling to find someone who knows your obscure time and billing package if that person leaves.

CHAPTER SIXTEEN

Litigation Programs

THERE ARE SEVERAL PROGRAMS that automate certain litigation support functions, and while they offer different features, they fall into two general categories: case organization programs and courtroom presentation programs. Case organization programs are databases that are set up to analyze and manage facts and evidence. The common ones include LexisNexis Concordance (**http://law.lexisnexis.com/concordance**), LexisNexis CaseMap (**http://www.lexisnexis.com/casemap/casemap.aspx**), West Case Notebook (**http://west.thomson.com/products/services/case-notebook/default.aspx**), and Sanction Solutions Verdical (**www.verdictsystems.com/Software/Verdical**). Summation has been acquired by Access Data. The litigation support products many of you know, such as iBlaze, are still being offered by Access Data. The acquired products have been renamed (e.g., AD eDiscovery, AD ECA, and AD Summation) and are integrated solutions. Access Data is leveraging its forensic experience and merging e-discovery tools in an attempt to provide a total end-to-end solution. CaseMap is one of the most popular packages for solo and small firm lawyers, given its lower cost and ease of use.

Trial presentation programs manage and display electronic evidence, including exhibits, video and text depositions, sound files, and more. They facilitate quick access during trials and hearings and include on-the-fly annotation, such as highlighting and call-outs. Trial presentation programs include Sanction (**www.verdictsystems.com/Software/Sanction**), Trial Director (**www.indatacorp.com/Products/Trial/trialDirector.aspx**), and Visionary (**www.visionarylegal.com**). New to the scene are presentation packages for the iPad. Products such as TrialPad (**www.trialpad.com**) turn the iPad into a presentation tool for litigators. Most of the mentioned products have free downloads for a trial period or online demos. Although we do not review them in detail, they should be considered by lawyers with litigation practices.

CHAPTER SEVENTEEN

Document Management

DOCUMENT MANAGEMENT SOFTWARE SOLUTIONS can be relatively expensive for the solo or small firm operation. They tend to be used more for enterprise-size companies because of their cost and complexity. As the industry matures, vendors are merging the functions of document management, content management, and knowledge management. This is especially true as electronic files are becoming a critical component of discovery. You may see applications described as document management systems, content management systems, knowledge management systems, or even enterprise content management systems. Just because a vendor chooses to describe its product in a particular way doesn't mean there is anything unique or special about it. In general, all of the terms previously mentioned are used for applications that organize information.

The main purpose of a document management system is to organize information into a useable and searchable form. How many times have you looked for a file or document but couldn't remember the name or location? A document management system allows for fast and easy access to the data, whether in paper or electronic form. It also provides access control and enforceability of rules. As an example, perhaps one of your rules is that every document has a specific category (programmed ahead of time) tagged to it. This makes for consistency and removes the human error in typing or misspelling the category tag.

DocuShare

We will mention just a few of the products that are available, but understand that document management systems are not generally designed for small-scale operations. Xerox's DocuShare (**http://docushare.xerox.com**) has been around for many years. Pricing is available directly from Xerox or through partners. There is now an entry-level version of DocuShare available for small office installations, which starts at several thousands of dollars. The current version (DocuShare 6.5) requires a 64-bit server, which would significantly increase costs if you don't have one available. DocuShare may be a viable alternative, especially if you already have a Xerox copier that you could use for scanning documents.

iManage

It is really hard to stay current with a product that changes names and companies so many times over its life. A couple of years ago we knew it as Interwoven. Today the product is known as Autonomy iManage Worksite. Like DocuShare, expect to pay thousands of dollars for this system. It is a highly regarded document management environment (if you can remember the name) but is also geared more toward the intermediate to large-scale firms.

Worldox

The most popular and most used document management system for solos and small firm operations is Worldox (**www.worldox.com**). Worldox is licensed on a concurrent user basis and not per seat. The cost for Worldox GX2 is $395 per concurrent user, which makes it very affordable for solo and small firms, especially since there are no minimum seat purchase requirements. Annual maintenance is $84 per license and is mandatory for new orders. No separate server is required, and the indexer can be run on any workstation-class computer. The computer resource requirements for Worldox are very light when compared to other document management systems. The application is very robust and easy to use, hence its popularity within the legal community.

Case management systems (see Chapter 14, Case Management) are also used to provide a certain level of document management. Your electronic files are referenced to a client or client matter, making them easily accessible at the click of a mouse. A key point to remember about true document management applications is their stringent enforcement of the classification rules. The user must use the system within the configured rules, which sometimes frustrates people because of the rigid requirements. In contrast, applications that are not specifically document management software aren't restrictive or mandatory. The danger is that data may be lost or misfiled when the rules are not stringently enforced. Worldox is an excellent choice for document management, as it integrates with almost every case management system available. It is consistently well reviewed by legal software experts.

Acrobat

Many solo and small firm offices are equipped with Adobe's Acrobat product. The later versions of Acrobat provide the ability to manage documents. The collaboration components within Acrobat are used to organize and reference files in a manner similar to other document management systems.

Web-Based

Web-based document management systems are becoming very popular. The cost per user is typically more than if you purchased the product for use within your firm, but you save on the hardware and internal support costs. The vendor provides the back-end hardware and software for the management of your documents. The nice part about Web-based document management systems is that the information is accessible from any computer with an Internet connection. The bad part is that the vendor is holding your data, and you are subject to the reliability of the Internet connection. If you elect to use one of the online document management systems, be aware of the security precautions for client data that is being held by a third party. At a minimum, make sure that the connection for accessing the documents is encrypted and that the data is stored in an encrypted form on the provider's equipment. You should also make sure that you have a copy of the data in your hands to avoid being "held hostage" by the third-party provider. And yes, we've seen that happen.

NetDocuments is a popular SaaS provider for document management. Many lawyers, small to large, have had great experiences with NetDocuments. We have heard lawyers say that it was very easy to install and configure. In one case, a lawyer converted his firm (tens of thousands of documents) over to NetDocuments in a weekend all by himself. NetDocuments provides all of the features you would expect in a document management system in addition to matter-centric workspaces, e-mail management, collaboration, and mobile access.

There are three versions of NetDocuments. The Basic version is $20 per month per user, and it is $30 per month per user for the Professional version. There is a base volume of storage allowed per user, with overage fees beyond the allowance. The Professional+ Edition includes e-mail management and costs $38 per user per month. Your actual costs will vary depending on the selected package, since there are fees for e-mail management (except Professional+), local document storage, third-party integrations, extranet services, etc. We encourage you to take advantage of the 30-day free trial prior to making any financial commitment, as implementing NetDocuments can be a challenging project.

Plain Folders

Finally, a very simple form of document management for solo and small firms is to follow a standard folder and file naming convention along with search software (see Chapter 25, Utilities). Besides the cost for search software, this is a very low-cost solution. Typically, folders are named on a per-client or client-matter basis. Files are then given a very descriptive name, such as <client name>, followed by the file purpose and sometimes the date. As an example, "Rothburg request for admissions.doc" would be the file name for your request for admissions in the Rothburg matter. This is a very manageable method to organize data when you are small. As your practice grows, search software may be needed to assist in finding particular files pertaining to specific issues.

Searching

Search software such as dtSearch or X1 (see Chapter 25, Utilities) can be used to index the files within your client folders so that you can quickly find the document pertaining to the request for electronic evidence or some other specific document on a partner's Motorola cell phone.

If you are considering the purchase of a document management system, Worldox is an excellent first choice. We have implemented this software many times, and clients are always happy with it. No matter what product you are considering, see whether there is a trial version available, or at least participate in a demo of the product to determine if it meets your firm's needs.

CHAPTER EIGHTEEN

Document Assembly

Essentially, document assembly software automates the creation of legal documents that are used repeatedly. This would include such documents as wills, leases, contracts, and letters. You can think of document assembly as templates that can be used over and over. This shortens the time for document preparation and increases the efficiency of your practice. If you use flat fees, document assembly can be a godsend.

Document assembly software can be specialized for a particular industry or can be generic. As an example, specialized document assembly software is typically used in estate planning and tax preparation. In those situations, the user answers questions in a survey type of form, and then the required documents are generated using the answers provided. If you've ever used one of the personal income tax programs (e.g., TurboTax, TaxCut), you've seen how document assembly works. You may see the term "document automation," but it means the same thing as document assembly for our discussion.

HotDocs

In law firms, the top three document assembly packages are HotDocs, ProDoc, and AIA Contract Documents. HotDocs (**www.hotdocs.com**) is the most popular document assembly software by a very large margin. HotDocs is a very powerful solution and comes in several "flavors." There are two desktop versions and a server-based edition. HotDocs Developer (desktop-based) is the global standard for document automation and allows you to convert word processing documents and PDF forms into templates. You create a template and determine what text to include or exclude, depending on the answers entered by the user. This is the survey-type entry that was described earlier. The presentation walks you through the questions to gather the data needed to generate the document. The current version supports Microsoft Word 2010 and Corel WordPerfect X5. It also includes PDF Advantage, the forms automation toolset. PDF Advantage turns PDF documents (e.g., loan applications, IRS forms, court documents) into an automated HotDocs template. HotDocs User is the other desktop product and is used for organizing and accessing templates built with HotDocs Developer. You can choose to assemble the template with an existing answer file or create a new one on the fly.

As with other application software these days, HotDocs is available in a browser version, too. The product, HotDocs Server 10, allows for document assembly using a standard web browser. This is particularly helpful for remote users and means you can deploy templates via the Internet.

Hotdocs isn't getting any points with us these days. Pricing for HotDocs is no longer publicly available—it was removed with the new release of HotDocs 10. You will need to contact one of the HotDocs partners to obtain pricing information.

ProDoc

ProDoc (**www.prodoc.com**) is another document assembly application that is a legal resource from Thomson Reuters. One of the interesting features of ProDoc is how the licensing works. ProDoc is licensed on a subscription basis. The basic subscription license allows for usage on three computers or three concurrent users. If you install ProDoc on a network, the licensing enforces the three concurrent user limit. You can only install ProDoc on three computers if they are stand-alone and not running in a network installation. The software is licensed for a single firm at a location. If you share office space with another firm, then each firm needs to purchase its own subscription to ProDoc. Pricing is easily determined from ProDoc's website. Just pump in the type of firm and number of users.

The ProDoc forms are state specific and currently only available for California, Florida, Massachusetts, New York, and Texas. There is also a national package available as a supplement library with links to parent

BTS (Business Transactions Solution) forms on Westlaw. There are various document assembly subscriptions available for the supported states. Be sure to check the website to see what modules are contained in each package and that your particular practice area is covered.

AIA Contract Documents

AIA Contract Documents (**http://www.aia.org/docs_default**) is a specialty package used for design and construction projects, so it's an excellent product for those dealing with construction law. In fact, the product was developed specifically with the law in mind. The generated documents conform to the laws in effect at the time of creation. Also, the AIA documents are intended for nationwide use and are not restricted to specific states. A new, single-seat license that allows for unlimited documents is $969 a year. There are licensing choices for small, medium, and large firms. Small firms have choices of 100, 300, or unlimited documents. Medium and large firms have unlimited document options. The choices for medium and large firms range from an unlimited five-seat license for $3,449 up to an unlimited 50-seat license for $29,699.

HotDocs is the clear recommendation for solo and small firm lawyers wanting to embark on document assembly. As a generic package, it is very well suited for any type of law practice. HotDocs integrates with many document management and practice management packages. There are many choices for technical support, including wiki, forum, and documentation. HotDocs resellers are the primary method for consulting and product acquisition. We just wish the company was more transparent with its pricing. Be sure to request the 30-day trial and see if you can save some consulting expense by developing templates on your own.

CHAPTER NINETEEN

Cloud Computing and SaaS

To SaaS OR NOT to SaaS? That is the question. . . .

There is much marketing hype over SaaS (software as a service) offerings. Essentially, SaaS is a different way to spell ASP (application service provider). Even Wikipedia confirms this renamed offering. To make it easy for readers to understand, imagine that you don't own a copy of Microsoft Office; you simply go to a site on the Internet, where you are, by subscription, allowed to use Office. The resulting data is held by the provider, not you.

The traditional client/server model puts total control in the hands of the law firm. The data is held internally, and access is controlled by the firm. You can choose to encrypt the data locally, which we recommend, or leave it in plain text. Either way, it is within the technology walls of the law firm and not directly accessible by any third party.

In contrast, the SaaS model puts your data in the hands of a third party. This is not necessarily a bad thing, but do you really know if the information is safe? Your contract with the provider may specify that the data be stored in encrypted form, but what if a disgruntled employee has access to tools that allow him or her to decrypt the data and sell it to the other side in a major litigation?

When you contract with an SaaS provider, you are required to accept the service as it delivers it to you. This means that any upgrades or bug fixes will be implemented by the provider. Sound like a good thing? Just ask Ben Schorr, CEO of Roland Schorr, an IT support and management company based in Hawaii, and author of *The Lawyer's Guide to Microsoft Word*

2010 and *The Lawyer's Guide to Microsoft Outlook 2007*, both published by the American Bar Association:

> One of my concerns about SaaS is the double-edged sword called "upgrades." A selling point of SaaS products is that the vendor just transparently updates it in the background, and you don't have to worry about it. Monday morning you log in and . . . "Oh, look, new features!" But what if you don't like those new features?
>
> What if you're on a tight deadline and Google decides to do a massive upgrade to Google Docs? Do you have time to get yourself and your staff up to speed on how the new version works? With Microsoft Office, you upgrade when you're good and ready. We do quite a bit of work with firms all over the country, in fact, helping them plan and approach that migration. Training their staff, preparing for the various consequences of the rollout, making sure their ancillary apps and add-ins are ready to support the new version. (Want some fun? Tell a managing partner that the new version of her e-mail app is NOT compatible with her case management system . . . the day AFTER she upgrades.)
>
> With SaaS, you don't generally get that. You may get no warning at all that features, user interface (UI), behaviors are about to change. You certainly aren't going to get a chance to use it before your staff does so that you can get up to speed on it and be ready to answer questions when the 9:15 messenger run is waiting to go and the documents still aren't printed (unless you want to sign into the SaaS app at 3 a.m., I guess).
>
> Hey, it's great that somebody else manages your upgrades and updates. That's usually a good thing. But it's not always a good thing. Unpredictability is not a quality I value in my mission-critical apps.

Enough said. Besides the data security and access concerns for the SaaS model, the financial stability of the provider should be a major consideration, especially in these uncertain economic times. The last thing you need is to have the provider go out of business. Even if you have adequate notice, the cost to migrate your data to another provider or bring it back in-house can be significant. This brings us to the topic of exit strategy. At some point, you will likely want to bring the function back within your IT control or move to another provider. The contract should provide for specific costs and timetables to facilitate the move.

Another issue is the stability of the communications network. By design, you are dependent on the speed and quality of your Internet connection. Smart firms will have dual network connections to the Internet, although this will mean an increase in cost over what is normally installed at the firm. The Internet connection must be available at all times; otherwise, you will not have access to your data. There aren't many judges who are sympathetic to your problems if you miss a filing date because your Internet connection went down. And Internet connections, as we've all miserably learned, do sometimes go down—and always without notice.

To be fair, let's look at the upsides of SaaS . . . and yes, there are a few.

There can be some financial advantage to contracting service to a third-party provider. Your investment in hardware and software is minimized, since you are really only passing keyboard, mouse, and screen data over the communications link or accessing the application via a web browser. The actual processing occurs at the SaaS provider. All configuration and data hosting are external to your firm's infrastructure. Costs for the SaaS model can be based on the number of users or the amount of data storage volume. Either way, it is fairly easy to identify and budget for the cost of the service, which is a big selling point for a lot of firms. However, to get these "stable" price points, the contract terms are typically three to five years. This means that the firm must make a pretty long commitment to using the SaaS model and the specific provider.

Another advantage to the SaaS model is the rapid reaction time to changes. It is very fast to add new users or increase the amount of space for data storage. By the same measure, it is very fast to decrease the number of users or storage space. This means that you are more flexible in controlling your costs. If your firm is in contraction mode, you can reduce expenses, assuming that the contract doesn't tie you to a minimum amount. Many firms like the mobility aspect of the SaaS model, since they can access the applications from any machine with an Internet browser. Typically, there isn't anything special that needs to be installed on the client computer. The user needs only a browser and perhaps some type of plug-in to access the SaaS application. This means that it is easy to gain access to the firm's data from the office, home, or an Internet café in the Bahamas.

Too often, all costs and all risks are not considered when analyzing an SaaS solution. The SaaS ballyhoo has drowned out all reasonable objections. Clearly, we are not big fans at the present time, especially for law firms. Client/server solutions can be clearly defined from implementation through the life of the solution. You control the implementation, configuration, and ongoing costs. While you can contractually specify some costs with SaaS, future upgrades and exit conversions may tip the financial decision.

Bottom line: We recommend that most of you keep control of your own data. It will be cheaper and less risky in the long run. If you still feel that you need to investigate and research SaaS vendors, we describe a few in this book. We just ask that you do it carefully and ask the right questions before making your decision. We are listening to arguments that some SaaS providers actually offer better security than law firms themselves. There's some truth in that, to be sure, and we are moving (slowly) in the direction of recommending SaaS with proven providers with good track records. Finally, be sure to check with your bar, as several states now have opinions regarding the usage (and requirements) of cloud computing. If you're wondering how states are dealing with the cloud from an ethical perspective, the general view is that it is acceptable to use the cloud as long as you investigate the provider, particularly making sure that confidential client data will be adequately protected.

CHAPTER TWENTY

Collaboration

COLLABORATION MAY OR MAY not be at the top of your list, especially if you are a solo lawyer. However, we're sure that you will have occasion to deal with other lawyers or even have a need to collaborate with your clients on a case. There are some great technology solutions to allow for collaboration—and solutions are multiplying week by week. These are just a few of the primary tools that are available for sharing information and working in a collaborative mode.

Social networking is a collaboration area that is gaining in popularity. Facebook has won the social networking war and is now being used extensively for business purposes. Twitter and LinkedIn are also very popular, and we're keeping an eye on Google+ to see if it gains traction, and it looks like it is, with CBS news reporting in late 2011 that it now has more than 10 million users. Some lawyers are getting business through social networking sites, and others are raising their visibility with potential clients or colleagues who might provide referrals. Still others have obtained opportunities to write or speak on their area of expertise. See Chapter 26 on social media for more information on how lawyers are using these new applications.

Google Docs

Probably one of the most well known of the collaboration tools is Google Docs, which can create documents, spreadsheets, and presentations. The popularity of this SaaS product is no doubt due to the fact that it carries the favorite price tag of all lawyers—it is completely free. The application allows you to work on a document, spreadsheet, presentation, or drawing with others and see the modifications in real time. You just use the web browser on your computer with your Internet connection. There are even enhanced features, which you may not be aware of.

You do need to have a Google ID to use Google Docs. Just go to **http://docs.google.com** and enter your login information. You can also create an account from the main entry page. Besides creating your files from scratch, Google Docs allows you to upload files that you've already created on your computer. In January 2010, Google announced that you could upload any file type to Google Docs, but you can only convert certain file types to work within it. Documents and spreadsheets can be exported and saved on your computer in .doc, .xls, .csv, .ods, .odt, .pdf, .rtf, and .html file formats. Google Docs also supports drag and drop in the current version as well as folder uploads, so you are not limited to one file at a time. If you use Chrome as your web browser, just point to the folder and upload it. If you use a browser other than Chrome, you will need to enable Java support and download an applet to support the folder upload ability.

By default, files are not shared until you make them shareable. This is certainly the preferred security policy and keeps your data private unless you make a conscious decision to share the information. Once you've created or uploaded the file to Google, you configure how the file is shared or, as Google calls it, you determine the visibility options. Google's visibility options include "Private," "Anyone with the link" and "Public on the web." "Private" is just that: private. As mentioned, this is the default visibility setting. A document that is set to "Anyone with the link" is like an unlisted phone number. This means that the data will not be visible unless you know the URL or are just plain lucky in guessing what it is. "Public on the web" means that the document is available to anyone and may get indexed by search engines.

Besides the visibility, you can also change what a user can do with the data. The creator of the document is tagged as the owner and can obviously do anything. If you define specific people to have access to the file, the choices for access are "Can edit," "Can comment," and "Can view." This gives you some level of granularity in the access and visibility options.

As a practical point, multiple people can collaborate on a file, and everyone doesn't need to have the same software or version. You can go online and create a file to start the process. Once completed, perhaps you download the file as a .doc file, since you use Word as your word processor. Another person downloads the .rtf version that he read into an old version of WordPerfect, and a third person downloads the .odt version because she uses OpenOffice. Each person downloads the same information, but in a different file format to match what they use on their computer.

The current version of Google Docs now supports mobility options. As smartphones become the computing platform of choice, Google has developed methods to get to your information. You can view documents on virtually any smartphone that supports html. Currently, you can only edit your information from a device running Android 2.2 or higher or an Apple device running iOS 3 or above. By default, the document will come up in "Mobile" view when it is opened on a mobile device. You can switch to "Desktop" view if you want to change the font or color of the text. We're sure iPad users will be bouncing back and forth between the two modes.

The caution with Google Docs is that the data is being held by a third party. Obviously, you would not want to use it to work on highly proprietary information, such as a patent application. Even though you can control who has access to the files and what they can do, Google still holds the "keys" to all of the data. Google has had some highly publicized security issues over a period of years, so it is wise to consider what data you store there.

Acrobat

Today, more and more lawyers have Acrobat (**www.adobe.com/products/acrobat**), especially if they do e-filing of court documents. Acrobat allows for collaboration with PDF documents, so you can conduct shared document reviews that allow the participants to view one another's comments. All three Acrobat versions (Standard, Pro, and Suite) allow for this type of collaboration. Acrobat X Standard is currently $299, Pro is $449, and Suite is $1,199. Acrobat X Suite combines Acrobat X Pro and Adobe Photoshop CS5 with rich media applications. Lawyers should opt for the Pro version, primarily for the enhanced security, Bates stamping, and redaction ability. Acrobat X Pro allows you to create a document that your clients may find useful. It allows Adobe Reader (the free reader version) users to participate in reviews with complete commenting and markup tools, including sticky notes, highlighter, lines, shapes, and stamps. This means that your clients (or other lawyers, for that matter) don't have to purchase Acrobat to collaborate with you. This feature is not available with Acrobat X Standard, hence the recommendation to purchase the Pro version. Consider purchasing Acrobat 8 Professional, especially if you can find it at a much reduced cost, since it is two versions back. Version X is the current version, but there aren't any significant enhancements for the legal profession over those legal-specific functions that are included in Acrobat 8 Professional.

An additional option is to buy a copy of Acrobat 7 Standard on the Internet for around $45 (sometimes you can find it on eBay for around $30). You then go to the Adobe site and purchase the Acrobat X Pro upgrade for $199. This means you walk away with Acrobat X for around $245 instead of the $449 retail price. That's a real bargain and would more than pay for this book. The audiences we speak to continue to report that this is one of their favorite tips.

Microsoft Word

Another collaboration tool is the "track changes" feature of Microsoft Word. With this tool, you can see the modifications of each user who modifies the document. The caveat is that the software must be configured to properly identify the user. Some preloaded Office installations have the user configured as something generic, like "Owner" or "Satisfied Customer," and not the user's name. You can see how your Office (2003 and prior) installation is configured by going to Tools > Options and selecting the User Information tab. Word 2007 users would click the Office button in the upper left, select the Word Options button at the bottom, and see the user information in the Popular menu choice. Word 2010 users select File and then the Options menu choice. Once this option is properly configured, the user information will show properly with the tracked changes. The user also has the ability to insert comments in addition to actually modifying the document contents. As a precaution, do not strip the metadata (as you might normally for confidentiality reasons) from the document if you are sending it to another party for collaboration. Removing the metadata also removes the tracked changes, so the recipient will not see the intended modifications. When you've got the document ready and want to send it to a client, then scrub the metadata.

SharePoint

SharePoint is Microsoft's solution for collaboration. Basically, SharePoint is a web-based server environment that allows the end-user to collaborate on data that is managed through a SharePoint server. There is no special client software needed, as access is accomplished via a browser.

SharePoint 2010 is considered to be expensive for most solo and small firm operations, especially for new installations. Besides the cost of the server hardware, you will need the server software and client access licenses (CALs). Microsoft has done it again and made licensing for SharePoint a totally confusing effort. The SharePoint Foundation server is free but has limited function. You may have to purchase only a server license, depending on how you want to use the product. CALs may also be needed depending on the type of information and access. There is even an option for enterprise CALs if you need a very robust and flexible SharePoint environment. Suffice it to say that it is all very complicated and can get rather expensive. If you need the services of a full-blown SharePoint server, you may want to consider some of the hosted solutions, which should be a lot more affordable for a solo or small firm office.

Microsoft is pushing SharePoint in a major way. It is thought that the current Public Folders function of Exchange will go away in future versions so that you are forced to go with a SharePoint installation to get the same features you currently get today with a base Exchange installation. We thought this was going to happen with the release of Exchange 2010, but we are happy to say that the Public Folders function is still there.

We've written about SharePoint in the last several editions of this book. Microsoft continues to hype it, but we don't see much traction in the real world. Fortune 100 companies may be embracing the product, but only one client has it installed, and we don't see that SharePoint is worth the expense. Many of the solo and small firm practitioners are using SaaS solutions instead of investing in a complex SharePoint environment. We agree with that direction and don't think SharePoint is going to change the world, as Microsoft has often predicted.

Office 365

Microsoft has finally introduced a product that may give Google a run for its money. Office 365 is really a web-based productivity suite that also contains some collaboration capabilities. The solution is a subscription-based service, so the out-of-pocket cash flow is very reasonable. There are several subscription plans available depending on the number of users and any advanced features that may be needed.

Solo and small firms will probably opt for Plan P, which is geared toward professionals and small businesses with up to 25 employees. The cost is $6 per month per user, which is very affordable. It includes access to e-mail, web conferencing, documents, and calendars. The Office Web Apps provide access to familiar products, such as Excel and Word, using a web browser. You can simultaneously edit documents over the Internet with other users and see the changes in real time. In a recent *Network World* survey, 65 percent of the respondents selected the Office 365 suite over Google Apps. Interested? Make sure you try the 30-day trial package; for $6 you wouldn't be throwing away a lot of money.

For much more on collaboration tools from two of the greatest experts in the country, see Dennis Kennedy and Tom Mighell's book, *The Lawyer's Guide to Collaboration Tools and Technologies* (ABA Law Practice Management Section, 2009), available at ABA's web store (**www.ShopABA.org**).

CHAPTER TWENTY-ONE

Remote Access

MOST LAWYERS ARE ROAD warriors today. If their entire office is not on their laptop, a good chunk of it is—and the rest is accessible through remote access. Whether in court, on vacation, traveling, or in a meeting, lawyers need access to their e-mail, calendar, appointments, and files. Some lawyers have discarded workstations entirely, using only their laptops and a docking station at work and tablets while on the move. Others have both a workstation and a laptop. The popularity of laptops has zoomed in the last decade, to the point where the lawyer without a laptop is a relative rarity. Our new mobile lawyers are now equipped with technologies that allow them to be as productive when on the road as they are in the office, minimizing downtime and keeping those billable hours (or productivity hours, in the case of the alternative billers) up. There is a strong expectation by many clients and colleagues that lawyers will be constantly accessible via e-mail—even, sadly, while on vacation. We privately joke (and lament) that vacations are times when our laptops get a nice view. So how do we stay in touch with the office?

Virtual Private Networking

A virtual private network (VPN) connection is a secure communications network tunneled through another network, such as the Internet. The VPN connection allows a network user to connect to the office when working remotely. The communications tunnel encrypts the data traffic between the remote user and the office network, maintaining the security of the information as it is passed back and forth. This is extremely important for law firms when their lawyers are working on client files while traveling or away from the office. Best of all, the VPN service software is included with Microsoft's server operating systems, and the VPN client software is included with Microsoft 2000, XP, Vista, and Windows 7 operating systems.

The average lawyer is likely to be dumbfounded when confronted with setting up a VPN, so this is best left to your IT consultant. However, it is not terribly expensive, and it offers terrific security for your data. The greatest advantage of VPNs is that they are multiuser, whereas others are one-on-one solutions.

GoToMyPC

GoToMyPC is a remote connection service that allows you to connect to your work computer when you are away from the office. This service is a great alternative if you're a solo practitioner or if your law firm does not have the ability to set up a VPN-type connection for remote users (if you don't have a server). Like a VPN connection, data communications between the client and the host are encrypted and secured. To connect to your work computer, software must be installed and running on the host machine (the computer you wish to connect to), and both the client and the host computers must have Internet access. The GoToMyPC website maintains contact with the host computer so the IP address of the host is always known. This is critical: This solution works even if the host has a dynamic Internet connection that will not remain constant. No configuration of the company firewall will need to be made to get GoToMyPC up and running.

GoToMyPC costs as little as $99 per year for one computer license and will need to be renewed yearly. There is a monthly plan, but the cost jumps to $10 a month. There is no limitation on how often you may connect to your host computer, and you are allowed to connect to your host computer from any computer. The software requires little setup and configuration and can be purchased online from GoToMyPCs website at **www.gotomypc.com**. This software is more costly than its competitors, so be sure to check out all of your available options before selecting which remote access solution to purchase.

LogMeIn

LogMeIn Pro is a remote access solution that is very similar to GoToMyPC. The software works the exact same way, with the service provider maintaining the IP addresses of host computers. This is a good solution for those firms with dynamic IP addresses. The service allows you to gain seamless and total access to your office PC from any computer with an Internet connection. To connect, a user logs into the LogMeIn website and the connection to the host computer is made automatically. Some of the features include remote printing, the ability to transfer and share files between the connected computers, and the ability to map network drives to your local computer. Just like GoToMyPC, this service is extremely secure, using 128- to 256-bit SSL end-to-end encryption. When compared to GoToMyPC, this remote access solution costs much less. A LogMeIn Pro subscription costs $69.95 per year for one computer license and will need to be renewed annually. The monthly plan costs $12.20, so the annual plan is recommended. This software can be purchased online from LogMeIn's website at **www.logmein.com**. We strongly recommend the use of this product for remote accessibility for its ease of use and setup.

TeamViewer

TeamViewer Business Edition is a remote access solution on steroids. It contains a number of features that are not available with LogMeIn and GoToMyPC, but it comes with a hefty price, although it's a one-time purchase. Just like the two remote access solutions described above, TeamViewer works flawlessly behind network firewalls and is a good solution for firms that use dynamic IP addresses. It also allows up to three people to connect to or view the same screen at once, allowing for small presentations or meetings, unlike GoToMyPC or LogMeIn, which allow only one connection at a time. Some of the additional features include:

- Up to three concurrent connections to the host computer
- Multiplatform support, including Mac OS X, Windows 7, and Linux computers
- Included communication tools that allow users to connect with each other through video chat or VoIP
- One-time charge for a lifetime license; no recurring yearly costs
- Easiest of the three to set up and run, and no browser needed to launch connection
- The ability to transfer files securely

TeamViewer can be purchased online from **www.teamviewer.com**, and a single lifetime business license for one computer costs $749.

Mobility Tips

Besides providing remote access solutions for the legal road warrior, we wanted to include some useful tips to think about before heading out on the road:

— Pack a surge protector. It doesn't matter what brand. You never know when you will need more than two outlets to power all of your devices and to protect your electronic devices from power surges and dirty electricity.

— Purchase a lock for your laptop. Ninety-nine percent of laptops have a Kensington security slot, and it's prudent to use it. Kensington locks, such as the MicroSaver DS Notebook Lock, can be purchased online from Kensington's website (**www.kensington.com**) for around $50. A small price to pay to keep your laptop secure.

— Pack a spare cell phone and tablet charger and sync cable. You shouldn't travel without either one.

— Pack an AC extension cable. This will come in handy when you are far away from a power outlet.

— Keep an AC power adapter for your laptop in your bag. You never know when you might need one.

— If you're traveling internationally, be sure to pack multiple converters so that you can connect your devices. In the United States, we operate on a system that runs at 120 volts. Be sure to check the voltage of the country you're visiting prior to leaving.

— Another tip for international travelers: Leave your cell phone at home. Roaming charges can be staggering, and can be initiated even if you're not actively using your phone.

— Keep appropriate video adapters with your laptop in your laptop bag. You never know when you might need to connect your laptop or tablet to a TV or projector for a presentation.

— Pack headphones to keep the noise out. Have you ever tried to be productive on an airplane? It's hard when the person next to you can't stop talking. Just plug in your headphones and your problem is solved. You can even listen to relaxing music while you work. For those who want wireless Bluetooth headphones, check out the Jabra BT8030 headphones, costing about $150, or the Sony DR-BT101, described earlier in the book; however, you won't be able to use these on an airplane because they are transmitting devices. For music aficionados, the Bose QuietComfort 3 headphones offer the top of the line in headphone technology and include the noise-canceling circuitry that you hear everyone talking about. The downside, though, is the price—very, very expensive at around $350.

—Back up your data to an external hard drive or the network server. If your laptop crashes or is stolen, you will want a backup of your most important files.

—Encrypt your hard drive and data. There are many software tools available to do this, such as PGP, TrueCrypt, and PC Guardian. In the event your laptop is lost or stolen, your data is protected. Configure a startup or BIOS password on your computer, if available. Again, this adds another layer of protection.

—If you have a tablet, be sure to password protect your device with a passphrase. PINs aren't as secure and can be easily cracked. On an iPad, a passphrase requirement on the Lock Screen will enable encryption of your data. On Android devices, you can encrypt your data as well through the configuration settings.

—If you have a smartphone with a data plan that allows device tethering, take advantage of the data service you have already paid for and tether your laptop or tablet with your smartphone for Internet service. Avoid paying daily hotel fees for an Internet connection if it's not provided free during the course of your stay. However, data overage charges from your wireless carrier can be expensive, so it's best not to stream the movie at the top of your Netflix queue while tethered.

—Encrypt your USB flash drives and external hard drives.

—Disable your wireless autoconnection feature within the Windows operating system. Most laptops with wireless cards will automatically connect to any unencrypted, open wireless network when your default connection is unavailable.

—Prior to leaving the office, make sure that your security software has the latest updates and definitions to protect your devices while you're away. The same applies to Windows Updates.

These are just a few of the recommendations that we have for the legal road warriors, all based on our own experiences traveling. We hope that you can learn from our mistakes.

CHAPTER TWENTY-TWO

Mobile Security

TECHNOLOGY ADVANCES IN THIS area have come at warp speed. Gone are the days when you carried around a 50-foot phone cord looking for an analog phone jack that could be used with the modem in your laptop and America Online. Being übergeeks, we then carried along a splitter, coupler, and additional phone cords so that we could work comfortably on the bed or desk while we traveled around the nation. No more. It's even difficult to purchase a modern-day laptop with a modem. Wireless, whether WiFi or with your cellular carrier, is the word these days. More and more hotels, motels, conference centers, coffee shops, book stores, cafes, etc., are offering wireless access solutions.

Software

Before we jump into the boring details, let's cover some solutions that should be on your laptop no matter what other technology you use for remote connectivity. It goes without saying that you should have some sort of all-in-one security solution installed on your laptop. It should be configured to check for automatic updates and to perform a periodic full scan (we do weekly scans) to catch anything that may have "landed" before the signatures were updated. It would be just your luck to catch a virus on day one and be the first kid on the block to suffer the effects. Normally, the all-in-one security products will contain security features like antivirus, antimalware, firewalls, spam control, and antiphishing. Don't leave home without it.

Encryption

Secure mobile computing must contain some method of encryption to protect valuable personal and client data. We prefer whole disk encryption. This means that everything on the hard drive is encrypted and kept secure. We don't have to remember to put files into special folders or on the encrypted virtual drive. All too often, humans are in a big hurry and may not save their data in the special protected encrypted areas, leaving the information vulnerable.

In addition, without whole disk encryption, artifacts of the decryption passphrase are stored in various places (e.g., master file table (MFT), Page File, temp files, unallocated space). Forensics can extract these artifacts and make it probable that the passphrase can be determined. Many of the newer laptops have built-in whole disk encryption. To state the obvious, make sure you enable the encryption or your data won't be protected. Also, encryption may be used in conjunction with biometric access. As an example, our laptops require a fingerprint swipe to power on. Failure at that point leaves the computer hard drive fully encrypted. A very comforting thought if laptop thieves, who constitute a large club these days, make off with your laptop. If you think we are being too cautious, bear in mind that a laptop is stolen every 53 seconds in the United States. PCWorld.com reported that more than 10,000 laptops were lost or stolen at U.S. airports per week, totaling almost 640,000 lost or stolen laptops each year. We mean it when we say, "Be careful out there." Also, don't forget to encrypt your USB flash drives. Unfortunately for us good guys, these devices are easily lost and almost always contain our most valuable data.

Wireless

What's next? We won't cover modem access in the traditional sense, since dial-up isn't desirable, effective, or even around these days. Wireless is the rage of all the road warriors. There are two basic types of wireless access you'll encounter. The first type is generically termed a "wireless hot spot" and is what you find at your local Starbucks, hotel, or at the airport. You may or may not have to pay for these wireless connection services. Many businesses are offering free wireless as a way to attract customers—heck, even McDonald's offers a free wireless hotspot. Most of these hot spots are unsecured and wide open. This means that it is possible for your confidential data to be viewed by the customer at the next table or the one sitting on the park bench outside the café.

Does this mean you shouldn't use any of these wireless clouds? If you have a choice, we would say these clouds are best avoided by those who are technology averse and don't understand how to operate securely in an unsecured cloud. Read on, and determine whether you can safely be trusted to do what follows.

See if there is an option to have a secure connection to the cloud. This would be indicated if you use **https://** (note the s, denoting "secure") as part of the URL. Typically, website connections are unsecured and do not provide an encrypted session like the **https://** connections do. Be especially careful if you have to pay for the wireless connection. Be wary when you are at the screens that have you input your credit card and billing information. *Do not* enter any of this sensitive information without an **https://** connection. Once you've established a connection to the wireless cloud, be sure to use your VPN or other secure (**https://**) access to protect your transmissions.

Also, when connecting to a secure website, if you're presented with an error message referencing an SSL certificate error or invalid certificate, proceed with extreme caution or don't proceed at all.

Some hotels may give you a wireless cloud that is already secured. Typically, these wireless implementations use WPA (Wi-Fi protected access) or WPA2 to secure your connection and data. The cloud will be visible to your computer, but you will be required to provide a password before your computer connects. Once connected, the data you transmit will be encrypted and secure.

One scheme we see all the time: You are in a hotel that requires you to pay for Internet access. But when you ask your computer to show "all available wireless networks," it will display something like "free public wireless" as a network name—or something else that sounds innocuous, usually using the word free to entice you. Beware—these are often data thieves offering up an insecure cloud for the sole purpose of making off with your data. You can get the "free Internet"—but at a terrible price. Never be tempted by these clouds.

AirCard

Another wireless connection method is commonly called an AirCard. These are cards that are used to connect to the high-speed wireless networks of cellular phone providers. The major technologies in use today are EV-DO and 3G/4G. Don't be swayed by the vendor claims for speed and availability. Make sure that you will be able to have service in those areas you travel to the most. Reliability is another consideration, as is whether you already have a cellular plan.

The AirCard itself is a hardware device that you can externally connect to your laptop or select as a built-in option when configuring a new computer system. External AirCards come in both USB or PC card formats. These cards can be used on any laptop with USB ports or PC Card slots. Some newer laptops and netbooks have the electrical circuitry built in, so no additional hardware is required. The built-in capability means you have nothing to lose, but it is "married" to the laptop and can't be transferred between machines. Further, you would also be stuck with a single cellular vendor, as each vendor's radio is different. The external AirCards can cost several hundred dollars, but most providers offer significant discounts. As an example, Sprint currently offers a USB antenna for no cost after discounts and rebates.

The service itself can be daily, monthly, or annually by subscription. The monthly plans measure the amount of data you transfer over the connection and charge you for any overage usage. Typically, the data plans limit your usage to about 10GB a month and will run between $30 and $80 per month. Be wary of any data plan that offers unlimited data, because if you read the fine print, they're really not unlimited and have some sort of data cap. Verizon offers a day pass, where you can get 24 hours of secure, high-speed connectivity for $15. If you are an occasional traveler, this may be all you need, though it is irritating to have to fill out the full information and credit card screen each time you want to use the service, which is currently required by Verizon.

Obviously, you will want to purchase a monthly plan if you travel a lot or will use the service for more than four days a month. The AirCard is the preferred wireless connection, as the data is secured from the very beginning. You don't have to worry about whether you have an **https://** session or not. The electronic circuitry itself and the cellular carrier provide a fully encrypted session immediately.

Also, it should be noted that if you have multiple devices that need Internet access, rather than purchasing a subscription for each device, which can be very costly, invest in something like the Verizon MiFi or other mobile hot spot. These devices create a local wireless network that can provide Internet access (over the cellular network) to up to five devices. The Verizon 4G MiFi starts at $49.99 with a two-year data plan.

Public Computer Usage

A word of warning here. Be very careful about using a public computer, such as those in the library or business center of a hotel. Even if you are only accessing your web-based e-mail account, the data is temporarily written to the local hard disk. There is also the risk that some keystroke logging software is installed on the computer, thereby capturing everything that you do on the machine.

Does that mean all public computers are off limits? Not at all. We are big fans of the IronKey hardware encrypted USB flash drive. Besides the drive encryption and secure management of passwords, the IronKey has portable applications that are intended to be used with public computers. As an example, there is a specially modified version of the Firefox browser that doesn't write any data to the computer. All data stays on the IronKey, thereby making it secure and keeping it with you when you leave. Of course, this does mean that the computer has to accept the insertion of USB devices. Some business center machines are locked down and do not allow USB devices to be inserted, because it is a security risk to the business—USB devices can be used to introduce malware to the machine or network. Though we have tipped our hat to those who secure their computers this way (it's absolutely the right thing to do), it has prevented us from using our IronKey several times.

Smartphones

Want to know what the most insecure smartphone on the market is? Apple isn't going to like us, but, arguably, it's the iPhone. It's pretty clear that the iPhone was designed as a consumer phone first, with security just an afterthought.

At a minimum, everybody should have a PIN code programmed into their phone to prevent unauthorized access, along with a fairly short time out period. It doesn't do much good to have an unlocking PIN and then have 30 minutes pass before the phone relocks. We know it's a pain to constantly punch in the unlock code, but that will keep your data from being accessed by prying eyes. Better yet, it will stop someone from installing spyware on your phone that can effectively trap all of your communications (voice calls, e-mail, text messages, etc.). For those devices that offer a passphrase alternative to the PIN, such as the iPad, this would be the preferred choice to secure your device. Why, you might ask? Because a passphrase can be longer than a PIN and can contain non-numeric values, strongly increasing the strength of the protection.

Besides PIN protecting your phone, make sure you encrypt any memory cards, or just don't store any sensitive data on them. We're talking about the SD, micro SD, etc., cards that you can insert into the smartphone to increase storage capacity. There are programs available for some models that allow you to encrypt the card contents. The point is that you don't want any confidential information to be accessible on the card if you lose your phone. The PIN will protect the phone access, but the "bad guy" will pop out the memory card and read it from his computer if it is not encrypted.

Finally, investigate the ability to wipe the data from the smartphone remotely if it is lost. Windows Phone 7, iPhone, and BlackBerry devices have this ability, with or without a cellular network. The iPhone is a little more vulnerable, because the PIN can be bypassed with some versions of the iOS. Remember that the remote wipe feature is for the memory within the phone itself and *not* the memory cards that we spoke about earlier.

Final Words

The options and requirements for mobile security have certainly changed quickly over the years. Talk to us in four years and we're sure the world will have changed again. For now, make sure that you are aware of all the issues to securely transfer your data and that you are not relying on "antique" knowledge. You must assume that there is absolutely no protection of the communication stream between your laptop and your remote device. We've seen hotel networks that didn't have a firewall, so all traffic was allowed to flow through. We immediately saw probing attacks on our computers, which were stopped by the firewalls on our laptops. It's the wild, wild West out there, and you're the only marshal in town. Good luck, Wyatt.

CHAPTER TWENTY-THREE

More from Apple

APART FROM THE INFORMATION conveyed previously about Mac laptops and desktops, we want to offer you additional data in light of the continued interest lawyers have shown in potentially switching to Mac computers. Most lawyers have never used a Mac, either in their personal life or for their job. Most are only familiar with the iPod or the very popular iPad 2. Some people may argue that Macs are ready for "prime time," to take on Windows-based PCs in the business setting. From a hardware standpoint, Macs are just as good as, if not better than, PCs. You can't really tell them apart since Macs made the switch to using Intel-based processors. The only difference now is the operating system, which is still the main obstacle for Macs gaining a greater piece of the pie in the business marketplace.

Frankly, the problem lies with software compatibility with Macs. Most law firms, no matter the size, use legal-specific software on a daily basis to do their jobs. Whether you're looking at case management, billing, trial-related or field-specific software, most vendors still do not make versions for Macs. But for lawyers who use a computer just for word processing, Internet research, filing motions, billing, and accounting, a Mac could suit these functions perfectly. Below, we discuss some Mac-specific hardware and software solutions that may come in handy if you are or want to become a Mac user.

Hardware

Apple iPad 2
Just when you thought the fanfare for the iPad couldn't get any noisier, Apple released the next updated version, the iPad 2. And this upgrade couldn't have come soon enough.

Very few technology devices have arrived with as much fanfare and excitement as the Apple iPad 2 did when it was released in March 2011. The iPad 2 includes a number of feature upgrades and enhancements that weren't present in the original iPad, which was the first tablet computer designed and developed by Apple, although technically it really isn't a tablet. The iPad 2 runs the same software as the iPhone and iPod and can be synchronized with iTunes just like any of the other iOS devices.

The iPad 2 has a 9.7-inch Multi-Touch, LED-backlit, IPS screen glass display, with a resolution of 1024 x 768 pixels (132 pixels per inch). The touch screen breaks away from the previous models of touch screen devices that required a user to press the screen with a stylus, as in the old days of Palm Pilots. An embedded three-axis accelerometer is used to determine the orientation of the device—portrait or landscape mode—and some apps and games take advantage of this feature.

The iPad 2 comes with a built-in Wi-Fi network card enabling the device to connect to wireless networks, and the 3G model comes with a broadband AirCard and GPS locator. The device also includes Bluetooth capability and a battery lasting up to 10 hours, even when continually surfing the Internet.

Some of the major criticisms of the iPad 2 are the lack of Flash support, expansion capability, and alternate input/output sources. Many industry analysts say that the lack of Flash support significantly cripples Apple products, since so many websites incorporate the technology. Even though the iPad 2 comes with a fair amount of embedded memory, there are no options to add storage in the form of memory expansion cards (e.g., SD, micro SD). Finally, there are no USB ports available, which significantly limits what connections may be added. As an example, your only current option is to print via Bluetooth or wireless printer or to use a Bluetooth keyboard. USB printers and keyboards are not an option. With the iOS 4.2 version release, Apple has included support for wireless printing over the local Wi-Fi network. The number of printers with AirPrint support continues to grow and includes a number of HP LaserJet and OfficeJet printer models. With the latest iOS 4.3 release, Apple has added display mirroring, which replicates the iPad's display over the video out connection, rather than the video out feature working only with selected applications.

The iPad 2 included a number of hardware advances over the first generation device, including:

- —Black-and-white and color options
- —Both AT&T and Verizon 3G models

—1 GHz dual-core Apple A5 processor
—Front and back facing camera
—Increased amount of memory

We have been quite pleased with the upgrades that Apple included with this model, but don't let the camera support fool you. Apple might have been better off not including the cameras given the poor quality and low resolution of the front and rear facing cameras. However, they did get something right. The increased processor speed and amount of memory make this device even faster and more responsive.

Today, this device is being used frequently by lawyers for court or meetings, rather than lugging around a laptop. Originally thought to compete against e-book devices such as the Kindle or Nook, the iPad has actually established a new class of devices to compete against smartphones, netbooks, and smaller laptops. Lawyers are drawn to the functionality and portability of the device, and we believe that interest will only increase as future generations are released. The iPad can be purchased directly online from the Apple Store (**store.apple.com**) starting at $499 for the 16GB WiFi-only model.

Apple iPad 2

Tom Mighell, an attorney and iPad expert, has two wonderful books available to assist attorneys who need help in understanding how to best utilize the iPad in their practice of law. The two books, *iPad in One Hour for Lawyers*, and *iPad Apps in One Hour for Lawyers*, can be purchased directly from the ABA's bookstore, and should be considered an invaluable resource for attorneys who are looking to 'test drive' their iPads at work.

AirPort Extreme

Apple's AirPort Extreme is its wireless solution for home, school, and business. The wireless router plugs directly into your cable or DSL modem and connects users wirelessly to the Internet. This router supports the 802.11a/b/g/n protocols. The wireless router supports NAT, DHCP, and VPN passthrough, allowing users the capability of connecting to their office network from home. The AirPort Extreme comes with built-in security features, such as a NAT firewall, Wi-Fi Protected Access, WPA/WPA2 and WEP encryption, and MAC address filtering. The router contains a GB Ethernet WAN port for connecting to a cable or DSL modem and three GB Ethernet LAN ports for connecting computers or networking devices. The built-in USB is provided to connect a printer or hard drive to be shared to users on the local network. The AirPort Extreme is both Mac and Windows compatible and comes bundled with software, power cord, and documentation. The AirPort Extreme can be purchased directly online from the Apple Store (**store.apple.com**) for $179.

Apple's AirPort Extreme

AirPort Express

The AirPort Express Base Station is a portable wireless router, perfect for taking with you while on the road. The small wireless router is extremely portable, about the size of a postcard, and weighs less than 7.5 ounces. The router supports the 802.11a/b/g/n protocols. This wireless device is great for hotels, supplying your laptop with wireless Internet so you can surf from any location in the room. The device has a built-in USB port for connecting a shared printer and an Ethernet port for connecting to your DSL and cable modem or your local network. The built-in wireless security supports WPA/WPA2, WEP, NAT, MAC address filtering, and time-based access control. The AirPort Express Base Station is both Mac and Windows compatible and comes bundled with the necessary software to get your computer connected to the wireless network. The AirPort Express Base Station can be purchased directly online from the Apple Store (**store.apple.com**) for $99.

Apple's AirPort Express Base Station with 802.11n and AirTunes

Time Capsule

Looking for a solution to automatically back up your files? Time Capsule works seamlessly with Time Machine, backup software included with the Mac OS X Lion operating system. Time Capsule is simply a wireless router with a built-in hard drive used for storing backups of your files. Using the Time Machine backup software, the application will back up your files and folders automatically, without user intervention. The data is backed up over the local wireless network to the Time Capsule hardware device. Time Capsule can be purchased and used solely as a backup solution, or it can also provide wireless Internet connectivity to your local network. It has the same built-in features and functionality as AirPort Extreme. Time Capsule is offered in two models with storage capacities of 2 and 3TB. The Time Capsule can be purchased directly online from the Apple Store (**store.apple.com**) starting at $299 for the 2TB model.

Apple's Time Capsule

Apple Thunderbolt Display

The Apple Thunderbolt Display is a model line of high-definition (HD) flat-panel LCD monitors offering 27 inches of diagonal viewing area. Its widescreen format makes this monitor a perfect display for legal professionals, providing enough real estate to display two or more documents side-by-side. The display is compatible with any Thunderbolt-enabled Mac notebook and desktop and supports resolutions up to 2560 by 1440 pixels.

The monitor has a 1,000:1 contrast ratio, 12 milliseconds response time, and a screen with an antiglare coating. The monitor has three USB 2.0 ports and can be purchased with an optional VESA wall mount. The monitor also includes a built-in FaceTime HD camera with microphone and 2.1 speaker system. The monitor even includes an ambient light sensor that can automatically adjust the brightness of the LCD display. The monitor also includes a GB Ethernet port, a Thunderbolt port, and a FireWire 800 port. The Apple Thunderbolt Display can be purchased directly online from the Apple Store (**store.apple.com**) for $999.

Apple Thunderbolt Display

Apple Wireless Keyboard

The Apple wireless keyboard uses Bluetooth wireless technology, eliminating the need for obstructive and unfriendly wires to connect your keyboard to your computer. The wireless keyboard comes in a low-profile anodized aluminum frame that matches the Apple theme. The keyboard contains function keys for one-touch access to Mac features and has power-management features to conserve the battery when not in use. The Apple wireless keyboard requires Mac OS X version 10.6.8 or later and takes two AA batteries, but can also be used with the iPad. It can be purchased directly online from the Apple Store (**store.apple.com**) for $69.

Apple's Wireless Keyboard

Apple Magic Mouse

Like the Apple wireless keyboard, the Magic Mouse uses Bluetooth wireless technology to connect the mouse to your computer. Laser tracking allows you to use the mouse on a number of surfaces while maintaining the precision and accuracy of tracking movement. The mouse uses touch-sensitive technology to detect both right and left clicks, and the innovative scrolling ball allows for 360-degree scrolling capabilities. The mouse is powered with two AA batteries and, when paired with the Apple wireless keyboard, allows you to work wire free at your desk. The Apple Magic Mouse can be purchased directly online from the Apple Store (**store.apple.com**) for $69.

Apple's Magic Mouse

Apple iPod

By far Apple's most successful hardware device, the iPod has sold over 200 million units since its creation in 2001. The portable digital-file-playing devices are by far the most popular handheld devices in use today, and some models can be used to play and shoot video, take pictures, play podcasts, and even play games. All models are capable of playing music. The iPod is available in four models: Shuffle, Nano, Classic, and Touch. Recent rumors are that Apple will discontinue manufacturing the Shuffle and Classic versions of the iPod. We should know if this is true by the time this book makes it to print. The iPod Shuffle is the smallest, with no display screen, and is available in a 2GB size. The Shuffle allows you to shake the device in certain positions to change the song, play the songs in order, or shuffle the order. The newest version also includes a new VoiceOver function that will tell you the song or artist you're listening to. The iPod Shuffle costs $49 and is available in five different colors.

The iPod Classic is the throwback to the original iPod with the circular wheel and comes in both black and white. The main feature of this device is capacity. It has 160GB of storage space, which can store a vast quantity of music, video, and podcasts. This device can even be used to play games. The iPod Classic costs $249 and is available only with a 160GB storage capacity. There is actually a hard disk in this version, so it won't work well while you exercise.

The iPod Nano is one of Apple's more popular devices. The current version of the Nano includes a radio tuner with live pause functionality, VoiceOver, and even a pedometer. You can enhance your workout experience with special Nike shoes that interface to the Nano. The iPod Nano is offered in seven bright colors, in both 8 and 16GB models, and costs $149 or $179, depending on the storage capacity. Flash memory is used in the Nano, making it ideal for workouts at the gym.

The iPod Touch is probably the most versatile iPod, providing users with a way to listen to music, watch videos, and play games as well as surf the Internet and check their e-mail. The latest version includes FaceTime, a video calling application, and a Retina display. The iPod Touch has a 3.5-inch diagonal color display, a touch-screen interface, and is available in 8, 32, and 64GB sizes. The iPod Touch even has a built-in Wi-Fi network adapter supporting 802.11b/g/n network connections. The device also includes Bluetooth support. The 8GB model costs $229, the 32GB model costs $299, and the 64GB model costs $399.

All of the iPod devices can be purchased online from the Apple Store or at your local electronics retailer. All of the devices are both Windows and Mac compatible, and they connect to your computer using a USB connection.

Available iPod Models

Software

Microsoft Office 2008 for Macs: Business Edition

We often are asked, "Can I open Microsoft Office documents on a Mac computer?" The short answer is yes, with Microsoft Office 2008 for Mac. This Microsoft product is the latest version of the productivity suite for the Mac platform. Microsoft Office 2008 includes Microsoft Word, Excel, PowerPoint, and Entourage, all for the Mac computer. Word, Excel, and PowerPoint are compatible with their Windows counterparts. Entourage is like Outlook, an e-mail client for Macs. Entourage includes support for Microsoft Exchange Server, so getting your corporate e-mail on your Mac is no longer an issue. The Business Edition also includes Microsoft Live Workspace Support, for sharing files and collaborating on projects from any location with an Internet connection; Microsoft Windows SharePoint Services, to store and share documents in one secure location; and Entourage 2008 Web Services Edition, to allow you to stay in sync with all of your mobile devices. Finally, Remote Desktop for Mac 2 lets you connect from your Mac to a Windows-based computer to access files and programs.

Microsoft Office 2008 for Macs Business Edition require Mac OS X version 10.4.9 or later and is available in both a Standard and an Upgrade Edition. Microsoft Office 2008 can be purchased online from the Apple Store (**store.apple.com**) for $249.95 for the Upgrade Edition and $399.95 for the Standard Edition.

Microsoft Office for Mac 2011 is now out and includes better compatibility across platforms, improved collaboration tools, and an improved user interface. The latest version also scraps Entourage for Outlook, which will provide Mac users with the ability to import Microsoft Outlook PST files. Visual Basic support returns as well, which is a must-have for those running macro-based applications. Users can also store files online using their SkyDrive folder, which provides secure access to edit or share your work from anywhere with free Office web apps.

Office for Mac 2011 requires Mac OS X v. 10.5.8 or later and is available only in a 32-bit version. A single license for this product can be purchased online from the Apple Store (**store.apple.com**) for $199.95.

Microsoft Office for Mac 2011

Toast 11 Titanium by Roxio

Toast 11 Titanium is the latest version of Roxio's long-running, disc-burning software for the Mac. With this software you can burn video or data to CDs or DVDs. This version gives users the ability to burn high-definition video to Blu-ray and HD-DVD. Toast even allows a user to capture streaming audio from any website and then transfer the audio to an iPod. The software has built-in basic features, such as the ability to compress, convert, and compile video in most formats, along with backup software that can be scheduled to back up your data. Features new to this version include the ability to extract clips from any DVD video and convert them to a format of your choice, convert audiobook CDs for playback on iPod devices, and build your MP3 library with automatic capture and tagging of Internet audio. Also included with this feature is a full version of Adobe Photoshop Elements 9.

Roxio Toast 11 Titanium

The software can be purchased online from Roxio's website (**www.roxio.com**) for $129.99.

Norton Internet Security for Mac

Every Mac user needs to protect his or her computer from viruses and other threats. Using antivirus protection on a Mac is no longer an option but rather a necessity. Norton Internet Security has an edition specifically for Mac computers that offers protection from the latest viruses, spyware, rootkits, and other web-based attacks. Norton Internet Security is compatible with OS X v. 10.4.11 and newer systems and runs natively on Intel- and PowerPC-based Mac systems. The antivirus protection can automatically scan and clean downloaded e-mail files and attachments and provide real-time protection and removal of viruses and other threats.

Some users say there are no viruses or threats for a Mac. Not so. Just look at how many systems were infected with the MacDefender virus this past year. It was such a problem that Apple released a security patch just to address this threat. There are many other documented viruses that are specific to Macs and many more that are operating system–independent. The message here is to get and install an antivirus or security solution. You should never use a computer on your business or home network without the proper security protection, even if it's a Mac. Norton Internet Security can be purchased online directly from Symantec's website (**www.symantec.com**) for $55.99 for a one-year subscription.

Norton Internet Security For Mac

Intuit Quicken Essentials and QuickBooks 2011 for Mac

Quicken for Mac offers a complete personal financial management package, providing immediate access to your accounts from a single location. By using Quicken, you can better organize your financial information and easily track your finances. Quicken Essentials provides an easy way to track and enter expenses without launching the entire application through the new QuickEntry Dashboard Widget. The software will run only on Intel-based Macs using 10.5.8 (Leopard), 10.6.2 (Snow Leopard), or 10.7 (Lion). Quicken Essentials is a brand new product, and several of the previous features do not exist. One key difference is that you cannot export your data from Quicken Essentials. Users can now export their basic tax information to TurboTax and other applications that can read a TXF file. Quicken Essentials for Mac is the latest version of the software from Intuit that is available for purchase on its website (**www.intuit.com**; $49.99).

QuickBooks, another financial and accounting package from Intuit, has an edition for Macs. QuickBooks 2012 for Macs can be used to organize your business finances. This software package can be used to track and manage your business expenses, invoicing, and payroll from a single financial application. QuickBooks for Macs can synchronize your contacts directly with the Mac OS X Address Book and set reminders in iCal. In addition, you can back up your data directly to your MobileMe account. This software is compatible with Mac OS X v. 10.6.7, v. 10.7, or higher.

Some of the new features of QuickBooks 2012 for Macs include:

—Newly redesigned sales forms

—Can add online banking transactions in batches

—Improved Search function

—Can invoice for projects in phases with Progress invoicing

—Can create multiple time sheets with one click

QuickBooks 2012 for Macs can be purchased online from Intuit's QuickBooks website (**www.quickbooks.com**) for $229.95 for a new license, $199.95 to upgrade. Two- and three-user versions are also available.

PGP Whole Disk Encryption 10 for Mac OS X

PGP Corporation (now owned by Symantec), a leading vendor of hard disk encryption software, has released a version of its hard disk encryption suite for the Mac computer. PGP Whole Disk Encryption software provides comprehensive, nonstop disk encryption for Macs, securing data on desktops, laptops, and removable devices. A user name and passphrase are required in order to decrypt the contents of the hard disk, protecting the data from unauthorized access. PGP Whole Disk Encryption 10 requires Mac OS X 10.5 or 10.6 and only runs on Intel-based Macs. PGP Whole Disk Encryption can be used to provide quick, cost-effective data protection for information on hard drives and removable media. Any lawyer using a Mac laptop should definitely have this software installed to protect sensitive and confidential information.

PGP Whole Disk Encryption 10 for Mac OS X software can be purchased online directly from PGP's website (**www.pgp.com**) for $139 for a single license with one-year upgrade assurance.

Apple iTunes

If you've ever owned an iPod, then you're certainly familiar with iTunes. iTunes is Apple Software's most popular product, mainly because it's necessary to manage your digital library on your iPod, iPhone, iPad, or other Apple iOS device. The newest version of iTunes allows users to download more content with their purchased artist's songs, such as the album cover, band pictures, and even song lyrics. Using the Home Sharing feature, users can share their digital libraries with up to five authorized computers in their house, allowing you to share purchased music files across multiple computer systems. Apple now allows you to view what music your friends are downloading and listening to, as well as the ability to follow your favorite artists. For users of the iPad, using the iBooks app, users can download books from the iTunes store directly to their device.

The new iTunes in the Cloud beta provides users with the ability to access their music, shows, apps, and books from multiple devices without the need to synchronize.

Using the iTunes Store, users can download apps, music, videos, podcasts, and more and then synchronize them to their devices, such as the iPad or iPhone. Users can subscribe to podcasts, and the iTunes application can download the latest shows as they're made available without any user input. We use this feature a lot when it comes to managing the legal technology podcasts we constantly monitor and to which we subscribe.

iTunes is available as a free download for Mac OS X and Windows XP/Vista/7 from Apple's website.

CHAPTER TWENTY-FOUR

Unified Messaging and Telecommunications

UNIFIED MESSAGING IS THE delivery of traditional voice communications into your e-mail box. This would include the delivery of facsimile transmissions as well. Unified messaging systems began to appear around 2001 and were fairly unsuccessful for the first couple of years. Now they are stable and actually work. This means that you can now monitor your communications constantly from (potentially) one location. This is a blessing and a curse, but it is now becoming a service that many clients expect you to have.

The simplest way to implement unified messaging is to have it integrated with your phone system. Some small firms may not even have a phone system, and we'll address that issue in a moment. Many of the newer PBX (private branch exchange) systems are incorporating a voicemail card directly into the telephone system chassis. Stand-alone voicemail systems are also an alternative for larger office environments.

For budget purposes, plan on spending around $3,000 for a voicemail system with unified messaging. As is true for most technology solutions, your mileage may vary. There are a lot of different ways that vendors implement unified messaging. Some are better than others, and, frankly, some are nothing more than kludge workarounds to make their systems sound more robust than they really are. Our recommendation is to stick with well-known vendors of communication equipment. You really can't go wrong with suppliers such as Cisco, NEC, Toshiba, etc.

There are companies that resell unified messaging solutions, thereby saving you the investment in hardware and software. These solutions are typically available for a monthly fee, and you may have to commit to a multiyear contract to obtain the service. Also, you are stuck with whatever features and methods the vendor provides. As an example, you may not like the file format for a fax delivery into your inbox, but you'll have no choice but to accept what they give you. Another concern is that all of your communications will be going through a third party. This means that your phone calls actually route through their system before being delivered to your location. In that way, they can capture a voicemail message or fax and repackage it for delivery to your e-mail address. We are generally not fans of having client data move through third-party providers and would recommend that you first investigate "owned" systems that you can control. While a price tag of $3,000 isn't cheap, the value is so great that a good number of solos and small firms have made the leap, and the numbers grow monthly.

We'll attempt to cover some of the concerns and questions you should have when considering whether to implement a unified messaging solution. These issues are related to equipment that is provided as part of your telephone communication system. The first issue is what communications the system handles. Can it do both voice messages and fax transmissions, or just one? Even though most systems will handle both voicemail and fax, most firms use only the voice capability and route the faxes to a dedicated fax machine or printer rather than to a specific person's inbox.

So how do you want the voice messages delivered? Most firms will elect to send only an e-mail notification that a voicemail message has been received. This configuration saves bandwidth because the message itself is not transmitted to the e-mail client and stays on the voicemail server until you retrieve it. This is hardly convenient if you are traveling. In fact, some telephone systems are configured not to allow remote connections, even for voicemail retrieval, as a security measure. There are a lot of lawyers who use BlackBerry devices. A large number of older BlackBerry devices cannot play sound files, so sending the message to your phone is pointless. However, the newer BlackBerry models can play audio files. Make sure that your portable device can play back the file format for your voicemail if you elect to deliver the message to your inbox. As an example, the iPad 2 doesn't play back .WAV files, which is the format of our unified message system. The other alternative is to deliver the actual message to your inbox. Obviously, this uses a lot more bandwidth, especially if you are delivering it to a cell phone that also receives your e-mail. You'd better have an unlimited data plan for your cell phone if you elect this configuration or a data plan that can cover your traffic load.

Another question for your PBX provider is how it handles the message delivery itself. Is it forwarded to your inbox and then deleted from the voicemail system? That means there is only one copy of it, and you'll never know you received a message if it gets trapped or trashed by your spam filter. If the original stays on the voicemail system and a copy gets delivered to your inbox, does the message light stay lit on your phone? You may not want this, but then again you may want a visual indication that a voice message was delivered.

How does the vendor identify the voice message in your inbox? Is the "From: address" something that is easily recognizable as the phone system, or does it come from you? What does the subject line contain? It is particularly helpful if the caller ID shows in the subject line, but not all vendors package messages that way. How is the voice message delivered to your e-mail system? Do you have to have a user ID and password configured on your voicemail box that is consistent with your network credentials? If so, you have the issue of constantly synchronizing your logon credentials with the telephone system. Many phone systems only accept numbers as a password, so you can't even use letters (forget capitals). This restriction may render your integration unacceptable.

Finally, how do you retrieve your messages? Are they delivered as a standard audio attachment to an e-mail message? This is certainly preferred, since you don't need any special software to listen to the message. Some of the lower cost (and kludge) solutions require that you install a software add-on to your e-mail client to listen to the voice message. This solution won't work if you are trying to deliver the voicemail to your cell phone. Another problem deals with specific software versions. You must make sure that any potential voicemail system will be compatible with your firm's e-mail solution, so if you have questions regarding what versions of Microsoft Exchange and Outlook the voicemail system is compatible with, make sure you ask your vendor before you make the investment. As you can see, having specialized software is not a recommended solution. Better to have the voice message packaged as a standard (not proprietary) audio file attachment. That way you can even retrieve your voicemail using a web browser from an Internet café while on vacation in Rio.

If all of this has given you a headache, don't worry. Make sure your IT consultant reads this chapter—he or she can answer all the questions for you. But make no mistake about it: No one who has successfully implemented unified messaging has ever discarded it. The value of unified messaging is phenomenal—being able to access your voicemail on your cell phone is a remarkable enhancement. You need never worry again about being out of touch. If you prefer not to give clients your home or cell phone number, you'll still get their messages. We cannot count the number of times that having voicemail sent to our cell phones has been worth its weight in diamonds.

Google Voice

For those lawyers constantly on the road, a free service you might find useful is Google Voice. If you'd rather not give out your personal cell phone number to your pesky clients, who always have emergencies regardless of the time, then this service might be for you. Google Voice allows you to select a phone number local to your area that forwards inbound phone calls to your other personal phone numbers. This service allows you to provide your clients with a phone number (not your personal number), screen incoming phone calls, and receive voicemails left on the Google Voice phone number in your e-mail inbox. You can specify what e-mail address you would like the voicemails forwarded to. Google Voice will even transcribe your voicemails to text and provide them in the body of the e-mail, allowing users to read the content before they choose to listen to the messages. Google Voice also allows users to receive and record phone conversations (be mindful of the laws in your state if you do this), index and search voicemails, and set up conference calls.

If you are currently a Sprint customer, you can take advantage of the Google Voice features without changing your phone number. Be sure to review the help section at the Google Voice site (**www.google.com/voice**) to see exactly what features you get by integrating your Sprint account with Google Voice.

Voice over Internet Protocol (VoIP)

In its most basic definition, VoIP is a family of technologies for delivery of voice communications over Internet protocol networks, such as the Internet. VoIP systems are digital and can run both voice and data systems over the same network, reducing investment in infrastructure. Corporate usage of VoIP phone systems has increased dramatically over the past few years, replacing the traditional copper-wire telephone systems that we all used in the past.

VoIP systems are primarily aimed at providing users with unified communications, delivering all services (voice, fax, voicemails, and e-mail) to a single location. VoIP systems are generally more flexible and less costly to implement than your standard copper-wire systems, and they can integrate easily with most existing data network infrastructures.

Security used to be a major concern for VoIP systems. That concern has been greatly reduced. It appears that vendors have finally overcome the performance hit associated with encrypting the voice traffic. You would be hard pressed to find a current vendor that sends voice traffic in an unencrypted stream. This means you'll sleep a little better knowing that your voice traffic travels in secure encrypted channels. That doesn't mean that your VoIP traffic isn't subject to hacking. In fact, security guru Bruce Schneier has published several blog posts describing how to hack a VoIP data stream. His latest post discusses how it is possible to even ". . . *identify the phrases spoken within encrypted VoIP calls* when the audio is encoded using variable bit rate codecs." Sound scary? The reality is that your calls probably aren't subject to interception, especially if you take prudent steps to control access to the VoIP network and equipment.

Because the underlying IP network that a VoIP system uses is unreliable, it's not uncommon to experience latency or jitteriness when making a call using a VoIP phone system, especially to off-site destinations. Once your voice packet hits the already congested Internet, you are no longer in control of how fast your data gets to where it's going, and that's what causes the delays. Using a VoIP system on the same data network as your computer system might tremendously slow down how fast you can access your server and case management applications because of all the data traffic on your local network. Be sure your existing data network and Internet connection are capable of handling the increase in load before implementing a VoIP system. If you have to upgrade existing hardware or the speed of your Internet connection, those are hidden costs that you might not be aware of and that you will have to plan for. Also, implementing an MPLS (Multiprotocol Label Switching) network gives you the option of configuring QoS (Quality of Service), where you can give the voice traffic a higher priority. MPLS networks are not cheap and tend to be used in larger firms with multiple office locations. Frankly, we think MPLS is overkill and too expensive for a solo or small firm considering VoIP.

And last, VoIP systems are susceptible to power failures and outages. Unlike analog phones that get their power directly from the copper phone lines, VoIP systems need electricity to operate, just like your computer system. You better have an analog phone line as a backup, or at least a cell phone.

VoIP phone systems have their pros and cons when compared to other digital phone systems. Be sure to ask your vendor the right questions to determine which type of system is right for you. And be wary of those vendors and check their references. We have seen a lot of VoIP installations that caused major-league heartburn for the law firms that undertook them. Not only have hidden costs pushed their budgets far beyond the original numbers, but vendors tend not to plan for redundancy or to warn of the potential downsides of VoIP. We have had both happy and unhappy VoIP clients, so we're not saying, "Don't do it," but be aware that this is not the right choice for everyone.

High-Speed Internet

None of our lawyers/clients ever complain that their Internet connection is too fast. We have collectively almost forgotten how slow the Internet used to be and how patiently we had to wait for our screens to load. High-speed Internet is now a requirement for solos and small law firms. High-speed Internet has all but replaced dial-up Internet connections because of the low cost and fast connection speeds. Why continue to wait for web pages to load and attachments to open if you don't have to? Few creatures are more impatient than lawyers, and virtually all of them have jumped to high-speed Internet within the past few years.

High-speed Internet connections are available from your local Internet service provider (ISP) and usually are provided over a cable, DSL, or fiber optic connection. These high-speed connections offer download speeds in excess of 25MB/s and varying upload speeds depending on the provider and the service tier to which you've subscribed. If your firm hosts its own services, such as e-mail or a website, static IP addresses can be obtained from your local provider with these types of connections. The ISP may charge more to issue your business a static IP address than if you just required a dynamically leased IP address. High-speed Internet access connectivity generally will cost $75–$200 per month.

If your firm requires a larger amount of bandwidth due to the number of users sharing the Internet connection or for web-based applications, your local ISP may be able to provide a connection type that meets your requirements. Some examples of upgraded service connections are referred to as T1 or fractional T1 connections and can cost hundreds of dollars per month. These types of connections also require longer service agreements and usually include a large setup cost. They do have the advantage of a service level agreement (SLA), which means that the connection must be repaired within a particular time and must be available a high percentage of the time. DSL or cable modem connections do not carry an SLA, so repair times could be several days during an outage. T1 circuits are becoming less and less popular, even though they are very reliable and guarantee bandwidth. A full T1 provides only 1.544 megabits per second (Mbps) up and down and typically will cost $300–$500 per month. Compare this to other broadband services (cable or DSL), where you can get 30 Mbps download and 5 Mbps upload for less than $200 a month.

If available in your area, a speedy alternative to a T1 is fiber optics. Fiber to the curb, such as Verizon FiOS, can offer business subscribers increasingly faster Internet connections at a much lower cost. Check with your local service providers to see if such a connection is currently available. In general, solos and small firms are well served by cable and DSL to meet their Internet connection needs.

Another option for Internet access is from your cellular provider. Mobile broadband Internet access has gained steam lately and is becoming a growing trend with mobile lawyers. Plus, it's a good way to avoid having to pay those outrageous prices for Internet access that hotels charge nowadays. You may have heard the terms 3G, 4G, etc., used to identify mobile broadband. For about $60 a month, your cellular provider can provide you with Internet access when on the road. If you've purchased a laptop recently, you might already have a broadband card installed. For everyone else, most providers will throw in the broadband card for no cost when you sign up for their service. Even iPad and smartphone users are using mobile broadband as part of their data plans.

CHAPTER TWENTY-FIVE

Utilities

WHAT WE ALL NEED is Batman's belt, with a full repository of tricks that we can draw upon at any moment to perform the myriad tasks associated with the practice of law. Failing that, we must acknowledge that it is impossible to list all of the utilities that a solo or small firm might find useful. There are so many great selections and just as many opinions as to what makes one utility more valuable than another.

The threshold question is, what constitutes a utility? For our purposes, we will consider a utility to be some software application that takes data and manipulates it for a specific purpose. That allows us a lot of latitude.

The challenge is to list utilities that offer a unique purpose for the solo and small firm lawyer. We have used many of these utilities ourselves and have had some great suggestions from our friends and colleagues. If you don't see your favorite utility here, just drop us a line and perhaps it will be listed in the next edition of the book.

X1

How often do you find yourself frantically searching your computer for a file only to discover that you have no clue *where* you saved it? It's happened to all of us, and the problem is compounded when you have copies of the same file saved in multiple locations. What a headache.

To relieve some of the stress, we recommend that lawyers use a product called X1. X1 is a piece of software that enables users to search for and instantly find information, while keeping the resulting file in its native format. No more messy conversions. X1 allows users to search for any file, whether located within their e-mail on the local computer, a network share, or removable storage drive. This software currently supports more than 500 file types in their native format and layout and can even search for data within multiple Microsoft Outlook PST files and Lotus Notes without having to mount the files.

The X1 program displays the search results as you type, similar to the new Google Instant Search, which allows users to modify their search query in real time. The advanced searching options allow users to search multiple e-mail metadata fields, such as From, To, and Subject, as well as to sort the resulting files by any of the file properties.

The X1 program is a powerful search tool that includes a number of advanced features, such as support for searching inside compressed ZIP files and RSS feeds, as well as a number of export options, such as exporting the search results to a folder or Microsoft Outlook PST file. The product is even administrator-friendly, supporting integration with Active Directory and Group Policy, for ease of deployment and flexibility in its configuration.

Prior to installing, you will need to make sure that you have enough storage space for the search index this program will create, which is roughly 20 percent of the total volume of files indexed. X1 supports Microsoft Windows XP, Vista, and 7 (32- or 64-bit) operating systems; Microsoft Outlook XP/2003/2007/2010 (32-bit); Microsoft Outlook Express 6.x; Mozilla Thunderbird 1.5/2.x/3.x; and IBM Lotus Notes and Domino 6.5x to 8.x e-mail clients. This product doesn't currently support the 64-bit version of Microsoft Outlook 2010 but does support the 32-bit version.

The X1 Professional Client software costs $49.95 per license and can be purchased with varying levels of support. To view or purchase this product, visit **www.x1.com**.

dtSearch

dtSearch is another powerful search tool that has been used by lawyers for many years, dating back to the early MS-DOS days. This product has come a long way and remains one of our favorite and most popular searching tools.

dtSearch is offered in a number of different versions, but solo and small firms should consider only the following versions:

- Desktop with Spider
- Network with Spider

The Desktop with Spider version is perfect for solo lawyers that need to be able to instantly search their client files on a single computer, although it can also be configured to index network drives. The Network with Spider version allows multiple users to search the same search index, which is a must when working in a multiuser networking environment.

The dtSearch products include support for full-text searching as well as the ability to search a number of common metadata fields, along with Unicode support. The product highlights search hits in most web-based file formats, such as XML and HTML, while keeping the format and layout of the page, including graphics and embedded hyperlinks. dtSearch also displays search hits in other popular file types, such as documents, spreadsheets, database files, and e-mails. The built-in spider can add website content to the searchable database, including secure, password-protected websites. The ability to index and search website content is a great feature for those lawyers involved in cases or matters involving e-discovery.

Like other full-text search applications, dtSearch uses a large volume of disk space to store its search index, requiring approximately one-third of the total volume of files indexed. The software states that a single index file can handle more than a terabyte of indexed text, which is a lot of files. dtSearch supports Windows 2000/XP/Visa/7 (both 32- and 64-bit versions) operating systems and even has a version for Linux. Just recently, dtSearch added support for the Microsoft Outlook 2010 64-bit e-mail client. Also new in the latest version is the ability to highlight search hits within PDF files retrieved after a search using Adobe Acrobat and Reader X.

dtSearch Desktop with Spider can be purchased on its website (**www.dtsearch.com**) for $199 per license. dtSearch Network with Spider can also be purchased at a cost of $160 per license for 5 to 24 users or $140 per license for 25 to 99 users. Further discounts are offered for purchases of more than 100 licenses.

Credenza

Are you looking for a way to enhance your ability to run and manage your law firm using just a single piece of software? It can be done, believe it or not, with Microsoft Outlook and a small add-in named Credenza. Surprisingly, many lawyers use Microsoft Outlook for their case management solution rather than purchasing a separate application for the job. To make your Outlook management easier, you should consider Credenza.

Credenza is a legal-practice management solution that integrates with Microsoft Outlook and allows legal professionals to manage their firms more effectively. Credenza allows you to:

- Create and open a file for each client matter or case
- Track time spent on individual e-mails and flags messages that may have been missed or forgotten
- Keep and make notes regarding phone calls, voicemails, and other messages
- View a complete chronology of a file
- Conflict check, automate inbox controls and the ability to share information with other users

Previously, Credenza offered only a free trial version to its potential users. Now, it offers a Basic version of the program that is free to download and use. The Pro version can be purchased and downloaded from the Credenza Software website at **www.credenzasoft.com** and costs $24.95 per month.

To determine which version of the software is right for you, you can view the Basic features here: **http://www.credenzasoft.com/basic.html**.

You can view the Pro features here: **http://www.credenzasoft.com/pro.html**.

Outlook Send Assistant

Concerned about inadvertently sending an e-mail message to an unintended recipient? If so, we have the tool for you. It is a must-have utility for every Microsoft Outlook user. Outlook Send Assistant (**www.payneconsulting.com/products/outlooksendassistant/**) is a small tool that packs a big punch. Here are some of the features of this simple and elegant tool:

> —Determines if there is an external e-mail address contained in the TO, CC, or BCC recipient list; confirms if the user would like to edit the e-mail or continue sending. (BCC works with internal or external addresses.)

— Notifies recipient of BCC status and prevents related disclosure.

— Checks for firm distribution lists to verify that the user meant to include recipients in the e-mail.

— Designates global address list (GAL) distribution lists as automatically trusted.

— Any GAL distribution list can be set up to prompt with a desired message that you can specify. For example, if you have a distribution list that goes to the entire firm, Outlook Send Assistant can prompt the user to verify that he or she really wants to send the message to the entire firm.

— Can also prompt regarding whether the user would like to include any kind of disclaimer message directing users to his or her website, etc., and place the appropriate text at the bottom of the e-mail message.

— Detect Reply To All usage and prompt the user by asking if he or she would actually like to reply to all recipients (customizable with any firm-specific language).

— Automatically add a Marketing, Circular 230 Disclosure, SEC, SPAM warnings, and security disclaimers to e-mail messages

Outlook Send Assistant works within Outlook 2000 and above, including Outlook 2010 (32-bit). Some of the features, such as the disclaimer message, require that Outlook be configured with HTML-type messages. That doesn't bother us since that's how we're already configured. Otherwise, plain text format is also supported. The cost is $15–$40 per seat, depending on the number of licenses purchased.

GreenPrint

GreenPrint Technologies (**www.printgreener.com**) has a software product, GreenPrint, that eliminates unwanted pages from your printing jobs, saving you ink, toner, paper, money, and trees. The software intercepts your print jobs and highlights unnecessary pages that can be removed, such as blank pages. How many times have you printed a web page that prints on two pages of paper, with only a single line of text on the second page? Usually the second page contains only a URL, logo, or banner ad. No longer will these wasted pages need to be printed. The Enterprise Edition includes such additional features as the GreenPrint Advisor, a tool to help your firm select low-cost printers, and GreenPrint Analytics, a powerful reporting tool documenting your firm's true savings.

GreenPrint makes recommendations about pages that should be removed from the print job and prompts the user for approval before the job is sent to the printer. There is a free edition of the software for home use, an edition for home and small office use, and an Enterprise Edition for businesses. The free edition for home use is ad supported. The Home and SOHO edition costs $19 per computer. You have to contact the vendor to get pricing for the Enterprise Edition. The product works with XP/Vista/7, Citrix, and Mac OS X 10.4/10.5/10.6/10.7.

Winscribe for the Legal Profession

Winscribe, a leading developer of dictation software, has a made a product specifically for the legal profession that allows dictations to be automatically transcribed, converting recorded words to text. Automating the process saves both time and money, increasing the efficiency of your employees. It marks the end of the "listen . . . type" era. Now your employees can spend their time doing something more productive and billable. Winscribe can even integrate with existing applications, such as your document management system, streamlining your workflow process. As the creator of the dictations, you can manage and monitor the status of your work, as well as retrieve jobs for review and editing.

Another innovative feature of this software is that it supports a wide range of input from recordings made on telephones, PCs and laptops, digital handheld devices, PDAs, BlackBerrys, iPhone or Windows Mobile devices. With the Winscribe Mobility Suite, the days of carrying around a digital recorder may be over. Now you can install mobile software on your smartphone to record dictations and transfer the files wirelessly to your firm's network. As always, client confidentiality is an extremely important issue. Winscribe protects dictations through the encryption of the files and through the implementation of a secure file transfer process. Winscribe has been vetted by the experts and found worthy. This product is available on Winscribe's website at **www.winscribe.com**, and can be purchased as an in-house package or an on-demand Software as a Service (SaaS) over the web.

Eyejot

What a slogan: "Video mail in a blink." Is video the future of e-mail? So long, text. If so, Eyejot has got it right. Eyejot is a comprehensive, client-free, online video-messaging platform ideal for both personal and business communications. Users can sign up for the service by creating a free account, which allows an unlimited number of five-minute video e-mail messages and provides support for both RSS feeds and iTunes. If you can send an e-mail, then you can send an Eyejot.

The Free account keeps your video messages for up to one month, allows you to send the video message to any e-mail address (not just an Eyejot account), and, if needed, provides code for you to embed the Eyejot widget on your website. However, the Free account is ad supported.

To send a video message, once an account has been created, a user must log into his or her account, upload the video, and then click the Send button. That's it, plain and simple. The software requires no client installation and works with all major web browsers. For those users who require more, there is a Pro account for $29.95 per year that allows you to upload videos, provides an enhanced mobile inbox, and is advertising free.

There is also a Pro+ account subscription for $99.95 per year that is advertising free and allows you to attach other documents to your video messages as well as customize your own message templates. Users can purchase and create an Eyejot account online at **www.eyejot.com**.

YouSendIt

What a wonderful resource to transmit large file attachments without charge. There are several service packages, one of which is free. The free offering, called Lite, can transmit an attachment that is up to 50MB in size. The Lite package also provides a user with 2GB of online storage space, mobile access, and a Desktop Sync application. Since a lot of ISPs limit the size of attachments, YouSendIt is a great alternative to "push" the occasional large attachment. The service works by creating an account at **yousendit.com** and actually uploading the file to the YouSendIt service. You provide the e-mail addresses for the recipient(s), and an e-mail message is sent with a hyperlink that allows for the download of the file from the YouSendIt site. If you have a need to regularly transmit very large attachments, especially those larger than 50MB, YouSendIt provides several pay services to accomplish this. The paid services provide enhancements such as e-mail support, longer availability for file downloads, reports, advanced security options, and more bandwidth for downloads. We have found this resource to be invaluable for sending conference attendees copies of our PowerPoint presentations, which tend to be quite large because of the graphics. Don't forget to encrypt your data prior to uploading it to YouSendIt's servers, if it is confidential in nature. This terrific utility may be found at **http://www.yousendit.com**.

Copy2Contact

Copy2Contact, formerly Anagram, is a piece of software that allows you to "sweep" text from an e-mail message and create a record within Outlook. You can sweep contact information that the sender has added in his or her message footer and instantly create an Outlook contact. The software is not limited just to the creation of contacts. You can "grab" text and create calendar entries, to-do items, and even tasks. The text can originate from anywhere. Copy2Contact will create the contact, calendar entry, task, etc., in your personal folder area, which is fine for most solos. If you have a Microsoft Exchange server with Public Folders, records generated by this program will not go directly to the Public Folder. You will have to move the data from your personal folder if the intended destination is a Public Folder. Copy2Contact is currently available for Google Apps, Salesforce.com, Microsoft Outlook, Netsuite, and Palm Desktop. Copy2Contact is compatible will all Windows-based systems, including Windows 7. The program also has a version available for BlackBerry and iPhone devices.

The base Copy2Contact for Outlook product costs $39.95 for a single user. There is a 14-day trial version to make sure that Copy2Contact will work on your computer and perform according to your expectations. Make sure you download and try the trial before you spend the money; however, we're sure (especially you solo lawyers) that you'll be typing in your credit card number shortly after your first use of Copy2Contact.

TwInbox

Are you a Twitter junkie? We've found a program that integrates with Microsoft Outlook that allows you to update your Twitter status directly from Outlook. TwInbox (**www.techhit.com/TwInbox/twitter_plugin_outlook.html**), a free add-on for Microsoft Outlook, allows you to receive your friend updates, archive, manage, group, and search your tweets in the same way that you manage your e-mail. Some of the additional features of this tiny program include allowing users to search and track keywords, group tweets by sender or topic, and upload and post picture files and Outlook e-mail attachments. A newly added feature also allows users to manage multiple Twitter accounts from directly within Microsoft Outlook. This product is free—why not give it a try?

TweetDeck

If you're a Twitter user and prefer not to tweet from within Microsoft Outlook or from the Twitter website, then this program might be for you. TweetDeck, another free utility, helps you organize Twitter and those you are following. You can group people so that you can concentrate on "special" individuals whose tweets are more important to you. This helps you reduce the noise level of Twitter and focuses attention on specific tweets. It also includes a URL "shortener." TweetDeck does require the installation of Adobe Air, which needs full administrative access to your hard disk. This is somewhat of a security hole, especially if the "bad guys" start to attack Air installations. So be sure to keep your Adobe products fully updated. This is a wonderful "dashboard" for managing Twitter—we know because we use it. Tweetdeck is available for download at **http://tweetdeck.com**.

TinyURL

Have you ever wanted to give somebody a reference link only to discover that it is about 400 characters long and contains all kinds of goofy characters and non-word representations? Probably the biggest problem is the breaking up of the URL link, especially when the e-mail is viewed as text formatted. The last thing you want to do is have the recipient cut and paste the various parts of the URL back together. TinyURL stores the complete URL on its servers and provides a very small URL instead. The user selects the smaller TinyURL, which translates and redirects to the much larger one. This is a free service to make the posting of long URLs easier—especially handy for Twitter! If you're a frequent user of TinyURL, there's even a toolbar for your browser that you can install to make the service more accessible. It is available at **http://tinyurl.com**.

IrfanView

Do you have some graphic files for a construction case that you can't seem to view? Or a video or sound file for a wrongful termination case and don't know how to play it? IrfanView (**www.irfanview.com**) is a wonderful software application that can view a very large number of different graphic file formats and can play several audio and video formats. IrfanView is compatible with all Windows-based systems, but not Mac or Linux. IrfanView is free only for home use, so you can't legally use it for your law practice unless you pay money. IrfanView makes it easy to be on the right side of the copyright laws by charging a mere $12 to use the product in a commercial setting.

Some of the common file types and formats that IrfanView supports include:

—JPG
—TIF
—GIF
—MPG
—MP3
—AVI
—WMA

DBAN

Darik's Boot and Nuke is a free program that can be used to securely wipe the contents of your hard drive. DBAN is an open-source project that can be downloaded from **www.dban.org**. DBAN will automatically and permanently delete the contents of any hard disk it can detect. DBAN also allows the wiping of multiple hard disks at the same time. We all love "free," and this program is the perfect complement to any lawyer's software tool chest. You will use DBAN to wipe the data contents from your hard drives and USB flash drives so that your confidential client information cannot be recovered. We have all read stories of customer data being found on hard drives purchased on eBay. Make sure that you wipe any media that may contain information you don't want someone else to recover. Could the National Security Agency recover something wiped with DBAN? Frankly, we think that's another urban legend, and we've never—ever—seen evidence of it. It's free, it's safe, and it helps you comply with your ethical duty to keep your client data confidential. When you're getting ready to donate or ditch your old computers, this is an invaluable tool.

SimplyFile

Long ago, we realized how much time we were losing each day carefully dragging and dropping e-mail into the correct Outlook folder, often accidentally filing messages in a folder below or a folder above the intended destination. Maddening.

With the SimplyFile software, each e-mail will display the name of the folder SimplyFile believes it belongs in. After it initially indexes and "learns" your filing system (and be patient, because it may run for several hours and impact system performance), it is correct more than 90 percent of the time. If it has guessed wrong, there is a QuickPick feature. Open it, and you'll likely find that the correct folder is near the top of the list of possibilities presented. If not, you can just type in the first few letters of the folder and it will appear. Most of the time, you'll just be clicking "file" and it's done. It can also turn e-mail into a calendar or a task. Marvelous. Authors Nelson and Simek regarded this product as their "find of the year" from 2009. The current version is compatible with Outlook 2010. This product does not work with Outlook Express.

SimplyFile may be purchased (or there's a 30-day free trial) at www.techhit.com/SimplyFile/. The cost for a single license is $49.95.

Shred 2

PC Magazine has a free utility that is designed to wipe specific files or disk areas. Shred 2 "officially" runs under Windows 95, 98, 2000, ME, NT 4.0, and XP. Don't worry, we are successfully running it on Windows 7 systems, too. If you want to wipe the recycle bin, then you'll need an updated .DLL file, which is discussed in the article about Shred 2 at www.pcmag.com/article2/0,1895,13352,00.asp. The software can selectively wipe files or folders and can be configured to do multiple wipes of the same area if you are particularly paranoid. This utility is especially useful in removing data remnants of files and their associated file slack, which can be forensically recovered if wiping did not occur. The nice part about having a file/folder wiping utility is that data can be selectively eradicated from your computer without having to wipe the entire hard disk and having to reload the operating system and all of the applications. Remember, though, you cannot recover the file once it is wiped, so pay attention when you're clicking that mouse.

SnagIt

No lawyer should be without a screen-capture program. SnagIt 10 is a screen-capture utility that can capture anything on your desktop. You can capture a specific window, a defined area, a specific object (e.g., the title bar), or a multitude of other things. There are over 40 ways to capture the information you want to preserve. A screen-capture application is a great tool to "grab" images to place in a motion or brief that show exactly what is shown on the computer screen. This is particularly handy when you want only a specific area of the screen. SnagIt can output the "snagged" image to a multitude of formats as well. SnagIt costs $49.95 for a single license version, with discounts for multiple copies. There is a 30-day trial version available, so you can see whether it fits your needs prior to purchase. It is available from **www.techsmith.com/screen-capture.asp** and now works on all Windows 32- and 64-bit operating systems, and there is a Mac version as well.

If you are using Windows 7, you should try the Snipping Tool before deciding to purchase a third-party application for your screen-grabbing needs. The Snipping Tool is included by default and is Microsoft's version of a screen-grabbing utility that allows you to save the captured data to a file or copy it to the Clipboard, which is handy when creating PowerPoint slides.

FavBackup 2.0.2

If you're like us, then you probably have multiple browsers installed on your computer. If you're looking at upgrading your computer to Windows 7, this tool provides an easy way to back up and restore your web browser settings and other data. FavBackup (**www.favbrowser.com/backup**) is a free utility and supports Internet Explorer 6–8; Firefox 2–6; Opera 9–11.5; Safari 3 and 4; Google Chrome 1–15; and Flock 2–2.5. This is definitely a tool to keep in your tool chest.

If you are a Google Chrome user, you can use the Bookmark Sync feature, which makes it easy to keep the same set of bookmarks on multiple computers. When enabled, the bookmarks or favorites will be stored online in your Google Account and will be automatically synched with each computer you use where this feature is enabled. No need to back up or transfer them manually. Again, the only potential roadblock is that a Google Mail account is required.

QuickView Plus

Spend a little more money and get a utility that can view more than 300 file formats, including Microsoft Office 2010 and Corel WordPerfect Office X3. That's what you get when you purchase QuickView Plus 11. The file support comes without the need for the native application, potentially saving you the costs of having to purchase a license for a product just to view a file. QuickView Plus maintains the formatting of the files you view so you can view and print files as they were originally created and meant to be seen. This is a great application to view file formats, especially from your electronic discovery cases. You can handle e-mail attachments and various "obscure" software packages that you've probably never heard of. QuickView Plus is compatible with Microsoft Windows computer systems.

At $49 for a single download license of the standard edition, it is a perfect complement to IrfanView. QuickView Plus is available for purchase and download at **http://www.avantstar.com**, and a fully functional evaluation copy of the product is offered for 30 days. The professional edition adds advanced viewing, searching, etc., and starts at $495 for five licenses.

Sam Spade

The name of this utility, obviously, is meant to evoke Humphrey Bogart in *The Maltese Falcon*. Indeed, this utility can perform some gumshoe functions, such as troubleshooting and dealing with Internet communications. However, the most useful function of this free utility is the ability to decode e-mail headers so that anyone can decipher the cryptic entries in a readable English form. Unfortunately, the original site for Sam Spade is down and no longer active. The good news is that there are several websites that have the latest version (1.14) available for download. This product hasn't been updated in the past five years and most likely never will be again.

For instructions on how to use the application, the SANS Institute has a great white paper on the matter that can be downloaded here: **http://www.sans.org/reading_room/whitepapers/tools/sam-spade_934**.

As we move forward into the world of electronic evidence, having the ability to decode e-mail headers is an invaluable asset to help ascertain where an e-mail "really" came from. Mind you, there are ways to hide for the world's miscreants, but Sam Spade can provide you with a lot of helpful information. Just do a Google search for "Sam Spade" and you will find several download locations on the first page of the results.

Karen's Power Tools

One of the greatest collections of utilities that we have found is a CD that contains more than 30 utilities and over 100 articles and newsletters. The CD is only $29.95 and includes a license for commercial usage. One of the most powerful programs from Karen's Power Tools is called Hasher. Hasher calculates the hash values for text strings, disk files, or groups of files. Hasher can calculate the MD5, SHA-1, SHA-224, SHA-256, SHA-384, and SHA-512 hash values. This is very valuable in determining if a file or data has been changed. It is very common for the hash value to be provided along with the data file itself, thereby aiding in maintaining authenticity. You will find Hasher to be indispensable in calculating hash values for electronic evidence. For those of you who haven't the slightest clue what a hash value is, think of it as a "digital fingerprint" and you've got the basic idea. There are other valuable utilities on the CD, which can be ordered at **www.karenware.com**. All of Karen's tools are compatible with Windows-based systems, including Windows 7.

Unfortunately, Karen passed away last year, so there will no longer be any updates distributed. Her utilities are still available and her family has announced that they will continue to provide them as long as there is interest and value to users.

Metadata Assistant

Our favorite metadata analysis and removal tool is Metadata Assistant by Payne Group (**www.payneconsulting.com/products/metadataretail**). Metadata Assistant integrates with your Microsoft Office installation and is particularly valuable when sending file attachments. The product will display a dialog box asking if you want to clean the attachment or just send it as is. As we mentioned previously, don't clean the metadata if you are collaborating on a document with another person, as it will remove the tracked changes. Metadata Assistant can also convert the attachment to PDF on the fly.

Metadata Assistant is extremely flexible and works with Word, Excel, and PowerPoint versions from 97 to 2010. It has e-mail integration with Outlook 2000 and higher, Groupwise 6.5 and higher (in version 2; version 3 support coming soon), and Lotus Notes 7 and 8. Version 2 integrates with Interwoven/iManage, Hummingbird, and Worldox document management systems. Version 3 integrates with OpenText DM 5.2, Worldox GX/GX2, Autonomy iManage 8.2 and 8.5, and NetDocuments R1-2010 and R2 document management systems. The 2.0 version is designed for Office 2007 and lower and is available directly from the Payne Group for $80 per license.

You can also remove metadata by converting the file to PDF. This does not remove all of the metadata, but it does remove a large portion of it and leaves only what are typically considered innocuous values. Microsoft also provides the ability to analyze and remove a document's properties in Microsoft Office 2010. However, some values that it leaves behind are still viewable by third-party products like Metadata Assistant.

The Payne Group also has version 3 of Metadata Assistant available. Version 3 works with Office 2010, and it's also compatible with Windows 7. The price has gone up slightly to $89 per copy. So what's new in this release? First off, there's a new interface and faster processing. You can now clean Office files that are stored as ZIP attachments. There is Unicode support and the ability to clean embedded Office attachments in Outlook. These are just a few of the new features for an already robust product.

No lawyer should be without a metadata scrubber to ensure removal of potential confidential data. Some states are even addressing the removal of metadata in their ethics opinions. Whether you are required to scrub metadata or not, Metadata Assistant is an absolute must-have utility for your practice.

Livescribe Pulse Smartpen

The Livescribe Pulse Smartpen is a device that can record a user's written notes along with the accompanying audio. The Smartpen can transmit the data to a computer via USB cable, allowing a user to view digitalized notes and recorded audio. The pen has an infrared camera that records 72 images per second to track the spatial movement of the device on the provided sheets of dot paper, the required use of which is one of the only downsides of the product. Users can now purchase their own dot paper, notebooks, and lined and unlined journals compatible with the Smartpen.

Using the bundled Livescribe Desktop software, users can manage written notes and recordings but cannot convert notes to text because the software lacks OCR capabilities. However, using the software's PDF export capabilities, you could always OCR the exported PDF files using Adobe Acrobat.

The Smartpen, just like a computer, can be updated with new firmware and software and is currently offered with 2 or 4GB of storage capacity. The Smartpen is compatible with Microsoft Windows XP SP3, Vista, and Windows 7, and also Macs OS X 10.5.5 or newer. A pretty slick tech toy, even for those who are aren't absentminded. Now, what were we about to do?

YouMail

Tired of the standard voicemail options provided by your cellular carrier? Looking for more advanced features? YouMail (**www.youmail.com**) is like Google Voice, without the extra phone number. YouMail provides a visual voicemail client for your smartphone that offers personalization of voicemail greetings based on the caller, voicemail sharing, caller blocking, and receiving voicemail alerts by e-mail and text. You can even organize your voicemails into folders and download them to MP3 format.

When a call doesn't get answered, the forwarded call is then transferred to your YouMail voicemail box rather than to your cellular provider's voicemail box. For an extra $4.99 per month, YouMail will transcribe and e-mail up to 20 of your voicemails to you per month.

Users who want to try out the service can sign up for a free account, which allows access to the stored voicemails through the online website or any of YouMail's apps. The account provides the user with the ability to store up to 100 voicemail messages and has a time limit of up to two minutes per voicemail recording.

SmartDraw VP

SmartDraw Legal Edition has been merged with the VP version of the software, which is a powerful software tool that allows lawyers to create sharp, professional-looking diagrams and trial exhibits with relative ease.

It's a must-have for your software arsenal. The tool, more robust than Microsoft PowerPoint, can be used to create time lines, estate planning diagrams, accident reconstruction, crime scene layouts, and more. The look and feel of the software is similar to Microsoft Office, and creating diagrams from the provided templates is simple. The Legal Edition provides specialized templates for the legal profession—over 1,000 of them—and if you can't find one to use, you can create your own. SmartDraw comes with more than 20,000 symbols and shapes to choose from, giving you the power to dynamically re-create that crucial event in your case. SmartDraw provides a number of export options, allowing users to save their work in a variety of formats, such as PDF, DOC, XLS, WPD, or JPG. SmartDraw does a good job as an alternative product to Microsoft Visio or Project, and at a fraction of the cost.

The latest update to SmartDraw VP includes a totally new user interface, powerful new print controls, new templates for brainstorming and project planning, and enhanced Visual Process Management functionality.

SmartDraw Standard VP can be purchased directly from the website (**www.smartdraw.com**) for $197 for a single-user license. A trial edition is also available for download for those users who wish to test drive the software before purchasing.

CaseSoft TimeMap 5

Another great time line–generating utility is CaseSoft's TimeMap. TimeMap is a time line–graphing tool that can be used to create polished time line graphs for trial exhibits, presentations, and professional documents. TimeMap can be integrated with CaseMap or used on its own. Data can be directly imported into the application from Microsoft Excel, Summation, Concordance, Microsoft Access, or almost any other spreadsheet or database program, eliminating the need to manually enter data. As data is entered into the program, TimeMap will automatically generate a proportional time scale and allows the user to adjust it if necessary. Once your time line graph has been generated, you can present the time line using TimeMap's Presentation Mode, or you can embed the time line directly into your PowerPoint or Sanction presentation. TimeMap 5 includes new features such as vertical time lines, additional time line templates, a new PDF writer, and enhanced integration with presentation software. The latest version also includes a new Spreadsheet view, global find-and-replace option, expanded images, and improved date display tools. TimeMap 5 supports Microsoft Windows 2000/XP/Vista and

Windows 7 and can be purchased directly from Casesoft's website at **www.casesoft.com**. A full-featured 30-day trial edition is also available for download for those users who wish to give the software a test run before purchasing.

Evernote

Have trouble remembering everything? We sure do. That's why we use Evernote. Evernote (**www.evernote.com**) makes it easy to remember things big and small, allowing you to capture everything you see when using your computer, cell phone, or mobile device. Using the program, you can clip a web page, snap a photo, or grab a screenshot and upload it to Evernote. Once uploaded, everything you capture is automatically processed, indexed, and made searchable. Of course, you can add your own tags and labels to your notes. Evernote will even scan handwritten notes and make the content searchable. There is a limitless number of ways to use this program, whether for play or work. Since all of the data you capture and tag is uploaded to your Evernote account, these files are accessible from all of your devices.

Evernote can integrate with your web browser, or you can install a small application on both Mac OS X and Windows-based computers, or your iPhone/iPod Touch, iPad, BlackBerry, Palm Pre/Palm Pixi, Android, Android tablet, or Windows Phone 7 smartphone. To sign up for a free account, visit Evernote's website at **www.evernote.com**.

WinRAR

WinRAR is an application for compressing data. WinZip is a very popular program as well, but WinRAR has some distinct advantages. WinRAR is faster than WinZip and provides smaller files. It can also create compressed archives that are much larger than WinZip. We see WinRAR used for transmitting large amounts of data. Data production as part of a discovery request would be one place to use WinRAR. WinRAR supports all popular compression formats (RAR, ZIP, CAB, ARJ, LZH, ACE, TAR, GZip, UUE, ISO, BZIP2, Z, and 7-Zip). This is a valuable tool for sending data via the Web as well.

WinRAR is available in 32- and 64-bit versions. The cost is $29 per license, and it is available directly from the website at **www.win-rar.com**.

CHAPTER TWENTY-SIX

Navigating a Minefield: Social Media and the Law

LOVE IT OR HATE it, social media is here to stay. By July of 2011, there were more than 750 million people on Facebook worldwide. The total represents approximately the population of the United States, Mexico, and France. This collective mass shares over 30 billion pieces of content each month.[1] MySpace, now largely made up of young people, still boasts a respectable 100 million monthly active users around the globe,[2] and Twitter, once the new kid on the block, has around 200 million users, who post over 155 million tweets every day.[3] Finally, LinkedIn has more than 100 million members in over 200 countries and territories around the world.[4] Of course, these are only some of the more popular examples; new social media sites literally pop up overnight. Google+ is now reporting more than 10 million users and it looks like it is gaining some traction in the marketplace.

Despite staid reputations, lawyers have embraced social media to a degree that parallels their dramatic spread among society at large. In fact, a 2008 Networks for Counsel Survey by LexisNexis Martindale-Hubbell revealed that approximately 50 percent of lawyers belong to online social networks; by 2009, that figure had jumped to 86 percent of lawyers between the ages of 25 and 35 and 66 percent of those age 46 or older.[5]

---

[1] **http://www.facebook.com/press/info.php?statistics** (last visited Aug. 3, 2011).
[2] **http://www.myspace.com/pressroom/fact-sheet/** (last visited Aug. 3, 2011).
[3] **https://business.twitter.com/basics/what-is-twitter** (last visited Aug. 3, 2011).
[4] **http://press.linkedin.com/about** (last visited Aug. 3, 2011).
[5] *See* "2008 Networks for Counsel Study: Online Networking in the Legal Community," Leader Networks, **http://www.slideshare.net/vdimauro/networks-for-counsel-study** (last visited Sept. 13, 2010); "2009 Networks for Counsel Study: A Global Study of the Legal Industry's Adoption of Online Professional Networking, Preferences, Usage and Future Predictions, **www.leadernetworks.com/.../Networks_for_Counsel_2009.pdf** (last visited Sept. 13, 2010).

Judges have also joined the social networking soiree, though perhaps more slowly.

Undoubtedly, the brave new world of social media offers lawyers and judges new ways to stay connected with colleagues, to remain up to speed with the latest news in their respective fields, to reach out to prospective clients, and to do their jobs more effectively. But all too often members of the legal profession have been blinded by the potential golden opportunities that social media present and have barreled headlong into the unknown, only to stumble into a landscape full of hidden land mines. While we are by no means arguing that social media is inherently worthless (on the contrary, we believe that, when used correctly, social media is a wonderful tool with unparalleled potential), we would caution lawyers and judges to tread carefully and watch their virtual footsteps.

Introduction to Social Media Tools

Social media is tools. And, as with any tool, you have to pick the right one for the job. With all the options out there, it can be overwhelming and almost impossible if you don't know where to begin. To help, here is a brief account of the popular social media sites lawyers frequent and how they use them.

Blogs

A blog, or "blawg," is an "online journal that discusses opinions or reflections on various topics and usually provides a mechanism for readers to comment."[6] Blogs are typically, but not always, written by one person, updated fairly regularly, and encompass a particular topic or interest. Usually, blog posts are arranged in chronological order, with the most recent additions featured most prominently. Generally speaking, lawyers have used blogs to increase their visibility, demonstrate their legal expertise, and interact with and influence others. By and large, blogs have formed the heart of the social media strategy of many lawyers because postings in other media often contain links to a blog for more in-depth discussion.

Social Networking Sites

In their simplest form, social networking sites are Web-based services that allow users to construct a public or semi-public profile, which they can

---

[6]Debra L. Bruce, *Social Media 101 for Lawyers*, Texas Bar Journal p. 1 (March 2010).

then share with other users with whom they have a connection. Users can then view their connections and those made by others who frequent the site. What makes these sites unique is not that they allow individuals to meet new people, but rather that they enable users to articulate and make visible their social networks. Both individual lawyers and law firms have embraced social networking sites as a means to increase their visibility and reconnect with friends or clients. They participate in discussion groups, announce events and achievements, and incorporate other forms of social media. A few of the most popular sites and their features are described in more detail below.

Facebook is the champion of social networking. Its approximately 750 million active members post thoughts, status updates, pictures, or videos to their own personal profile page. Members are permitted to make public comments on the wall of the profiles of their "friends"—other members with whom they have agreed to connect. Over time, Facebook has added a number of other features, such as an instant messaging service and "Marketplace," which lets users post free classified ads. What's important to keep in mind is that Facebook makes a large portion of its money in the same way many other Web-based companies do: by serving ads. Unlike Google, which is able to generate ads based on a user's past search results, Facebook has to show ads that will generate an interest in a particular product or service. Traditionally, these "guesses" have translated into an incredibly low rate of click-through, but Facebook has a plan. Their new Open Graph program is designed to gauge, measure, and record your behavior across the entire Internet, effectively giving Facebook a golden ticket to an unparalleled amount of marketing data about their users' demographics and interests. Thus, although the PR people at Facebook may boast about recent increased privacy changes, privacy and Facebook's business model will always remain at odds. Thus, it is in Facebook's best interest to have a user's browsing habits, likes, and interests as publicly accessible as possible, because ads that are tied to a user's interests are more likely to generate increased revenues.

Take, for example, Facebook's recent decision to allow its third-party app developers API access to users' addresses and phone numbers. Although the social networking site stated that developers must be individually approved by the users themselves and that they would only be able to access an individual user's address and phone number, many security researchers pointed out that it would be quite easy for shady developers to get in on the action. In fact, security research firm Sophos stated that Facebook app developers have already managed to trick users into giving them access to personal data and noted that this move will only make Facebook more dangerous.

Similarly, the social networking giant stoked fresh concerns from privacy advocates and lawmakers by rolling out technology that uses facial recognition to identify people in photos on its website. Facebook claims that the technology was designed to help its users mark friends in photos as they upload them to the social-networking site, but privacy advocates have proclaimed that this technology goes over the line. This potential privacy problem has been further aggravated by Facebook's decision to enable the face-recognition tool for all users by default. Massachusetts Representative Edward J. Markey said Facebook ought to have made the technology optional for users, noting that "if this new feature is as useful as Facebook claims, it should be able to stand on its own, without an automatic sign-up that changes users' privacy settings without their permission." Good luck with that, as Facebook has a long standing reputation for modifying a user's configuration without notice.

Another popular site with lawyers is LinkedIn, a smaller but more business-oriented social networking site. Basically, a LinkedIn profile is the equivalent to a "resume on steroids."[7] Users can post status updates, invite people to link to them, and publish their blogs. The site also provides a jobs posting section where users can post and peruse various employment opportunities. Like Facebook, LinkedIn incorporates a business model that is not necessarily privacy-friendly. Unlike Facebook, LinkedIn's business model is not primarily focused on advertising revenue, although it is a considerable portion of revenues. Instead, LinkedIn provides access to its social networking users for a fee. The more money you pay, the more users of the service you can contact. There are now heated debates online about whether LinkedIn or Facebook is the greater enemy of privacy, with most of the votes going to Facebook.

Then there is the fallen king of social networking, MySpace. As Facebook continued to grow in popularity and capture more and more of the social networking crowd, MySpace rebranded its image to appeal to "self-expressive, creative under-35-year-olds who are into games, music, and movies."[8] The site now focuses on user home pages that are abundant with live personal content as well as providing a heavy-duty entertainment news service for music, celebrities, and youth-oriented movies. This new niche mar-

---

[7] *Id.*
[8] Jon Schwartz, "Once-fading MySpace Focuses on a Youthful Incarnation," USA Today, **http://www.usatoday.com/tech/techinvestor/corporatenews/2010-03-10-myspace10_CV_N.htm** (last visited on Sept. 13, 2010).

keting scares many lawyers away. Some feel that this isn't the right market in which to solicit new clients. Others argue that a social network focused on games, music, and movies is no place to post legal information. And, like all the other social networking sites, the mighty dollar, not the user's privacy concerns, guide MySpace's business decisions.

Last is the newest iteration of the social networking platform, Google+. Google's latest leap into the social media craze is similar to many of the above-listed social media sites, though the Internet search giant has added a few "tweaks"[9] to set it apart from other social networking sites like Facebook and LinkedIn. However, it remains to be seen whether *this* social networking attempt will fare better than any of Google's other attempts at social media, which have resoundingly flopped. In March 2011, the Federal Trade Commission announced a settlement with Google regarding its Buzz social-networking service that requires the search giant to develop a comprehensive privacy program and submit to regular audits of its privacy policies.[10] And there was Google Wave, which allowed users to share images and other media in real time. It was terminated in August 2010, only a year after its debut.

Social Messaging Sites

The newest craze in social media is social messaging sites. These sites are perhaps best described as a cross between blogging and instant messaging. These sites have been considered one of the fastest ways for individuals to get up-to-the-minute news, because users often are able to post short little blurbs from their smartphones.

You've probably heard of Twitter. Twitter started off as a micro-blogging site, but it has quickly grown to encompass the essence of social messaging. Twitter allows its users to send and read other user messages called "tweets"—text-based posts limited to 140 characters (unless you use a third-party application to extend your tweets) displayed on the author's profile page.[11] Users may subscribe to other authors' tweets or search a word to find any tweet containing that word. Typically, Twitter users share infor-

---

[9] Google+ begins with "Circles," which helps, according to the Internet search giant, compartmentalize all the people in your life. Once you have your friends sorted into Circles, users then can use "Sparks" to connect with other users about topics that interest both individuals. In addition, Google+ also features "Hangouts," a video-chat option, which allows for live multi-person video conversations.

[10] The Google Agreement Containing consent order is available on the FTC website at **http://www.ftc.gov/os/caselist/1023136/110330googlebuzzagreeorder.pdf**.

[11] Daniel Nathans, "What is a Tweet?," **http://webtrends.about.com/od/glossary/g/what-is-a-tweet.htm** (last visited on Sept.13, 2010).

mation with links to blog posts or articles for more in-depth discussions and "retweet" to their followers anything they find interesting, amusing, or informative. Lawyers have recently realized that they can, through Twitter, build a reputation for expertise through their tweets as well as create valuable relationships with potential clients and referral sources they would not otherwise interact with regularly. One of the most concerning aspects of Twitter is the fact that a "tweet" never dies. Once posted, it very well might come back to haunt you. And all public tweets are now archived in the Library of Congress—enough to give a prudent lawyer pause.

The "Social Media Effect"

One of the most interesting areas of social media's impact on the legal world is what we have dubbed the "social media effect." Today, it is amazing how easily and quickly information is disseminated to society at large. Often, in the case of newsworthy trials, this means that society can, and often does, voice its opinion (whether right or wrong) on the outcome of a case. One need only look to the recent Casey Anthony trial to see this far-reaching effect. As one social media expert and consultant explained:

> Social media has allowed everyone an instant megaphone on the Internet, to express, argue and form opinions instantly. In the old days, we used to watch a newscast or read a news story. Now we get things so quickly that we are immediately reacting and feeling passionate.

If the Casey Anthony trial proves anything, this new "online jury" does not appear shy about sharing their opinions and feelings on the trial or on the parties. Numerous blog, Facebook, and Twitter posts were created during and after the trial, each expressing the commenter's opinion on the "correct" outcome of the case. This all begs the question: Do any of these communications affect the proceedings inside the courtroom? A recent study has found that many people view peer-to-peer opinions as the most credible, and thus they have more influence on users of the Internet today. As a result, reviews and online opinions have become the source to get authentic, objective (sometimes) news, making the relationship between social media and the legal system a complicated courtship, to say the least. Certainly, we believe that online reputations have the ability to impact court cases and provide jurors with an incentive to "get it right"—or at least take into account what society might think is the right outcome. In the end, recent events prove that social media will play an integral role in society's perception of major trials, and it appears that the legal system will have a difficult time controlling all of the evidence and news that is released before, during, and long after the verdict.

Social Media's Impact on E-Discovery: The Gift and the Curse

If someone had said five years ago that lawyers would scan the Internet for relevant evidence in litigation, he or she might have been greeted with skepticism. Yet today the Internet—and especially social media—has led to mountains of evidence. This has caused some lawyers to sing its praises and others to curse it. For lawyers searching for that golden nugget of information, social media do indeed present a "golden" opportunity. However, for lawyers forced to respond to numerous e-discovery requests, social media is creating new headaches for corporate compliance and legal professionals worldwide.

An Explosion of Evidence

As social media use has exploded in its popularity, so too has the legal use of information mined from these sites. In fact, according to a study performed by the American Academy of Matrimonial Lawyers, 81 percent of its members have used or faced evidence plucked from Facebook, MySpace, Twitter, and other social networking sites; i.e., social media have basically become a divorce lawyer's best friend.[12] And it doesn't stop there. Investigators, lawyers, and employers are finding photos and other information online that can become evidence in criminal and civil cases—or simply a reason not to hire someone.

For instance, several Twitter posts between two young men may become pivotal evidence in a murder trial. Apparently, what started out as a simple Twitter beef between Kwame Dancy and Jameg Blake spilled over to the streets, where Dancy was tragically gunned down just feet from his home. According to the police, the two had a rocky relationship, and the Twitter messages they posted only made it worse. Hours before the shooting, Dancy taunted Blake with a tweet: "N——s is lookin for u don't think I won't give up ya address for a price betta chill asap!" Now this message, along with many others, may be subpoenaed to bolster the theory that there was bad blood between the two men.

---

[12] *See* "Big Surge in Social Networking Evidence Say Survey of Nation's Top Divorce Lawyers," http://www.aaml.org/go/about-the-academy/press/press-releases/big-surge-in-social-networking-evidence-says-survey-of-nations-top-divorce-lawyers (last visited Sept. 13, 2010).

Likewise, in two recent employment discrimination cases, social media evidence discovered on the social networking site LinkedIn took center stage.[13] In both cases, the plaintiffs had claimed that they were improperly terminated from their casino jobs after Harrah's had purchased the casinos. To contradict their claims, the defendants introduced testimony of the plaintiffs' supervisors, who had stated that they were not Harrah's employees but rather employees for some other company. The plaintiffs, however, were able to disprove this testimony by introducing into evidence the supervisors' LinkedIn page, where the individuals had listed "Harrah's" as their employer.

In almost any personal injury case, social media evidence could be the proverbial "smoking gun." If you post online pictures or videos of events, activities, or vacations, an insurance company (or defense counsel) might use those to show that you are engaging in various physical activities, which would tend to discredit the injury that you allegedly suffered. Similarly, if you post comments about certain activities or subjects related to the accident at issue, those too could be used to challenge your truthfulness. We've seen several recent cases in which the courts have held that such information is admissible if relevant.[14]

"Discovering" the Headache of Social Media

Is social media just another type of electronically stored information (ESI) and therefore governed by the Rules of Civil Procedure? Yes and no. While the nature of social media data is very similar to other types of ESI, the actual practicalities of how you gather that data, preserve it, and produce it are very different.

For starters, while it is fairly easy to pinpoint and retrieve traditional ESI, such as Word documents, spreadsheets, and e-mail messages, the same cannot be said about information posted on social media sites. For one, the information posted may be physically stored on the user's computer but not, or in the case of a corporate client, the company's servers. It may not even be on the social media site's own servers, but rather may be located in leased cloud storage or even portable mobile devices. If this is the case, the retrieval of the requested data may be difficult, and thus it must sometimes be obtained through a third party if it is not possible to compel the user himself or herself to provide the data.

---

[13] *See, Blayde v. Harrah's Entertainment*, 08-cv-02798 (W.D. Tenn.; Dec. 17, 2010); *Branson v. Harrah's Tunica Corporation*, 2:08-cv-02804, (W.D. Tenn.; June 3, 2011).

[14] *See supra* notes 15-29 and accompanying text.

Obtaining Evidence: The Discoverability of Social Media Evidence

What is discoverable as social media evidence? A recent line of cases has provided some insight into what is discoverable, albeit the distinction between discoverable and nondiscoverable social media evidence is still hazy at best. On one hand, it suffices to say that the "old discovery rules" (those relating to paper discovery) still apply with similar force in the social media context. However, several subtle distinctions can cause considerable headaches when contemplating the discovery of social media evidence.

Take, for example, a New York case, *Romano v. Steelcase, Inc.*,[15] where the defendant sought to discover the plaintiff's current and past Facebook and MySpace pages and accounts, including deleted information, in the belief that information posted there was inconsistent with her injury claims. The plaintiff objected to the defendant's request, arguing, among other things, that her expectation of privacy trumped the defendant's need for access to the evidence. After first establishing that the information sought was clearly relevant to the plaintiff's personal injury claim, the court found that production of her MySpace and Facebook entries would not violate her right to privacy, and that any such concerns were outweighed by the defendant's need for the information. Specifically, the court noted that both Facebook and MySpace informed users that they were not guaranteed complete privacy; MySpace went so far as to warn users that their profiles and MySpace forums are *public* spaces. Concluding, the court stated:

> [W]hen Plaintiff created her Facebook and MySpace Accounts, she consented to the fact that her personal information would be shared with others, notwithstanding her privacy setting. Indeed that is the very nature and purpose of these social networking sites else they would cease to exist. Since Plaintiff knew that her information may become publicly available, she cannot now claim that she had a reasonable expectation of privacy. As recently set forth by commentators regarding privacy and social networking sites, given the millions of users, "[i]n this environment, privacy is no longer grounded in reasonable expectations, but rather in some theoretical protocol better known as wishful thinking."[16]

---

[15] 2010 WL 3703242 (N.Y. Sup. Ct., Sept. 21, 2010).
[16] *Id.* at 6.

The court ordered the plaintiff to allow the defendant access to the requested information.

Similarly, in *EEOC v. Simply Storage Mgmt., LLC*,[17] the court considered a defendant's request for production of all SNS (social networking sites) content on two claimants' online profiles. Like the plaintiff in *Romano*, the underlying objection to the production was that it would improperly infringe upon the claimants' privacy and cause embarrassment. The defendant responded to this contention by noting that the information was proper because the plaintiff, EEOC, had placed the emotional health of the claimants at issue beyond the typical "garden variety emotional distress claims"[18] and that "the nature of the injuries . . . alleged implicates all of [claimants'] social communications (i.e., all their Facebook and MySpace content)."[19] Here, the court stated that while the "discovery of SNS requires the application of basic discovery principles in a novel context," the true nature of the challenge before it was to "define appropriately broad limits—but limits nevertheless—on the discoverability of social communications . . . and to do so in a way that provides meaningful direction to the parties."[20]

Turning to the privacy concerns proffered by the plaintiff, the court determined that the claimants' expectation and intent that their SNS communications would be maintained as private was not a legitimate basis for prohibiting discovery; that SNS content must be produced when relevant to the claim or defense in a case; and that the proper scope of discovery was wider than communications that directly reference the matters alleged. The court determined that the proper scope in the instant case was:

> [A]ny profiles, postings, or messages (including status updates, wall comments, causes joined, groups joined, activity streams, blog entries) and SNS applications for claimants . . . that reveal, refer, or relate to any emotion, feeling or mental state, as well as communications that reveal, refer, or relate to events that could reasonably be expected to produce significant emotion, feeling or mental state.[21]

In addition, the court also ordered the production of any third-party communications to claimants if they placed the claimants' own communica-

---

[17] No. 1:09-cv-1223-WTL-DML (S.D. Ind. May 11, 2010).
[18] *Id.* at 3.
[19] *Id.* at 5.
[20] *Id.*
[21] *Id.* at 9-10.

tions in context. Finally, the court required the production of photographs of the claimants because the context of a picture and the claimants' appearance might provide insight into the claimants' emotional or mental status. Wrapping up its discussion, the court once again turned to the issue of privacy. The court acknowledged the possibility of embarrassment but reasoned that this is the inevitable result of alleging these sorts of injuries and explained that this concern was outweighed by the fact that the production here would be of information claimants had already shared.

One of the most recent cases, *Zimmerman v. Weis Markets, Inc.*,[22] traces the decisions discussed above. In *Zimmerman*, the plaintiff sought damages for a workplace accident that had left him with a scarred leg. In support of his case, the plaintiff had testified in his deposition that he was embarrassed by the scar, would not wear shorts, and had diminished enjoyment of life. During a brief review of the plaintiff's Facebook and MySpace profiles, however, defense counsel found that the plaintiff had posted photographs of himself wearing shorts and going about normal activities. As such, defense counsel sought access to all nonpublic portions of the plaintiff's social media pages, which was vehemently opposed by the plaintiff based on his privacy interests. Taking up the issue, the court sided with the defendants and ordered the plaintiff to disclose his social media passwords and user names. In so doing, the court reasoned that the plaintiff's public postings on the social media sites in question included a discussion of his injury, which was clearly relevant to his claim of serious and permanent impairment. Further, these public postings were construed as sufficient to demonstrate that his non-public postings would contain additional relevant information about his injury. The court also stated that the plaintiff's choice to bring this issue to trial, as well as his (perhaps none too smart) decision to share information about his injury online, meant that he could not have any reasonable expectation of media privacy.

The source of the evidence is very important. In *Crispin v. Christian Audiger, Inc.*,[23] the court granted reconsideration of a magistrate judge's decision to deny the plaintiff's motion to quash subpoenas issued to several social networking sites that sought disclosure of the plaintiff's subscriber information and communications relevant to the underlying dispute. Of particular importance, the court analyzed the applicability of the Stored Communications Act (SCA) to the social networking sites at issue. Here, the court noted that provisions of the SCA applied to "providers" of communication

---

[22] No. CV-09-1535, 2011 WL 2065410 (Pa. Comm. Pl. May 19, 2011).
[23] 2010 WL 2293238 (C.D. Cal. May 26, 2010).

services and the information they possess concerning entities and individuals.[24] For information to be afforded protection from disclosure under the SCA, a provider must either be an "ECS" or an "RCS" provider.[25] As pointed out by the court, the SCA has defined an ECS provider as any service that provides its users with the ability to send or receive wire or electronic communications. Conversely, the court explained that the statute has defined RCS as "the provision to the public of computer storage or process services by means of an electronic communications system and deserving of a lesser standard of protection concerning communications."[26]

Applying these definitions in the instant case, the court found that all of these social networking sites qualified as ECS providers because they provided message delivery services, and also as RCS providers because they offered message storage services.[27] As an interesting aside, some commentators have suggested that because electronic communications typically combine both services—message delivery and message storage—the ECS and RCS definitions in the SCA may have become a distinction without a difference.

After determining the SCA to be applicable, the court then turned to whether the information requested in the subpoena was public or private, the latter of which is protected from disclosure by the SCA while the former is not. The court in *Crispin* held that the web mail and e-mail communications sought were inherently private because these messages were not readily accessible to the public or, at most, were available to only a select few individuals. As such, the court reversed the magistrate judge's order with respect to the social networking subpoenas to the extent that they sought private e-mail messages. However, with respect to the Facebook wall postings and MySpace comments, the court determined that there was not enough evidence on record to make a determination as to whether these wall postings and comments constituted private communications. Accordingly, the court ordered a new evidentiary hearing regarding those portions of the subpoenas that sought Facebook wall postings and MySpace comments.

---

[24] *Id.* at 4.
[25] *Id.*
[26] *Id.*
[27] In support of its conclusion, the court cited examples of ECS, including basic e-mail services and private electronic bulletin board services. Further, the court recognized that an RCS provider offered longer-term storage or processing services, more or less like a virtual filing cabinet. Finally, the court noted that Microsoft was an example of both an ECS and RCS because it provided both e-mail delivery and storage services through its Hotmail website.

We're not real fans of the *Crispin* court's decision. The court's holding appears to appreciably restrict a civil litigant's ability to obtain potential evidence that can only be described as a proverbial "smoking gun" by extending the protections of the SCA to private communications sent through a social networking or web hosting site. Moreover, the 1986 law doesn't "fit" very well in the modern content—the court seems to be hammering a square peg into a round hole. How many "friends" are on the "private" part of a social media site before the distinction between public and private is lost, especially where all the friends are free to do whatever they want with the content? Since the case was one of first impression, the decision is not binding on other courts. It will be interesting to see how other courts react—and it would be helpful if Congress would retool a law whose time is long gone.

Getting Your Evidence In: Jumping the Authentication Hurdle

Once a lawyer has jumped the first hurdle and determined exactly what social media information can be discovered, the next hurdle that he or she must surmount is actually getting that information admitted into evidence. Fortunately, courts have provided some guidance into the issues that may arise here. For the most part, the courts have been fairly consistent in applying the traditional rules of evidence in this area, but there have been some notable exceptions worth mentioning. As always, one should consult the governing law in his or her particular jurisdiction to prevent an embarrassing and potentially costly hiccup at trial.

One feature that draws many individuals to social media sites and to the Internet generally is the level of anonymity. Anyone can set up an account under a false name, and information on a "legitimate" site can be manipulated. This feature, however, has given lawyers countless evidentiary headaches, and courts have responded by requiring electronic evidence to be authenticated prior to being admitted in evidence. Generally speaking, many courts have required that the requesting party provide evidence such that a reasonable jury could find that the exhibit is what the party claims it to be. Importantly, the court in *State v. Bell*[28] specifically pointed out that the evidentiary support necessary for admissibility was "quite low." The court admitted several MySpace entries, finding that sufficient authentication included testimony from the proponent that (1) he had knowledge of defendant's e-mail address and MySpace user name, (2) the printouts appeared to be accurate records of his electronic commu-

---

[28] 882 N.E.2d 502 (2008).

nications with the defendant, and (3) the communications contained code words known only to the defendant and his alleged victims.

However, in *Griffin v. State*,[29] the Maryland Court of Appeals held that the potential for manipulation in the context of social media required greater scrutiny of the foundational authentication requirements than that of traditional records. Because the authentication of key electronic evidence based on a picture, birth date, and residence location alone provided an inadequate foundation, the court found the trial court committed reversible error, overturned the conviction, and remanded for a new trial. That being said, the court did suggest that testimony from the purported creator, a search of her computer, or information obtained directly from the social networking website could suffice to authenticate electronic evidence.

With that in mind, the admission of social media evidence becomes much easier when there is any admission from the witnesses, or at least an admission by the plaintiff or witness of the IP address, along with the IP logs that should be produced by the social networking sites. One thing is for certain: Given the number of cases that have recently addressed the issue, authentication and admissibility issues of social media evidence will in the future likely become as routine as the introduction of business records and paper documents.

A Solution to the Discovery Problem?

Given these complications, there really isn't a one-size-fits-all solution to the problem. Each social media request must be addressed in different ways. However, there are some steps lawyers can take to help avoid headaches and possible spoliation sanctions.

Responding to Social Media Discovery Requests

If your client is an organization, you should ensure that the company preserves any relevant records that are within its possession, custody, or control, as well as instruct all employees to preserve any related information held by third parties. Employees should also be told not to discuss the possibility of pending litigation, as it could cause parties of interest to engage in a massive dump and burn strategy. In the end, if you can show the court that you've done your best and documented all steps taken, that's really all you can be expected to do. Good faith goes a long way.

---

[29] 2011 WL 1586683 (Md. Apr. 28, 2011).

Individual clients should be mindful of what they post on Facebook and other social media sites and realize that something said or posted five years ago could one day come back to haunt them. Now, we're not telling you to have your clients jump on Facebook and delete all inculpatory statements or photographs or, heaven forbid, their accounts altogether, but lawyers might want to warn their clients to be wary of what they put online. Let's say that your client is embroiled in a hotly contested divorce and, during their college years, jokingly posted a picture on Facebook that showed him or her making threatening gestures or engaging in some questionable behavior. Whether your client likes it or not, that picture might very well find its way into the courtroom if it is deemed relevant to the pending litigation. Clients need to understand the implications of their online behavior.

Obtaining Relevant Social Media Evidence Ethically

As the line of cases mentioned above shows, courts are accepting social media evidence with greater frequency. Obviously, whether a court will accept social media evidence in *your* case depends on the facts at issue and whether the evidence was obtained ethically and pursuant to the rules of evidence. But, assuming that the evidence would be admissible at trial, most lawyers often don't know where to begin when searching for this type of evidence.

So how do you find or obtain information on social media sites? As an initial matter, lawyers must always consider the ethical implications of obtaining information from social media sites by deceptive means. Often, this involves a lawyer sending, or getting a third party to send, a "friend" request to an adverse witness's private social networking page in order to discover impeachment evidence. Recent opinions from the New York State, New York City, and Philadelphia Bar Associations ethics committees have addressed this particular issue and all three determined that any form of deception or trickery to gain access to a social networking page was objectionable.

Interestingly, the New York City Bar Opinion 2010-2 (2010) noted that a lawyer could, as long as he identifies himself using his real name and profile, request friend status. It appears, however, that none of the three opinions has a problem with publicly available information; the New York State Bar Association Opinion 843 (2010) concluded that a lawyer may ethically view and access Facebook and MySpace of a party other than the lawyer's client in litigation as long as the party's profile is available to all members in the network and the lawyer neither "friends" nor directs someone else to do so.

That aside, there is some information that can be ethically obtained without formal discovery. As stated in the New York State Bar Association Opinion 843, any profile or post from a party, witness, or judge that is public information is fair game. In fact, the court in *Moreno v. Hanford Sentinel, Inc.*, 172 Cal. App. 4th 1125 (Ct. App. 2009), found that a post on an unrestricted MySpace page was open to the public eye, and thus the plaintiff had no reasonable expectation of privacy. That means that a lawyer should always check and see whether any individuals related to the pending litigation have a public profile on any social networking sites. If so, the lawyer should arrange for an independent third party to periodically take screen shots of potentially relevant information if it becomes available.

If an individual has heightened security settings that will not allow general viewing of relevant information, the security settings must be respected. Remember, attempting to bypass these settings through deceptive conduct or trickery will likely run afoul of ethical rules and subject the lawyer to disciplinary action or sanctions. This leaves the usual discovery process.

Generally speaking, the basic discovery rules apply. Preservation issues will need to be discussed as soon as the lawsuit commences and again in Rule 26(f) Meet and Confer of the Federal Rules of Civil Procedure. A lawyer could take screen shots to capture images of content located on the site, but those images are static, and, as we are all well aware, content is added and changed constantly, so getting authoritative data that can be time-authenticated in court is an issue. This is best done by an independent third party, frequently an expert—and this sort of preservation is relatively inexpensive. Once preservation is addressed, lawyers should draft and send interrogatories to determine what sites, if any, a party uses and request any and all corresponding ISP addresses. The Request for Production is next on the list, which should be broadly construed to capture any information—including photographs, wall posts, video, etc.—on any issue related to the lawsuit. Here, recent amendments to the Federal Rules of Civil Procedure have addressed a party's requests for electronically stored information (ESI) and should cover any ESI requests from social networking sites. Rule 34 provides that "any party may serve on any other party a request (1) to produce . . . any electronically stored information—including . . . data or data complications stored in any medium from which information can be obtained. . . ." Obviously, these requests will likely be met with some resistance, as most of the information is either very personal or irrelevant. Thus, as a final note, any lawyer worth his or her salt will be prepared to respond to any objections to this type of evidence—specifically, those related to relevance, hearsay, and authentication.

So far we've been talking about requests to individuals, but what about subpoenas to a social networking site? If the site gives the okay and the opposing party does not object, then discovery is very straightforward and usually explained on the social media site. Many of the popular social media sites, such as MySpace, for instance, even provide a relatively straightforward guide for individuals seeking to obtain information from their site. Facebook is a different beast. It has installed a new feature for users to download their own information. This is Facebook's attempt to remove itself from the civil subpoena process. Facebook has changed its procedures for obtaining data if the download function isn't sufficient. All requests for Facebook records are sent to **subpoena@facebook.com**, by fax (650) 644-3229, or by mail to:

> Facebook, Inc.
> Attn: Security Department/Custodian of Records
> 1601 California Ave.
> Palo Alto, CA 94304
> Facebook suggests including the following:
> E-mail address, Facebook user ID (UID) and vanity URL (if any).

Will Facebook comply with a preservation request? Hard to say, but doubtful. A quote from the Facebook site, "Facebook preserves user content only in response to a valid law enforcement request," suggests that requests in civil proceedings aren't going to get very far.

Without a court order, your request will probably be met with an objection by the site or the opposing party on the grounds that the production of private information would violate the SCA.

A Law Enforcement Twist: Trolling Social Media for Haphazdard Tweets, Comments, or Photos

Lest we forget, lawyers are not the only individuals searching for information on social media sites. Law enforcement officials too, among others, have jumped on the social media bandwagon in the hopes that would-be criminals will post incriminating evidence that can be used against them in a criminal investigation or trial. And it appears that judges are willing to allow these law enforcement officials unfettered (and often without the user's knowledge) access to a user's account; since 2008, federal judges have authorized at least two dozen search warrants to search an individual's Facebook accounts. These warrants typically demand that Facebook turn over a user's "Neoprint" and "Photoprint"—terms that the social networking giant has used to describe a detailed package of profile and photo information that even a user can't obtain. According to Facebook, it holds only the same data that a user has access to, but this does not appear to be true based on the law enforcement documents we have seen. Many other social media sites, including MySpace, Twitter, and LinkedIn, have been ordered to turn over a user's personal data as well.

What makes the recent popularity of social media search warrants so notable is the fact that not one appears to have been challenged on the grounds that law enforcement violated the individual's Fourth Amendment protection against unlawful search and seizure. Some believe that the reason behind the lack of Constitutional challenges is that often the user is unaware that his or her profile has been searched in the first place. By law, neither Facebook nor the government is obligated to inform a user that their account has been searched, although prosecutors are required to disclose any material evidence they find to a defendant. Twitter and MySpace take a softer stance. These two companies have formally adopted a policy to notify users when law enforcement asks to search their profile. In our opinion, we expect to see Facebook's practices challenged in the future. As Eben Moglen, a cyberlaw professor at Columbia Law School, pointed out, Facebook searches demonstrate that courts are ill-equipped to safeguard privacy rights in an age of digital media. The solutions are not legal, they're technical.

One Wrong Step and Ka-Boom! Social Media Mishaps

As social media become increasingly popular, legal professionals have to be mindful of the ethical land mines strewn across the social media landscape. True, social media sites do not present new ethical challenges, but they have the potential to magnify and accelerate the ramifications of ethics violations. The informality and speed that characterize social media can contribute to errors and ethical transgressions. In addition, "social networks are public, easily searched, and permanently archived."[30] In other words, when things go wrong, it usually ends in a very big BOOM!

---

[30] James M. McCaulely, *Blogging and Social Networking for Lawyers: Ethical Pitfalls*, Virginia Lawyer, Volume 58 (February 2010).

Lesson 1: It's Called Confidentiality, Stupid!

Of all the rules of professional conduct, the rule regarding confidences is probably the one most lawyers are aware of (or at least they're aware that there is such a rule). American Bar Association Model Rule 1.6 states: "[a] lawyer shall not reveal information relating to the representation of a client."[31] This rule's broad mandate mandates that client information remain confidential and not be disclosed in any setting, including an informal electronic exchange. Pretty simple, right? Yet time and time again, lawyers slip up and post specific client information on the web.

Take, for example, the case of Kristine A. Peshek, an experienced Illinois assistant public defender, who decided one day to rant about several of her clients on her blog, "The Bardd Before the Bar—Irreverent Adventures in Life, Law, and Indigent Defense." She posted:

> #127409 (the client's jail identification number) This stupid kid is taking the rap for his drug-dealing dirtbag of an older brother because "he's not a snitch." My client is in college. Just goes to show you that higher education does not imply that you have any sense.[32]

In another instance, a client testified that she was drug-free and received just five days' jail time, and then complained to Ms. Peshek that she was using methadone and could not go five days without it. Obviously annoyed, Ms. Peshek posted that her reaction was "Huh? You want me to go back and tell the judge that you lied to him, you lied to the presentence investigator, you lied to me?"[33] When her supervisors became aware of her blogging, Ms. Peshek not only lost her job as a public defender but also was suspended from the practice of law for 60 days.

Judges too can find themselves in hot water for posting information about cases they preside over. After being called in on a Saturday to hear bail applications for defendants arrested the night before, a magistrate judge in England decided to tweet about his cases. For example, one tweet said, "1st defendant. Conspiracy to rob TSB of 500,000 pounds. Good start—wrong previous convictions presented."[34] The magistrate judge later concluded: "Finished hearing bail. 3 refused for planning robbery of

---

[31] Model Rule 1.6. Obviously, while many states have adopted either the model rule's wording verbatim or some similar iteration of the rule, it is important for a lawyer to know the exact wording of the rule in his or her jurisdiction.
[32] Peshak Blog.
[33] Id.
[34] Robert Ambrogi, "When What Happens Online Ends Up In Court," **http://www.ims-expertservices.com/newsletters/sept/when-what-happens-online-ends-up-in-court-091509.asp** (last visited on Sept. 13, 2010).

480,000 pounds from TSB in Dawley, Telford."[35] Once the magistrate judge learned that his tweeting ways were to be investigated by a judicial advisory committee, he chose instead to resign from the bench, although he maintained that he did nothing wrong.

Lesson 2: Do You Know Who Your Friends Are?

Perhaps some of the most entertaining stories about lawyers and judges stepping on social media land mines involve the decision to "friend" another legal professional or a client on a social networking site—often Facebook. While there is no law against one lawyer friending another, depending on the jurisdiction, judges are sometimes barred from friending a lawyer if there is a substantial likelihood that he or she may appear before that judge. In addition, lawyers and judges can run into trouble if they friend someone associated with a case that they are a part of. For instance, ABA Model Rule 4.2 provides that lawyers must be careful not to engage in inadvertent (or intentional) communications with persons known to be represented by counsel,[36] and ABA Model Rule 4.3 tells lawyers that communications with an unrepresented person cannot be untruthful or misleading.[37] Finally, even the most cautious lawyer or judge will sometimes slip up and post an unflattering comment or status update. In so doing, these legal professionals may not only violate several ethical rules, but also run the risk of being caught by a "friend" in a fib.

Let's start with some questionable friendships. In a meeting in chambers with the judge during a North Carolina child-custody matter, a conversation between the lawyers and the judge turned briefly to Facebook. While the wife's lawyer was a non-user, both the lawyer for the husband and the judge frequented the site. That evening, unbeknownst to opposing counsel, the judge friended the husband's lawyer. You can guess what happened next. As the trial proceeded, the judge and the lawyer exchanged comments about the case through their Facebook pages.[38] After the hear-

---

[35]*Id.*
[36]ABA Model R. Prof. Conduct 4.2 (2010).
[37]ABA Model R. Prof. Conduct 4.3 (2010).
[38]Part of the Facebook exchange between the judge and the lawyer involved the weight to be given testimony that one spouse had been unfaithful. During a meeting in chambers the day after the Judge Terry had friended lawyer Charles A. Schieck, Terry told the lawyers he believed the testimony but did not see that it made any difference in deciding custody. Schieck responded, "I will have to see if I can prove a negative." That evening, Schieck posted on his Facebook account, "How do I prove a negative?" Judge Terry saw it and responded that he had "two good parents to choose from." Schieck then posted another comment, noting that he had a "wise judge." The next day, the two shared additional messages on Facebook. In one, Schieck wrote, "I hope I'm in my last day of trial." Judge Terry responded, "You are in your last day of trial."

ing ended, the wife's lawyer eventually found out about the "friendship" and immediately moved for a new trial and for the judge's disqualification. The judge promptly removed himself from the case and the wife got a new trial. The judge got something too. He earned a public reprimand from the state's Judicial Standards Commission, in which he stated "he will not repeat such conduct in the future" and "will promptly read and familiarize himself with the Code of Judicial Conduct."[39]

This next story provides proof that lawyers might want take a moment and think before friending a fellow legal professional. A lawyer in Galveston, Texas, had asked the presiding judge, Susan Criss, for a continuance due to a death in her family. Unfortunately for the lawyer, Judge Criss was no social networking slouch. She quickly discovered that instead of grieving her recent loss, the lawyer had posted a string of status updates detailing her week of drinking, going out, and partying. Quite a different story from the sob story she told in court. As one would expect, when the judge informed the lawyer's senior partner of her misrepresentation, he was quite steamed. She did not get the continuance.

Lesson 3: Sometimes It's Not Good to "Tweet" Your Own Horn!
Another common area where a simple slip up can lead to big ethical trouble for a lawyer is advertisements. Each state has promulgated rules governing what lawyers can or cannot say. Lawyers often forget that these rules apply with the same force in the electronic world as in the paper context.

Many jurisdictions have a rule that states, in or way or another, that lawyers are either forbidden from holding themselves as experts (or specialists) in a certain field or must meet certain requirements in order to do so. This means that a lawyer could violate the applicable ethical rules by filling out the LinkedIn section called "specialties." Additionally, lawyers who post comments on Facebook or tweet about a huge win in the courtroom will likely violate the prohibition against advertising specific case results unless the post is followed by a disclaimer. In the case of Twitter, it is almost impossible to do this, as there is a 140-character limit.

Finally, a South Carolina Ethics Advisory Opinion states that a lawyer is responsible for any recommendations, endorsements, or ratings ascribed to that lawyer on a third-party Web site. If the lawyer is unable to monitor and remove or edit noncompliant statements, that lawyer must remove himself or herself from the web site. However, that same ethics committee

---

[39] *In the Matter of B. Carlton Terry, Jr.*, North Carolina Judicial Stds, Comm'n, No. 08-234 (April 1, 2009).

did note that a lawyer may use services, such as Groupon or LivingSocial, to offer discounts and deals on legal services *as long as* the method used complies with ethics rules for advertising and the rule on sharing of legal fees. There can be additional ethical pitfalls to avoid when using these services; specifically, a lawyer should make sure to clearly state the scope of representation that is covered in the "deal," route payments to the trust account if required, and be conscious of the duty to prospective clients. Before you start posting half-off estate planning coupons, be warned: North Carolina has issued a proposed ethics opinion that comes to the opposite result. Thus, it seems that different ethics committees view these services differently, and thus you might want to consult your state's advisory opinion first or, if no opinion exists, pose a hypothetical question and wait for a definitive answer.

Conclusion

Like so many things, social media can be a gift when wielded correctly, but a downright curse when used improperly or if the user is not familiar with the basic aspects of each social media platform. Undoubtedly, social media is the future, and, whether lawyers like it or not, they must quickly adapt or risk becoming as outdated as Windows 95. Many of the follies that have plagued lawyers and judges could be avoided simply by using a little common sense and basic legal know-how.

First, remember the "Mom" rule: Don't post anything that you wouldn't want your mother to see. While you can control the privacy setting on your account, you can't control what your friends do with photos or texts you have posted. This rule applies across the board—from lawyers to judges to the average Joe. Second, lawyers and judges need to think about their ethical obligations, which, contrary to popular belief, apply with the same force in the "virtual" world as in real life. Many of the issues highlighted above could have been avoided if the legal professional had simply asked, "Would this be permitted by the applicable ethical rules if it occurred in a face-to-face meeting or conversation?" If the answer is no, then the lawyer or judge probably should steer clear. Sanctions resulting from ethical breaches are increasing in number, and prudent lawyers will avoid being anywhere close to the line between ethical and unethical conduct.

CHAPTER TWENTY-SEVEN

The Paper LESS Office: Kicking the Paper Habit in the Era of the Cloud

by Ross L. Kodner, Esq.

WHO ISN'T STRUGGLING WITH an endless sea of paper that conspires to bury them? Who hasn't wasted an hour on any given day, putting all client work on hold, while they chase around the office looking for a paper matter file? The answer, if we're being honest with ourselves, is "all of us." Stop the madness and make finding, filing, and sharing files easier by going "paper less" rather than "paperless." Scanning paper documents as searchable PDFs and using a legal document management system lets you build and manage complete, contiguous electronic client matter files and, in the era of the cloud, access it from anywhere, any time.

> *First thing we do, let's kill all the paper.*
>
> —Will Shakespeare,
> if he were alive today

> *Paper, paper everywhere,*
> *Nor any page to find.*
> *Unless it's electronic paper in the cloud.*
>
> —Ross L. Kodner
> Continuing Thoughts on The Paper LESS Office

Note: I work as an independent technology consultant for law firms. As part of this work, my firm acts as a reseller for certain technology products. However, just as the authors have stated in the preface that the book contains their objective advice, I have strived to provide unbiased advice and product recommendations in this chapter.

The Paper LESS Office: Kicking the Paper Habit in the Era of the Cloud

ONE CONSTANT IN THE otherwise ever-changing world of legal technology is frustration with paper—piles and piles of paper that conspire to waste our otherwise productive and billable time. Piles of paper that cause untold angst as we chase around our offices and homes looking for documents that might exist only in electronic form. Exasperation when we realize that the client work we need to do at home one evening is just not going to happen, because our ability to work is dependent on the physical presence of the paper client file . . . which you forgot to take home. But there's good news: You may be able to get out from under all that paper.

For years, lawyers have been on a quest for the paperless office, but this concept may be the greatest lie of the technology age. Our offices will never be paperless, at least in the foreseeable future. Even if we reduce the amount of paper we generate, other people will continue to send us paper. Can you realistically walk into most courtrooms and present a paperless case to a jury? Probably not—at least not in most jurisdictions. Are your 50-year-old eyes comfortable with proofing a 60-page contract onscreen? Perhaps yes for some, but likely not for most of us. Early technology scanning was touted as the great answer, but it is not.

I Want It NOW! Or Sooner! Life in the Age of Instancy

Lawyers and legal professionals in all walks of practice—from SmallLaw to BigLaw, in corporate and government practice—all face the reality of this "Age of Instancy" in which we practice and live. Think of it this way: Twenty-five years ago, do you remember how extraordinary it seemed when the company then known as Federal Express promised that it could deliver a hard-copy document anywhere in the world by 10:30 the next morning? It seemed positively miraculous, didn't it? Today, 10:30 the next morning seems like an eternity to have to wait. How our perceptions of time and expectations of access to documents and other information have changed!

Today, while on the phone with a client across the continent, if the need to share a document arises, what do we do? Instinctively, and without need for any taxing conscious thought, we say, "No problem, I'll e-mail them while we're talking." A 5-megabyte collection of attachments zips across the ether and arrives in the client's e-mail inbox, almost before we can finish the sentence. Collaboration, orally and digitally, all happening virtually at the speed of light. Or even better, don't bother transferring it at all—use a web-based secure document repository, such as Dropbox (**www.dropbox.com**), Box.net (**www.box.net**), NetDocuments (**www.netdocuments.com**), or the Worldox/Web Mobile adjunct to the Worldox legal document/email management system (**www.worldox.com**).

In the last year, the rise of "Cloud Computing" has been meteoric. While the concept of cloud computing is shrouded in a fog of vagueness, it can generally be described as the ability to either run software functions or access data across the Internet, with many different ways of doing so. In terms of the concept of becoming "Paper LESS," one can look at several different "cloud" approaches, all focused on any place, any time, any system access to client and firm files. We'll explore these various approaches later in this chapter.

Instant access to information changes our expectations. Clients are "trained" to expect instantaneous everything. Instant access to documents, electronically delivered. Instant responses to questions they pose to their lawyers, such as when was that deposition scheduled? Or, how much do I have left of my retainer balance? Or, do you have the contact info for that financial forensic consultant you mentioned last week? Law practices that are not able to instantly respond to such "in conversation" queries quickly become labeled as "technopeasants." Effectively, such lawyers can be instantly branded by their clients as being both mechanically and substantively incompetent and, frankly, more of an irritant than a professional counselor to the client.

While the "Age of Instancy" may not be a positive development of the human experience, it is a fact of professional life. Woe unto the lawyer who fails to acknowledge this issue by putting him- or herself in the clients' shoes and understanding how true it is that the clients' perception is the only reality that counts. So what does this have to do with managing paper in our practices? Simply everything.

Paper: Endless Frustration and Expense

Paper is the bane of every law practice's existence. Paper wastes our time and costs us money. Paper files get lost and cost money to store—and yet more money to retrieve. Paper, used injudiciously, negatively impacts the environment. Paper tends to get coffee or lunch spilled on it in direct proportion to the importance and irreplaceability of the document. Paper isn't searchable in any efficient way compared to electronic searching abilities. In fact, there is a great corollary of life in law practice: "The more urgently one needs a paper client file, the less likely it is where it is supposed to be." Who hasn't experienced a day where an urgently needed paper file just doesn't turn up at all? The toll on profitability and client responsiveness, not to mention our personal sanity, is dramatic and negative. It makes sense to find practical ways to avoid this multidimensional self-infliction of pain.

Saving the Planet, Saving Your Sanity—More Paper is NOT the Way

Being environmentally conscious is no longer optional. The movement to become more "green" is now entrenched and continually sweeping across the worldwide business landscape. Clearly, generating more paper is the antithesis to being green, meaning that becoming Paper LESS in law practice is of paramount importance and can be the initial touchstone of a green initiative in any law firm or legal department.

Think about the environmental impact and the staggering carbon footprint involved in printing just a single sheet of paper:

- Trees are harvested, with considerable energy expended in their acquisition ("chopping it down"), transportation, the process of transforming trees into logs, from logs into wood chips, from wood chips into wood pulp, and then eventually into paper.
- Then the paper is packaged in . . . MORE PAPER!
- The paper is shipped to its retail location, then to the consumer.
- The paper is printed in a device—a printer or copier—that has its own significant environmental footprint and trail of anti-green shame.
- The printing system employed devours toner or ink—again, supplies carrying their own carbon imprint and anti-green burden.
- Eventually the paper is likely discarded, often bypassing a responsible recycling process and contributing to overfilled landfills.

Becoming Paper LESS in practice—generating far less paper or virtually no new paper—is a perfect way to jump-start a green initiative and creates myriad economic, functional, and client service–related benefits.

The Cost of Being in a Paper MORE Office

Think about this question: How much time do you or your staff waste in an average workday, either (a) looking for paper client files, or (b) looking for information you can find only in paper files? How many of you waste 15 minutes chasing paper? 30 minutes? An hour or more? How many of you have experienced days where the paper file never turns up? Or even worse, a staffer starts an expedition to seek out a missing, urgently needed paper file. After 15 minutes and no success, the lawyer then chases the staffer, who in turn is still chasing the file. So it ends up being 30 staff minutes and 15 lawyer minutes—a phenomenal waste of otherwise billable and productive time.

We can perform some quick legal business math to calculate the value of these endless paper chases. Presume a net realized billed rate of $200 per hour—a likely average for solo and small firm lawyers in private practice. Then presume a billable value of $60 per hour for legal assistants or paralegals. Assume three lawyers waste an average of 15 minutes per day chasing paper, and one legal assistant and one paralegal waste 30 minutes each day (more for staff, because they are often chasing paper on behalf of requesting lawyers). That common small firm scenario represents a total daily value of otherwise billable/productive time wasted of:

$150 per day for the lawyers

$60 per day for the staff

That translates to:

$750 per week for the lawyers, $3,000 per month, $36,000 per year

$300 per week for the staff, $1,200 per month, $14,400 per year

That represents more than $50,000 in otherwise billable/productive time for this firm. And make no mistake: The effect of $50,000 in revenue never coming back to this firm has precisely the same effect as writing out a $50,000+ check at the end of the year. A basic business operations lesson shows that a reduction of top-line gross revenue has precisely the same negative impact on bottom-line profit as writing a check for $50,000. A cardinal principle of business operations is that a firm does not actually have to generate a check to spend money. Money not coming in has the same effect as a check that draws down from a bank account.

That is the cost of being mired in a Paper MORE practice. A $50,000+ hit for a three-lawyer practice. Hardly inconsequential; in fact, a staggering drain of a law practice's only available "product inventory," its billable and productive time. In the current economy, where so many law practices are being squeezed to the limits of financial viability, no firm can afford to subsidize this level of uncaptured revenue.

With so much at stake in managing the paper chase, why have there been so many stories about failed attempts to go "paperless?" Whether a law practice down the street or some government agency that devoured millions of taxpayer dollars in a fruitless, multiyear paperless office project, failure or, at best, a mediocre outcome. Why is this the case? The reason is simple: No matter how much your practice or your company tries to reduce the paper it uses and generates, the rest of the "paper clueless" world (especially budget-challenged government agencies) will inundate you with paper. When you consider the number of companies whose livelihoods are derived from paper in some way (paper companies, copier and printer companies, printing consumable companies, etc.), the reality is clear: Paper will be with us for some time to come—perhaps forever. So is it hopeless? Are we doomed to be perpetual slaves to the printed page?

What if you never had to chase paper files around the office? What if you could find a way to have to touch paper files less often, or virtually never? What if you could "buy back" that wasted 15, 30, 60 or more minutes per day looking for paper necessary for you to serve your clients? What might that mean economically? Even if you took an especially conservative posture in terms of how you viewed the conversion of "wasted paper chasing" time into billable time and cut the above recovery calculation by 50 percent, that would still represent $25,000 per year in "found money," and that's not pocket change for a three-lawyer practice annually.

And what if the answer to this problem cost less than $10,000 in out-of-pocket costs for software, hardware, and consultative guidance (approximately $3,000 for software, $3,000 for desktop scanners, and $4,000 for planning, process-streamlining, installation, and training)?

In that 50 percent discounted conservative analysis, the first-year net yield is at least $15,000 ($25,000 in converted/recovered billable/productive time less $10,000 in out-of-pocket costs), and then at least $25,000 per year thereafter—a conservative five-year billable/productive net revenue increase of approximately $115,000 in exchange for an approximately $10,000 front-end investment. The best investment you ever make in your life could turn out to be the investment you make in your own law practice.

Another factor, while more subjective in measurement but equally tangible in perceived value, is the positive effect on everyone's psyche and mental well-being. The endless daily paper chases take a toll psychologically on lawyer and staffer. It is just plain stressful when a paper file eludes location and wastes time, usually at the most inopportune moment. The stress, frustration, and angst that missing paper files inflict on legal professionals may be difficult to quantify. Nevertheless, it is as real as the fact that the sun rises in the east. Stress lessens our effectiveness, drives away valuable employees, and affects our well-being, especially when we take it home and inflict our frustrations on our families. Modern law practice is complicated and taxing. Anything we can do to positively impact our stress levels while simultaneously filling our firm coffers is something we need to embrace.

Fragmented Client Files Defy Common Sense

Being paper-centric in practice brings another inherent anti-common-sense inefficiency. One of the core problems in working on client files is that they are always split into two locations. The documents we create are located internally on our PC systems. The client documents we receive from outside sources are stored in our paper filing systems. So, if you want to view all the correspondence on a client's file, you have to look in two separate places—on-screen for your own documents, and then you need to track down the paper file and rifle through it to view the externally generated letters. That is, of course, if no one happens to have that particular file in their briefcase at home. Who hasn't experienced the fallout from this irrational and illogical artificial fragmentation of our case files? This is most certainly not a "best practices" approach. It is a professional competence issue before it ever rises to the level of being a technology problem.

Stop the Madness: Become Paper LESS in Your Practice

You're still reading and slowly becoming a believer in some kind of Paper LESS Office—one where you can avoid wasting time in the paper chase that has haunted you for your entire career. The next question is, how does your practice become Paper LESS? Surprisingly easily. With a combination of scanning tools, the wonders of the universally accessible and compatible PDF file format, sound but simple procedures, and a document/e-mail management system, a law practice can undergo a Paper LESS transformation literally overnight. Let's see how.

How many of you have had bad scanning experiences over the years? Many of you, in all likelihood—and there's a logical reason for all the scanning frustrations of the past. Since the dawn of document scanning, the term "scanning" has been synonymous with "OCR" (optical character recognition). In other words, most people equated scanning with trying to use software to identify the characters on a page and turn the page into an editable word processing document. It was a good idea conceptually, but in practice, even with the best OCR technology available, the process is still far from perfect. For example, with 97 percent OCR accuracy, three incorrect characters out of every 100 could mean as many as 66 errors per page on average. And what if one of those errors is critical and not detected?

And then, even with the latest, greatest OCR software, running on new PCs literally dripping with computing horsepower and fast new scanners, the process is about as slow as watching water boil . . . or paint dry . . . or grass grow. How can that be? It's 2011, not 1990. The reason is that it is still very difficult to replicate the layout by applying codes, styles, and other formatting tools to produce a usable word processing document. And it is often surprisingly slow, turning that shiny new 40-page-per-minute scanner, effectively, into a five-page-per-minute unit. Go ahead and let out that primal scream—we have all been there and have all similarly suffered.

So stop the madness. The bottom line is that modern scanning should not be equated with OCR. Instead, scanning should be looked at simply as a way to turn physical into electronic paper—effectively to photocopy the documents, but not in the traditional way that copying produces a duplicate piece of paper. Rather, the document is photocopied to the computer screen, producing a precise duplicate of the scanned paper. You then store it as a searchable (or, as Adobe calls it, an "accessible") PDF file. Then use a document management system and well-thought-out document storage procedures with a smart file-naming convention to store the "electronic paper" in your electronic client file cabinet.

And if the on-screen document looks precisely the same as the original piece of paper, why would you ever waste time trying to locate the paper itself? You wouldn't. You would use your document management system to rapidly navigate through your electronic file cabinet, or use instant search technology to pinpoint the document and pull it up onto the screen. No more "Keystone Cops" episodes of staff chasing paper, lawyer chasing staffer. No more drain of otherwise billable or productive time. Instead of those endlessly amusing games of "who the heck has the Jones file," just click, click and you're working—billing time, making more money—*sans* all the paper-chase-related stress that previously dominated your days.

Taking that a step further, what this all yields is the ability to make all documents in your practice—of all types—completely portable. This gives you the ability to work anytime, from anyplace, when clients need you to work or you choose to work. And it also brings in the practical reality of "device independence." With web-based access (securely, of course) to complete and contiguous electronic document files, does it matter if it's a Windows laptop/netbook, an iPad, or even an iPhone, BlackBerry, or Droid smartphone you're using? Nope. It's such an exciting degree of flexibility in work habits, work timing, and work location that it could induce heart palpitations.

Getting Specific About Being Paper LESS

That's the essence of the Paper LESS Office process. Now let's get specific. What tools do we need? What processes make sense? How do we get from a Paper MORE Office to the Paper LESS Office?

Paper LESS Side Benefit: And when you close a Paper LESS file, it's already "electronic paper": you can store it in a convenient byte-sized package (sorry, pun intended).This is a far better alternative for closed file storage than the costly, space-hungry storage requirements for physical paper files, which usually end up commandeering an area the size of starter home.

With a concept that I developed first in 1995 and have since called the "Paper LESS Office," scanning is viewed as a way to turn physical paper into digital paper.[1] When documents are scanned as *images*, the process can be 20 times faster than the processing-intensive and error-ridden OCR approach. On screen, imaged documents that have been scanned as searchable PDFs look precisely like the originals.[2] Even handwriting, preprinted lines, and boxes scan perfectly.

One of my own clients, lawyer and litigator Dale Cottam, a partner with the firm of Hirst & Applegate in Cheyenne, Wyoming, explains how his firm uses the Paper LESS Office process:

> When staff and attorneys receive paper documents in the mail, they scan each one using a low-cost and efficient Fujitsu ScanSnap S500

---

[1] I first put forth the Paper LESS Office concept in an article of the same name in the now defunct *Law Office Computing* magazine in September 1995.
[2] This is a core part of the Paper LESS Office concept, wherein scanned documents stored as PDFs look precisely like the originals, but have searchable and even editable textual content.

scanner (a model since replaced by the new S1500, which includes Adobe Acrobat 9.0 Standard), which essentially is a "PDF machine." Every person at the firm—staff and attorneys—has a ScanSnap on his or her desk to make converting paper documents to electronic documents second nature.

Once scanned, the electronic documents are saved in the universally readable PDF format. With a click of the mouse and a few seconds per page processing time, the text in the electronic document is converted to searchable text. The original paper document is placed in an expandable file folder and, in most cases, never is touched again. In some instances, the original is mailed to the client.

The electronic documents are stored in the attorney's electronic in-box using the Worldox document management system,[3] or they are routed directly to the attorney via e-mail. Either way, a copy of the electronic document is saved on the firm's network server, which is backed up nightly.

Attorneys read the electronic documents on their computer monitors. If they are on the road, they can access the electronic documents through the firm's VPN (virtual private network), a high-speed remote connection.

Scanning Systems—What Works?

In terms of scanners, a critical success element is use of a combination of a centralized, higher-speed scanner or multifunction copier with scanning abilities as along with distributed, de-centralized individual desktop scanners. Why both? Why not just rely on that newly leased, monolithic, all-powerful, hulking multifunction copier/printer/scanner down the hall? After all, you're paying for it every month, and it's a wonderfully rapid, high-capacity scanner.

Here is why relying solely on that über-capable multifunction unit will ultimately cause your Paper LESS Office initiative to fail. Let's assume that you have a wire basket next to your super-duper multifunction device down the hall. Everyone puts their documents to be scanned in the bas-

---

[3] Worldox is a product of World Software Inc. (**www.worldox.com**)—one of the three leading legal-focused document/e-mail management and work-product retrieval systems, in addition to Interwoven (Interwoven, Inc., formerly known as iManage) and eDOCS (Open Text Corporation, formerly known as PC DOCS Open).

ket. Then every Tuesday and Thursday afternoon, your partner's 16-year-old daughter's boyfriend's cousin, 15-year-old "Nick," comes in to scan your documents. Now, think about that scenario for a moment. How could Nick, the high school scanning clerk, have any clue about where to store the documents or what to call them? You didn't have time to paper-clip a note to the document naming the client and matter to store the documents under and an equally descriptive file name. So the odds are, in spite of Nick's best efforts, you'll end up with a jumbled mess.

Instead, the approach that has proven itself in the field over many years places individual desktop direct-to-PDF scanners at EACH PC in the office, lawyers and staff alike. The idea is that inbound paper is distributed to the people who are familiar with the documents and who are familiar with the cases to which they belong. These people know where to store the documents and what to call the documents, because these are the cases they actually work on. Lawyers and staff will likely scan different types of documents. Lawyers may scan a few business cards collected at the Rotary Club meeting that represent prospective clients and possible referral sources. The same lawyer might scan a pertinent article from the latest issue of the *ABA Journal* or their local state bar magazine. Staff is likely to scan case related documents—incoming correspondence, pleadings received in the mail, etc.

With each person doing his or her own case-related scanning, the overall scanning burden is distributed, and it is accomplished contemporaneously. This yields electronic case files that are made whole in or near real time. This further means that any lawyer or staff looking at the electronic file onscreen can count on the file being current and complete. This encourages further reliance on the electronic file by maximizing trust in the new approach.

Of course, when a larger volume of paper comes in, such as several banker's boxes in response to a discovery request, no one will want to scan 10,000 pages at their 20-page-per-minute desktop scanner with the 25-sheet paper feeder. That is when the staffer trots down the hall and scans using that monster multifunction machine equipped with a high-capacity paper feeder and a blistering 60-page-per-minute scanning speed. But in this case, the key is that the person scanning is the staffer who is actually familiar with the case and knows where to store and how to name the electronic paper.

This combination of centralized and decentralized scanning resources is an approach that has proven itself. Throw into the mix using the right lawyer or staff resource to scan the documents—the people who best know their own files and their own documents. This works. One approach to the exclusion of the other has inevitably failed in firms that tried just the centralized approach alone.

In terms of USB port-connected desktop scanners, there are several capable products. A consistent favorite over the last several years has been the ScanSnap series from Fujitsu, a well-respected and entrenched producer of scanning systems. With a 20-page-per-minute scanning speed for the current S1500 and S1500M (the M standing for Mac version) and duplex capability (scans both sides in a single pass), this color-capable printer includes a 50-page feeder with an adjustable guide that can handle stock as small as a business card. The attraction of the ScanSnap series has been a combination of reliability, incredible ease of use via the famous "big green button," the inclusion of a full copy of Adobe Acrobat Standard 9.0 edition, and reasonable price—in the $425 range. While the current version of Acrobat is Acrobat X (the roman numeral for 10), Acrobat 9 is still highly functional, and if you wish to be more current, Adobe will let you upgrade from the bundled version to the current X Pro version (think: lots of legal-focused features like Bates stamping and secure redaction) for $199 directly from the Adobe website.

Other capable desktop scanners include other models from Fujitsu and from Visioneer, Xerox with its fast 50-page-per-minute Documate series, Canon, and Kodak, as well as Hewlett-Packard with its venerable ScanJet product line.

It's possible to take your Paper LESS Office totally mobile as well. Fujitsu extended its popular ScanSnap series to include the very portable model 1100 scanner (**http://tinyurl.com/ScanSnapS1100**). This is a tiny Windows-focused device, about the length of an egg carton but about 1/3 its depth. It weighs in at about 12 ounces and is powered by a USB cable connected to your computer of choice, so no bulky power brick. Unlike the desktop model, there is no document feeder in which to stack a pile of pages to scan. Rather, it is in the "high-touch" category, requiring you to insert one page at time. The ScanSnap Manager software controlling the scanner is smart enough to keep asking you to insert pages of any given document until you tell it you're finished. But like its big brother ScanSnap models, the newly scanned document will pop up in Adobe Acrobat, ready to organize and make part of your electronic client file. Perfect for toting in one's laptop bag and using it at a deposition, will signing, real estate closing, or at counsel's table.

PAPER LESS QUICK TIP: a common misconception is that if one scans at a higher resolution, the text recognition results will improve. In fact, often the opposite is true. Lower scanner resolution settings can yield better recognition. At higher resolutions, modern scanners have such capable optics that they can actually become "confused" by the fibers of the papers, which are incorrectly interpreted as characters. Set the resolution to 150–300 dpi for better text recognition results whether using OCR software or producing searchable PDF files.

Document Management Systems: The Electronic Glue Holding It Together

The critical element in the Paper LESS Office process is the use of document management technology. A dedicated, legal-focused document management software application or document management capability is the "digital glue" that holds the Paper LESS Office together.

There are four "traditional" legal document management systems (or perhaps five?) available as of this writing:

- Worldox GX2 from World Software, an update to the product released in September 2009 (**www.worldox.com**, available since the late 1980s after starting its life as a DOS application called Extend-a-File). While suitable for large firms and deployed in a number of BigLaw organizations, Worldox has traditionally dominated the small and mid-sized law practice marketplace. This has largely been the result of several factors, including lower cost to acquire and implement because it doesn't require a costly underlying SQL Server database infrastructure, and relative simplicity to implement and to maintain versus its BigLaw-oriented rivals. It integrates tightly with Microsoft Outlook for e-mail management and to many practice management systems, including Amicus Attorney (**www.amicusattorney.com**), PracticeMaster (**www.tabs3.com**), and LexisNexis TimeMatters and Total Practice Advantage (**www.timematters.com**).

- Autonomy iManage Worksite (**www.autonomy.com**), traditionally a larger-firm-oriented document management system that relies on a SQL Server database. This more expensive and more complex infrastructure makes this an impractical choice for SmallLaw.

- PC Docs from OpenText (formerly known as Hummingbird Docs) (**www.opentext.com**)—very similar to the Autonomy system as a BigLaw-oriented, SQL Server-based application; quite prevalent in large firms and virtually never seen in small firms.
- NetDocuments (**www.netdocuments.com**). A SaaS product (Software as a Service—in other words, an application that runs in a web browser with documents either stored on a third-party hosted storage system or on the firm's own web-accessible servers). SaaS brings its own range of questions and holds promise, but this product is not oriented to smaller firms in terms of pricing or its relative inability to directly integrate with SmallLaw practice management systems. NetDocuments has recently made inroads into the smaller firm marketplace with a $20 per user per month "Basic" membership for 10GB of base storage plus 1GB of additional storage for each user.

There are also approaches focused on using web-based secure document repositories—examples of cloud computing or SaaS offerings. These tend to be much more minimal in functionality compared to actual document/e-mail management software. Rather, they are focused more on universality of accessibility and device independence, storing documents in password-protected web folder systems for authorized users to share. Perhaps the best-known service of this type is DropBox (**www.dropbox.com**) (2GB free, 50GB $10 per month, 100GB $20 per month, or a new DropBox Team plan for $795 per year, including five user licenses and 350GB of shared storage. Additional DropBox Team user licenses are available for $125 per year, with additional storage priced at $200 for 100GB per year).

As to the traditionally locally installed systems, the Worldox GX2 (**www.worldox.com**) document management system, the most suitable of the above-listed applications for SmallLaw, organizes paper documents received in the mail and scanned as searchable PDFs; e-mails received with attachments (when used with Microsoft Outlook, an e-mail even with multiple attachments can be organized by Worldox in one step, rather than the usual daunting series of multiple-save steps otherwise required); and documents created within the office, regardless of which software program was used to create them (for example, Word, Word Perfect, Excel, Adobe Acrobat/PDFs, digital photos, voicemail files, etc.). The same Worldox interface is common to all file-saving processes, simplifying the approach and cutting the learning curve. Effectively, your electronic filing system can be set up and organized to precisely parallel your file cabinet/red-rope brown expandable file/manila folder–based paper system, making it easy for anyone to understand, regardless of whether they are a legal techno-pro or a techno-peasant. There is an adjunct module called Worldox Web/Mobile that extends the accessibility of Worldox-managed documents and e-mails to the web, securely, on Windows PCs, Macs, and iPads/Smartphones.

Most practice management software, programs such as Amicus Attorney, Tabs PracticeMaster, ProLaw (from Thomson-Reuters), TimeMatters (from LexisNexis), and others, incorporate some degree of document and e-mail management as well. Or, in the alternative, leading practice management systems typically integrate with leading legal document management systems. Which approach is best? The internalized document management functionality of a practice management application of the third-party, separate but integrated, dedicated document manager? The answers are specific to the unique document management approaches of each practice management system. But the bottom line for most firms is that the more robust features and the mandatory must-save-it-the-document-management's-way approach of third-party tools tend to prevail. Often built-in document management segments of practice management systems do not require that every document be saved to client case files. Experience shows that the failure to make this an automatically mandatory process results in people taking shortcuts and creating incomplete case files that cannot be relied on.

In essence, the document management system takes the scanned document-turned PDF and organizes it in this manner:

When one clicks the "File Save," or "File Save A" function in Acrobat, instead of the software's native file-management dialogue boxes appearing, the Worldox document management system pops up.

To save the file, one selects which "File Cabinet" (or in Worldox-speak, the "profile group"). Examples commonly include Client Documents, Forms & Templates, Firm Administration, and Personal Files.

Then one is presented with a Profile screen that allows the user, instead of having to navigate through an often mystifying and inconsistent Windows folder tree, to complete a set of fill-in-the-blanks for information such as the Client Name, the Matter Name, the type of document (i.e., correspondence, contracts, pleadings, etc.), who authored the document, and sometimes the historical date of the document, or a notation as to whether the document has been reviewed by a responsible party in the firm). These pieces of information are accessible very rapidly from quick-pick lists or even in a single-click approach that calls up a template called "Quick Profile" for oft-accessed client matters or subject files. All in all, much more concise and faster than common Windows navigation.

Fill in a plain-English name for the document, ideally following a logical file-naming convention agreed upon and consistently used by everyone in the firm, and click "ok." The scanned electronic paper is now organized and connected to the same cohesive, contiguous, and complete electronic matter file as are all the internally generated word processing files, spreadsheets, presentations, digital photos, downloaded PDFs, and e-mails with their attachments—a complete electronic case file.

Later, documents can be found by simply "checking the electronic file cabinet"—clicking to the Client, the Matter, and then an electronic version of the Manila folder. If it is not possible or efficient to locate the desired document by viewing the electronic file cabinet and then scanning the list of plain-English file names, the document can be found nearly instantly by searching for key text within the document itself using a word or phrase search similar to a query in Google, Lexis, or Westlaw. Worldox searches are infinitely faster than the brain-dead "File, Find" function in the Windows XP operating system and every bit as fast as the modern desktop search products such as Windows Desktop Search, Copernic, X1, and Google Desktop. Note that the Windows 7 operating system has an "instant search" function built-in—a carryover from its Vista predecessor (and frankly, one of the only positive aspects of Windows Vista). Mac users have long benefited from instant searching via the Spotlight feature of the Mac operating system.

Even a scanned document, which is otherwise just an "image" like a digital photo, can be located using key terms, provided that when it was scanned the image was converted to searchable text using Adobe Acrobat (version 7 and up to the current version 9, Standard/Professional/Extended edition, or an equivalent product that does automated batch conversions of scanned "image" PDFs into "searchable" PDFs, such as AquaForest's Autobahn DX (**www.aquaforest.com**), which can be set to find all new "image" PDFs stored during the day and convert them in an automated fashion into "searchable" PDFs versus the cumbersome, more manual/attended process using Adobe Acrobat itself, which can otherwise slow the scanning process considerably).

Okay, Now Let's Get to Our Documents from Anywhere, Any Time: The Paper LESS Cloud

It is impossible to overstate the nearly all-pervasive emphasis on cloud, or Internet-based computing today. It's a revolution that has swept all aspects of legal technology and the choices and options available to small firms, as well as practices of all sizes. But the challenge is defining what the cloud is and how it might meet (or not) the needs of any given practice.

The first step is demystifying the cloud computing concept. What exactly is it? Well, it's not an "it," it's a whole raft of "its." There are many different ways of accessing law practice information over the Internet, even more than the types of clouds that meteorologists categorize. Let's explore some of these approaches, looking at the Paper LESS suitability of each for small law practices.

1. **Web-Based Software (a/k/a SaaS—Software as a Service)**
   - The idea here is that the software you would use isn't installed on your own computer hardware. Rather, it's installed on a remote system somewhere else (that someone else owns) and you access its functionality and your firm's data it contains via a web browser. Some purists consider this the "real" cloud approach, since it has the least software impact on your own hardware. In fact, it doesn't matter what hardware you use, Windows or Mac, iPad or other tablet. If you have a high-speed Internet connection, you can work from any device, any time.
   - **Paper LESS Connection:** SaaS products such as practice managers Clio, RocketMatter, Advologix, Houdini, Esq., and Aderant Practice Manager include document management to varying degrees. Online document management such as NetDocuments, and also online document storage such as Dropbox, Box.net and SugarSync, are examples of web services with Paper LESS connections.
     - There are some potential disadvantages of the SaaS approach. Your ability to work depends on your ability to find a high-speed Internet connection. No connection, generally, no work.

2. **Rent-a-Cloud:**
   - Under this approach, you can use all the software you'd normally use on your own systems—practice managers like Tabs PracticeMaster, Amicus Attorney, or Time Matters, as well as document managers like Worldox. But instead of these programs running on your own network server, you can rent a server maintained by a third party and access it across the Internet cloud. This approach has all the benefits of running arguably more full-featured software that you may already own,

plus the benefit of not having to maintain your own server hardware, including having someone else back up your information to protect it and, most often, having someone else update the server's operating system software.

- As above, there are some potential disadvantages to this approach. Your ability to work depends on your ability to find a high-speed Internet connection. Generally, no connection, no work.
- There are also potential ethical issues related to giving control of confidential client information to a third party. These are likely a red herring, as there are long-standing accepted precedents for this approach—in particular, storing client files at third-party document warehouses.
- Costs. In the short run, startup costs are lower than buying one's own new server. There is little upfront cost other than possibly an IT consultant's assistance in migrating information from a traditional local system to a new web-based server. As an example, one could use a third-party server host, such as the well-known GoDaddy.com offering, where a dedicated Windows 2008 Server with 500GB of storage space costs about $300 per month and then about $6–$10 per month per user for hosting Microsoft Exchange Server to handle mail and calendars with Outlook. Over time, these costs add up and are more expensive in most cases than the third option below—having your own "cloud."
- **Paper LESS Connection:**
    - Works just like your present internal systems connecting to a Windows server, as is so commonly the case. So there are no changes in your present software; the only difference is that the server is somewhere else, and you use something called Windows RDC (Windows Remote Desktop Control) to access the information. This means that Macs can access the information also—an added benefit.

3. **Build Your Own Cloud:**
    - Under this approach, you would still have your own server, but if you're a Windows-using firm, as so many are, you can access all your firm's information and software across the Internet cloud by using something called Windows Terminal Services (TS) or the more modern iteration of it, called Windows RDC (Remote Desktop Control). Under this approach, anyone outside of the office can click an icon and get an office "desktop,"

and then work as if they were sitting in the office. This works even better with a relatively inexpensive piece of more capable remote access software, Citrix Fundamentals—considered the "king of remote access tools." For all intents and purposes, most readers can view Citrix as a layer on top of Windows RDC or Windows TS that just plain works faster and better and supports remote access by Windows and Mac computers, iPads, and other tablets, and also smartphones (to truly achieve the Independent(s) Day I spoke of in the Introduction to this year's edition of this book).

- Advantages are numerous—you maintain total control of your own systems but extend the reach of your Paper LESS Practice to any authorized user any time, any place they can get a high-speed Internet connection from many types of devices. Relatively low-cost addition to an existing Windows system: five users can access their system remotely via Citrix Fundamentals for about $2,000 in software cost and no ongoing subscription fees.

- Disadvantage: You own the hardware, and you have to maintain it. That means backing it up, updating the software systems yourself, and paying for IT support when there are specific operational problems.

4. **Scattered Cloudiness—Being Partly in the Cloud:**
   - One option is to put part of your practice, Paper LESS-wise, in the cloud. One way to do this is to outsource your mail server functions. If you're a Microsoft Outlook user, small firms can very cost-effectively outsource the underlying Microsoft Exchange Server functions to a third party. GoDaddy.com and Rackspace.com are two large and proven providers of these services. Users can use Outlook just as they may currently use it—integrating with a legal document manager such as Worldox GX2 to organize inbound/outbound e-mail and attachments to electronic case folders. From the technical end, the Exchange Server software, which isn't trivial to configure, support, and maintain, is provided by the third-party host—a very workable and usually very cost-effective situation for firms of all sizes.

   - Based on GoDaddy.com's Exchange Hosting options, a five-person law practice can avail itself of this service for $43 per month, providing a very generous 4GB per user in mailbox storage and also full Microsoft ActiveSync functionality for syncing with smartphones, iPads/tablets, etc., for lawyers on the go.

The Real World: Comments from the Trenches in the Paper Wars

Dale Cottam further observes from his perspective as a busy commercial litigator:

> In today's fast-paced technology world, many clients expect their attorneys to be at least at the same technical level of capability and proficiency as they are. With the relatively low cost of available scanning hardware and document management software, firms can keep up with their clients. Part of the cost of this technology will be offset by decreased expenses for postage and long-distance phone calls associated with faxing and increases in productivity. The level of stress involved in searching for lost files and documents is reduced dramatically.

Figure One demonstrates the real-world and practical advantages of electronic versus paper files. If you are considering moving from paper to electronic files but aren't sure how to start, here are a few suggestions:

Figure 1 Advantages of Electronic Versus Paper Files

Factor	Paper Files	Electronic Files
Active Case and Archival Storage	Paper is expensive to file, route, and store.	Electronic documents are cheap and convenient to store. If paper files are shredded after closure of a case, physical storage costs are cut dramatically, yet lawyers have all old file information accessible instantly via electronic searches. Archiving on the firm's server(s) takes the place of physical storage. Electronic paper can always be reduced to physical paper if ever needed.
Finding Lost Documents	Finding lost documents takes significant time—sometimes many hours, including relying on discussion with other lawyers and staff. If a document has been misfiled, it may never be found.	Searching for electronic documents is nearly instantaneous using a search engine contained within document management systems. A lawyer who previously wasted 15 minutes per day looking for paper files can easily recover valuable billable time by immediately locating "electronic paper" and not chasing paper files around the office. If this 15 minutes can be converted into billable time, the financial effect can be an additional $12,000 per year for a lawyer who bills an average of $200/hour.

Figure 1 Advantages of Electronic Versus Paper Files—(*Continued*)

Factor	Paper Files	Electronic Files
File Sharing	Collaborating on paper documents is cumbersome; copies must be made and routed at significant cost in terms of staff time and consumables, not to mention the negative environment impact.	Collaboration, revisions, remote access, and sharing of important information are very convenient when documents are stored electronically.
Remote Access	Paper documents must be mailed or faxed off-site. Or lawyers who need to work on files must remember to bring boxes of paper with them.	Electronic documents are available to lawyers and staff over secure remote connections or can be received via e-mail, enabling instantaneous access to every document on a single matter without regard to the location of the physical paper file. With device-independent approaches, documents of all types can be securely accessed from devices ranging from laptops to netbooks (Windows or Mac systems), iPads, and smartphones.
Protecting Client Files from Disaster	Irreplaceable paper documents are at risk for being destroyed by fire and natural disasters.	Electronic files are easily backed up and stored off-site and can be restored to the firm's network quickly. This is the first realistic way to protect client files from damage by fire and natural disasters.
Brief Banking	Tedious filing and organization must be used to quickly find relevant briefs in paper format. Most firms fail to keep it updated, so few people would ever trust it.	Electronic versions of briefs and memos can be located quickly using search engines and indexers that look for specific words or phrases. Finally, the mythical "brief bank" becomes usable, current, and reliable.
E-mail Management	To make a "complete" paper file, you would need to print every e-mail and attachment that is sent and received—sheer inefficient insanity.	The Paper LESS Office™ approach using the Worldox (or other) document management system allows you to save (via "profiling") a stand-alone e-mail or one with multiple attachments in a single step for both inbound and outbound messages. This results in a nearly miraculous answer to a spiraling issue of e-mail chaos that plagues so many law practices today. E-mails are merely correspondence—and they belong connected to the complete electronic case file, as opposed to being eternally buried in the bottomless hole of an inbox.

Make the commitment to the process of moving toward the Paper LESS goal. Give up on the pipe dream of being paperless; it's simply not realistic and will lead to inevitable disappointment. You're not going to rid your practice entirely of paper. The key is dedication, an emphasis on standardized and consistent procedures, and a commitment to educating your team about the "whys" (and not merely the "hows") they are making the shift to viewing electronic matter files as the primary, "sacred" and complete client file.

Ensure that your hardware is up to the demands of the increased amount of scanning, processing, and storage. This would be the ideal time to send your six-year-old PC stations to a virtual "assisted living center" and replace them with a set of contemporary desktop and laptop systems. Dual monitors (or even three displays) are very helpful for simultaneously scanning, storing, and viewing multiple programs. With a practice management system, your word processor(s), Acrobat, Outlook or another e-mailer, a time entry input application, and one or more web browsers, the productivity payoff is normally instantaneous. Network servers need the ability to store 1–5GB per lawyer per year. Having a reliable, multiple-level backup system[4] and testing it often with "mini test restores" is critical, as are all the normal recommended elements of a sound data backup process.

SIDENOTE: A Paper LESS Peripheral Benefit: Protecting Your "Paper"

One of the great weaknesses of any paper-centric system is the vulnerability of the medium. It is simply impossible, in any practical or realistic sense, to back up paper client and administrative files. If a hurricane's fury tears through a community, if an earthquake rends the ground beneath a law firm's building, if a fire incinerates a practice—paper client and administrative files, which may have no alternative media counterparts, are gone forever.

One of the unintended yet extraordinarily valuable byproducts of the Paper LESS Office process is that the protection of what would otherwise be at-risk paper files. Paper LESS electronic documents are "backup-able." They can be protected and stored off-site and even online in a geographi-

---

[4] *See* Ross's Great Truths About Data Backup, **http://www.tinyurl.com/kodner-on-backup**.

cally distant location. Lawyers have an ethical responsibility to practice competently. It takes no great intellectual leap to see that deploying a Paper LESS approach, combined with essential and sound data backup techniques that protect paper files and the ability of lawyers to serve their clients, may become part of the core definition of "competency" in law practice sooner rather than later.

Factor in cloud storage and incorporate a degree of automated data backup that could be tough for a small practice to achieve at the same level of reliability and sophistication.

Plan and test. Spending time planning as well as "pilot" testing systems and procedures, thus avoiding fits and starts before the Paper LESS concept is rolled out firmwide.

The Paper LESS Bottom Line . . .

A truly paperless office is never going to happen while any of us are alive. No matter how diligently you try to reduce or even eliminate the paper you generate, other people will send you paper for years to come. But to be sure, being Paper MORE in your practice is a one-way ticket to diminished profitability, diminished client responsiveness and diminished sanity. The good news for everyone is that a Paper LESS Office is rapidly and practically attainable. You can use less paper, have to find less paper, and touch paper less often, thereby becoming significantly more efficient, more profitable, more responsive to your clients, less stressed, and more environmentally responsible in your practice. Consideration of "cloud concepts" can further extend access to your Paper LESS files to your people anywhere they might be working, any time of the day, and open secure access to clients, co-counsel, and experts in an ethically compliant and secure manner. By employing a creative and common-sense approach to scanning, and by leveraging anti-paper PDF tools, you can transform your practice—and even the rest of your life—in every possible way.

Ross L. Kodner, a lawyer, is president and founder of MicroLaw, Inc., an international legal technology and law practice management consultancy based in Milwaukee and founded in 1985 at the dawn of the legal PC age. Along with Sharon Nelson and Jim Calloway, he is a co-author of the ABA Law Practice Management Section book *How Good Lawyers Survive Bad Times*, available at **www.tinyurl.com/how-good-lawyers**. His contributions to this 2012 edition represent his fourth annual effort. For a quarter century, Ross has been the principal of MicroLaw, Inc., serving private law firms and corporate and government legal departments worldwide. A former long-time member of the ABA TECHSHOW executive planning board, he also served four years as chair of the ABA Law Practice Management Section's Computer & Technology Division. Currently he is an ABA GP|Solo Division active member and both founded and served as co-chair of the Division's National Solo & Small Firm Conference, as well as founding and serving as first chair of the Wisconsin Solo & Small Firm Conference. Ross was the inaugural recipient of the John Lederer Award for Solo & Small Firm Service in Wisconsin in 2009. He is also a prolific author and CLE speaker, with over 400 published articles and more than 1,300 CLE sessions since the 1980s. He is also the only five-time Technolawyer Award winner, including the lifetime achievement "Legal Technology Consultant of the Year" award in 1999. Follow his writings weekly at his award-winning blawg, Ross Ipsa Loquitur (**www.rossipsa.com** and **www.microlaw.com**). As long as he can remember, his mottos have been "Friends don't let friends word process without Reveal Codes (even with Word)!" and Red Adair's famous statement, "If you think hiring an expert is expensive, try hiring an amateur." He can be reached via **rkodner@microlaw.com**, **www.microlaw.com**, and **www.rossipsa.com**.

CHAPTER TWENTY-EIGHT

Tomorrow in Legal Tech

> *I try to save clients money.*
> *I try to help them make sensible decisions.*
> *I try to keep them from being on the bleeding edge of technology.*
> *I try to keep them from making decisions that compromise their security.*
> *In an amazing number of cases, I fail, and they go headlong in the direction of their choice.*
> *When something goes wrong, they invariably blame me.*
> *And that is why I own an urn labeled "Ashes of Problem Clients."*
> —Sharon D. Nelson, President, Sensei Enterprises

As you might guess from the quote, I am a believer in technological change—when it's strategically sound. But we are seeing today a trend that we think will continue: Legal technology is now often driven by consumerism. Partners in law firms are demanding, and getting, the technology they desire, whether or not it makes any sense.

We see this particularly with smartphones. If a partner wants an iPhone, he or she gets it. Forget that it is evidence-rich and can be easily compromised if lost or stolen. Security goes by the wayside when someone in power barks loudly enough. More and more, we are seeing a wide variety of smartphones in use in a single firm, making the infrastructure harder to support and playing havoc with syncing different phones to computers.

Likewise, there is a press by some lawyers to have a Mac. There's nothing wrong with a Mac inherently, but it tends to be more expensive to support PCs and Macs in the same environment—something no one gives a thought to when they want the Mac.

Though we have occasionally run into smartphone policies, it hasn't been often, and we expect that to continue. Smartphone policies are essential. Believe us, if you're blocking social media sites on your network, folks are simply reaching for their smartphone to check their Facebook page. If you've blocked social media on firm smartphones, they'll simply use their personal cell phones. As data breaches continue to proliferate in law firms, we hope to see tighter policy and technological controls on smartphones.

One of the trends we are seeing is that the BlackBerry (in spite of its security) is losing ground in the marketplace. Author Simek is flatly predicting the demise of BlackBerry. Currently, the Droid rules (coming in at a very impressive 48 percent of market share), followed by the iPhone. One concern we have with Android phones is that because their architecture is open source, this may assist would-be writers of malware. Android is moving rapidly to natively support encryption, which will be a tremendous security boost—in fact, new models running "Ice Cream Sandwich" should be in place by the time you read these words. It will also merge the operating system for smartphones and tablets, much as Apple did for its iOS.

Smartphone malware is on the rise, and that will certainly continue as people increasingly use smartphones as a computer that happens to be able to make a phone call. More than 250,000 Droid users have been impacted by smartphone malware, which grew by 400 percent from October 2010 to March 2011. Expect it to keep on coming and to get more sophisticated. Lawyers will need to install reputable security software on their smartphones and to engage in safe computing habits.

Mobility has been one of the chief buzzwords of 2011, and with good cause. Lawyers are gobbling up any technology that will permit them to work remotely, whether they are at court or on the road. This has meant, for better or worse (mostly worse, from a security standpoint) that data is everywhere and that we cannot remember, much less manage, all the data we have spread around.

In the wired world, physical security was relatively easy to obtain, but now that we demand full access to our data from anywhere, security is a much bigger (and unsolved) issue. We are so dependent on mere connectivity that we are hopelessly lost without it. And what do we do when a third party holds our data and it is down? We are only beginning to scratch the surface of some of the problems that have cropped up as mobility becomes an integral part of legal technology.

As predicted, Windows 7 was indeed widely adopted over the last year. In spite of the soft recovery and the meltdown of summer/fall 2011, we are not seeing any drop in spending on IT, nor do we expect to. One lesson we learned during the recession of 2008 is that law firms need their computers to work. Spending there lessened a bit but not much. We are all so dependent on technology that we are prone to open our wallets even in tough times to stay competitive.

Social media continue to play a very important part in law firms, and increasingly law firms are embracing social media as a marketing tool, learning how to attract new clients and keep online relationships with current clients. We expect firms to get smarter and smarter about this over time and anticipate that more than a few lawyers will get in trouble for violating ethical rules in their use of social media. It seems as if it is just too tempting to trumpet victories in court without a disclaimer, to call oneself an expert or a specialist, and to step over the line of inadvertently forming a lawyer client relationship.

One question we are often asked is whether Google+ will challenge Facebook and LinkedIn. Though we are climbing out on a big limb here, we think the answer is no. Even though Google+ has a number of novel and intriguing features, there are two reasons why we don't see it catching its rivals. First, Google has stumbled badly every time it has tried to climb into the social media playpen. Secondly, Facebook and LinkedIn achieved critical mass some time back—and challengers are going to have a hard time getting users to switch platforms.

We've seen some our "early adopter" friends get on Google+ and sing its praises, but these are the kind of people who pant to be the first kid on their block to have every new tech toy. What would make us wrong? If the public gets fed up enough with Facebook and LinkedIn being carefree about privacy issues, they might seek a more private alternative. Maybe, but Google has had its share of privacy bungles too.

We recently recorded a podcast with Brett Burney called "All Things Apple for Lawyers" (available at ABA's Law Practice Management Section), so let's tackle that subject next. More and more lawyers are jumping on the Apple train, which continues to roar along. We were used to seeing a shift to Macs and the popularity of the iPhone, but the use of the iPad has really been stunning this year, and we don't foresee any slowdown in its popularity. Lawyers will be well advised, though, to seek out reliable lawyer experts before they go crazy buying law-related apps, many of which are of questionable worth and insecure.

While the iPad has major security issues and many lawyer functions require some kind of work-around, it is a great user device, and lawyers have glommed onto it. While many lawyers fundamentally use the iPad for games, e-mail, and the Internet, litigators have continued to find ways to use it in the courtroom, and we expect to see many more of them in courtrooms nationwide. But be forewarned: The iPad does not replace your laptop or your tablet. Still, the iPad 2 was a huge hit in 2011, and CLE seminars on its usage by lawyers surged to standing room only crowds.

What will happen to Apple now that Steve Jobs has departed? There is a lot of controversy swirling around this issue. We are, with some hesitation, thinking that Apple may plateau or even decline without the inspiration of Steve Jobs—but we are prepared to be wrong.

Virtual law firms continue to sprout up, along with some innovative technology to support them. The low overhead is alluring, to say the least, and that allows lawyers to price their services attractively. Likewise, most of the major law firms now offer alternative fee arrangements (AFAs), and we expect the rest to follow suit as clients demand more predictable pricing and greater value for their dollars. A cautionary note: If you are planning to invest in new time and billing software, make sure it can accommodate AFAs; many programs cannot.

Lawyer videos are still growing in popularity but not as fast as we had predicted. We hope the growth will accelerate, because our own experience is certainly testament to what videos can do. We currently have 48 videos online answering commonly asked (and therefore searched-on) questions. While most of the videos have modest viewing numbers, one has been viewed more than 110,000 times thus far. We are starting to see You Tube on our intake forms as the place where clients first found us. And Google, which owns You Tube, continues to give videos greater weight in its search rankings, so lawyers would be wise to think about making videos for search engine optimization and also to attract new clients. Without question, many people prefer to watch videos to have their questions answered, so the trick is really to have the right questions as the titles of your videos.

We've mentioned smartphone security before, but a trend we are now seeing is a growing number of external attacks on law firm networks. The FBI, which issued an advisory to law firms in 2009 that they were increasingly becoming the targets of hackers, sure appears to have been right. Rob Lee, a security specialist at Mandiant, estimated that 10 percent of the data breaches he investigated this year were at law firms.

While at one time it was primarily the largest firms that were targeted, the hackers are learning that smaller firms are softer targets. We have often heard small firms' lawyers express the sense that no one is interested in their data. Wrong, wrong, wrong. Your data is prime material for identity thieves—and spammers would love to add your computers to their botnets.

Where are the attacks coming from? In many cases, China. Rob Lee says that the Chinese don't waste their A-level hacking squads on law firms; the rookies can handle it. That doesn't say much for the state of law firm security, which clearly needs to be beefed up.

There is still no federal data breach law, but we do think one will be coming before too long, because it is difficult for anyone doing business in multiple states to abide by the very different data breach laws of the states—and Massachusetts is one of the toughest.

Cloud computing took off in 2011, and we expect that lawyers will still move to the cloud in droves in 2012. One by one, the state bars that have examined the ethics of cloud computing have basically said that cloud computing is okay as long as lawyers do their due diligence to make sure the data is properly secured. Our own experience is that lawyers tend to sign up with cloud providers without even reading the terms of the agreement.

It is critical to know where your data is. Recently, providers have begun assuring clients that their data will be held in the United States, which most clients prefer so that they don't have to deal with the varying privacy laws of other countries. It is also critical to make sure the data is encrypted in both storage and transmission. If you move your data, is there a charge? What's the process? Common-sense questions about security would go a long way toward helping a lawyer meet the ethical requirements, but we rarely see much in the way of due diligence when solos and small firms decide to move their data to the cloud. Dropbox is a case in point. We can't tell you the number of lawyers who jumped all over Dropbox, and you even heard the service recommended at CLE sessions. Not until recently did anybody appear to read the terms of service for Dropbox. It is now public knowledge that Dropbox will decrypt your data and turn it over to law enforcement if a valid warrant is served. That means that Dropbox has the keys to decrypt. So much for security.

In a 2011 study of law firms, 49 percent reported that the cloud had serious security and compliance issues, which tells us that lawyers may be slower than the general public to rush headlong into cloud computing.

By the time this book is published, Apple will have the iCloud up and running. According to Apple, it will bypass a PC and become the hub of your digital life. Any iOS device you buy will automatically sync to the iCloud. Will the iCloud make the PC obsolete? There are a lot of arguments on both sides. Our own sense is that the PC is unlikely to join the dinosaurs, but it may become a secondary device, with much more emphasis put on mobile devices. We'll have to save some of this discussion for next year when we see how the iCloud works out. Given Apple's ongoing security woes, this is one cloud we would advise folks to avoid.

Virtualization continues to move forward at firms of all sizes. The wonder of having multiple servers in one physical device has been amplified by cost and space savings. Remember the major security concern: You have one host providing security to every server in the device. That means that lawyers and security providers must be concerned with hardening the security of the host—still something that has not been achieved in many law firms.

We continue to see most solos backing up to an external hard drive, and many, concerned about disaster recovery and business continuity, are investing in BDRs (backup and disaster recovery devices), which can encrypt and back up data (every 15 minutes if you set it up that way) and then shoot it off for remote storage. They can even support a virtual server on the device itself. With these systems in place, if your air conditioner leaks and shorts out your Exchange server, recovery time is often just an hour or so. There are services that will monitor the health of your servers day and night, shooting you (or your IT provider) an e-mail or a phone call if something goes wrong. This means you'll never show up at work to find yourself out of business. The cost to join is $3,000–$4,000 for the hardware and less than $2 per GB per month for off-site storage. Even with the fog of uncertainty shrouding our economy, many firms have now made this move.

Author Nelson continues to evangelize for social media, which has helped brand her as an expert, attracted many journalists, and resulted in speaking invitations, new friendships, and business opportunities. Lawyers who are careful not to self-promote but to be helpful to others will continue to do well. Social media is clearly not going anywhere and have, in fact, become a vehicle for what one wag called "making oneself a little bit famous"— which is really all one needs to bring in new clients. The very best part? It's free, or almost free, and that is great for your marketing budget.

Just be mindful of the security issues surrounding social media sites and make sure you don't post anything you don't want to see in the paper the next day. And watch those privacy settings. Facebook is notorious for altering privacy settings or adding a new "feature" that is wide open by default. Check your privacy settings on a regular basis—at least every month or so.

As we predicted last year, there have been new developments in the intersection between social media and e-discovery. It is now clear that the Stored Communications Act bars Internet service providers from providing the substance of communications they hold, though you may be able to get time of connections, IP addresses, and similar non-content information.

Facebook, which was mightily sick of subpoenas, now has a "Download Your Account" feature so that users can produce their own social media evidence in e-discovery. Look for other social media sites to follow Facebook's lead.

In the e-discovery world, the two words "predictive coding" were the buzz phrase of the year as companies rushed to create code that could, to a reasonable certainty, screen out privileged documents and identify relevant ones, thereby curtailing the number of human reviewers required and the associated cost. It certainly is true that people get tired, have headaches, experience a bad day, and just get sloppy. Machines don't have that problem. But it's expensive to join this club; it will take six figures in most cases. While we expect most of the large vendors to offer predictive coding, it is not so clear that the smaller ones will follow, though some are promising to do so. To the extent predictive coding takes off, contract lawyers may be hit really hard in 2012.

Another e-discovery trend we are beginning to see is increased e-discovery readiness even in smaller firms. Court cases in 2011 have begun to suggest that judges are not only expecting "the big guys" to get themselves educated about e-discovery, but "the little guys" as well.

The uncertain economy will undoubtedly cause law firms to defer capital investment in IT, at least to some extent. Many lawyers are renegotiating contracts, outsourcing where it saves money, and enhancing efficiencies through technology to help the bottom line. Given the state of the global economy as we write, you can expect all of these trends to continue.

The New York State Bar Association issued a report in April 2011, *The Future of the Legal Profession*, which you can read at **http://www.nysba.org/AM/Template.cfm?Section=Task_Force_on_the_Future_of_the_Legal_Profession_Home&Template=/CM/ContentDisplay.cfm&ContentID=48108**

Though the report deals with many things, there is a separate section on technology. The bottom line is that technology changes rapidly (frustratingly so at times) but it can be used to manage data, help with case management and billing, and assist lawyers in finding a work-life balance.

To give a recent example from one legal entity we were helping, they sought a bid that would bring them enterprise content management—highly desirable, to be sure. But the bid called for a five-year completion. We threw up our hands in horror and explained that any technology project of this nature would be obsolete in five years. Legal tech just plain moves too quickly. They are now hoping to persuade the vendor to make it a three-year contract. Sometimes law firms are tempted by these long contracts because they have to pay less each year, but in the light of technology's rapid changes, the cost savings are often illusory. In a five-year contract, tech changes may force the scope to change along the way, increasing the price—or you need to suffer with the doggone thing because you paid a fortune for it, even though newer technology has passed it by.

One good suggestion here: If you're making some kind of major overhaul of your technology and soliciting bids, have a consultant who is not bidding review the bids. We are often engaged for that sort of independent review. It makes good sense, since we are not invested in the project, and the cost to do so is usually not terribly steep compared with the cost of the project.

So there we have it; it's a wrap for another year. We'll dust off our crystal ball again next year and see how we did this time around. We ate a little crow pie last year based on our predictions, but not much. However, we believe in humility and will be prepared to eat a bigger piece next year if required.

Appendix

AMERICAN BAR ASSOCIATION
STANDING COMMITTEE ON ETHICS AND PROFESSIONAL RESPONSIBILITY

Formal Opinion 10-457   **August 5, 2010**
Lawyer Websites

Websites have become a common means by which lawyers communicate with the public. Lawyers must not include misleading information on websites, must be mindful of the expectations created by the website, and must carefully manage inquiries invited through the website. Websites that invite inquiries may create a prospective client-lawyer relationship under Rule 1.18. Lawyers who respond to website-initiated inquiries about legal services should consider the possibility that Rule 1.18 may apply.[1]

---

[1] This opinion is based on the ABA MODEL RULES OF PROFESSIONAL CONDUCT as amended by the ABA House of Delegates through August 2010. The laws, court rules, regulations, rules of professional conduct, and opinions promulgated in individual jurisdictions are controlling.

**AMERICAN BAR ASSOCIATION STANDING COMMITTEE ON
ETHICS AND PROFESSIONAL RESPONSIBILITY**
321 N. Clark Street, Chicago, Illinois 60654-4714 Telephone (312) 988-5300
CHAIR: Robert Mundheim, New York, NY ■ Robert A. Creamer, Evanston, IL ■
Terrence M. Franklin, Los Angeles, CA ■ Paula J. Frederick, Atlanta, GA ■ Bruce A. Green, New York, NY ■ James M. McCauley, Richmond, VA ■ Susan R. Martyn, Toledo, OH ■
Mary Robinson, Downers Grove, IL ■ Philip H. Schaeffer, New York, NY ■
E. Norman Veasey, Wilmington, DE
CENTER FOR PROFESSIONAL RESPONSIBILITY: George A. Kuhlman, Ethics Counsel;
Eileen B. Libby, Associate Ethics Counsel
©2010 by the American Bar Association. All rights reserved.

I. Introduction

Many lawyers and law firms have established websites as a means of communicating with the public. A lawyer website can provide to anyone with Internet access a wide array of information about the law, legal institutions, and the value of legal services. Websites also offer lawyers a 24-hour marketing tool by calling attention to the particular qualifications of a lawyer or a law firm, explaining the scope of the legal services they provide and describing their clientele, and adding an electronic link to contact an individual lawyer.

The obvious benefit of this information can diminish or disappear if the website visitor misunderstands or is misled by website information and features. A website visitor might rely on general legal information to answer a personal legal question. Another might assume that a website's provision of direct electronic contact to a lawyer implies that the lawyer agrees to preserve the confidentiality of information disclosed by website visitors.

For lawyers, website marketing can give rise to the problem of unanticipated reliance or unexpected inquiries or information from website visitors seeking legal advice. This opinion addresses some of the ethical obligations that lawyers should address in considering the content and features of their websites.[2]

II. Website Content

A. Information about Lawyers, Their Law Firm, or Their Clients

Lawyer websites may provide biographical information about lawyers, including educational background, experience, area of practice, and contact information (telephone, facsimile, and e-mail address). A website also may add information about the law firm, such as its history, experience, and areas of practice, including general descriptions about prior engagements. More specific information about a lawyer or law firm's former or

---

[2] We do not deal here with website content generated by governmental lawyers or offices or by nonprofit law advocacy firms or organizations. *See, e.g., In re* Primus, 436 U.S. 412 (1978) (discussing how solicitation of prospective litigants by nonprofit organizations that engage in litigation as form of political expression and political association constitutes expressive and associational conduct entitled to First Amendment protection, which government may regulate only narrowly).

current clients, including clients' identities, matters handled, or results obtained, also might be included.

Any of this information constitutes a "communication about the lawyer or the lawyer's services" and is therefore subject to the requirements of Model Rule 7.1[3] as well as the prohibitions against false and misleading statements in Rules 8.4(c) (generally) and 4.1(a) (when representing clients). Together, these rules prohibit false, fraudulent or misleading statements of law or fact. Thus, no website communication may be false or misleading, or may omit facts such that the resulting statement is materially misleading. Rules 5.1 and 5.3 extend this obligation to managerial lawyers in law firms by obligating them to make reasonable efforts to ensure the firm has in place measures giving reasonable assurance that all firm lawyers and nonlawyer assistants will comply with the rules of professional conduct.

As applied to lawyer websites, these rules allow a lawyer to include accurate information that is not misleading about the lawyer and the lawyer's law firm, including contact information and information about the law practice.[4] To avoid misleading readers, this information should be updated on a regular basis.[5] Specific information that identifies current or former clients or the scope of their matters also may be disclosed, as long as the clients or former clients give informed consent[6] as required by

---

[3] *See, e.g.*, Ariz. State Bar Op. 97-04 (1997), *available at* **http://www.myazbar.org/Ethics/opinion view.cfm?id=480**; Cal. Standing Comm. on Prof'l Resp. and Conduct Formal Op. 2001-155, 2001 WL 34029609 (2001); Haw. Sup. Ct. Disc. Bd. Formal Op. 41 (2001), *available at* **http://www .odchawaii.com/FORMAL_WRITTEN_OPINIONS.html**; S.C. Bar Eth. Advisory Comm. Op. 04-06, 2004 WL 1520110 *1 (2004); Vt. Advisory Eth. Op. 2000-04, *available at* **http://www.vtbar.org/ Upload%20Files/WebPages/Lawyer%20Resources/aeopinions/Advisory%20Ethics%20 Opinions/Advertising/advertisin.htm**. Many state and local ethics opinions are published online can be accessed through the ABA Center for Professional Responsibility website at **http://www.abanet.org/cpr/links.html**.

[4] *See, e.g.*, N.C. State Bar Formal Eth. Op. 2009-6 (2009) (firm may provide case summaries on website, including accurate information about verdicts and settlements, as long as it adds specific information about factual and legal circumstances of cases [complexity, whether liability or damages were contested, whether opposing party was represented by counsel, firm's success in collecting judgment] in conjunction with appropriate disclaimer to preclude misleading prospective clients).

[5] *See, e.g.*, Mo. Bar Inf. Advisory Op. 20060005 (2006) (firm must remove lawyer's biographical information within reasonable time after lawyer leaves firm).

[6] *See, e.g.*, Ohio Advisory Op. 2000-6, 2000 WL 1872572 *5 (2000) (law firm may list client's name on firm website with client's informed consent). *See also* N.Y. Rule of Prof'l Conduct 7.1(b)(2) (2009) (lawyer may advertise name of regularly represented client, provided that client has given prior written consent).

Rules 1.6 (current clients) and 1.9 (former clients).[7] Website disclosure of client identifying information is not normally impliedly authorized because the disclosure is not being made to carry out the representation of a client, but to promote the lawyer or the law firm.[8]

B. Information about the Law

Lawyers have long offered legal information to the public in a variety of ways, such as by writing books or articles, giving talks to groups, or staffing legal hotlines. Lawyer websites also can assist the public in understanding the law and in identifying when and how to obtain legal services.[9] Legal information might include general information about the law applicable to a lawyer's area(s) of practice, as well as links to other websites, blogs, or forums with related information. Information may be presented in narrative form, in a "FAQ" (frequently asked questions) format, in a "Q & A" (question and answer) format, or in some other manner.[10]

Legal information, like information about a lawyer or the lawyer's services, must meet the requirements of Rules 7.1, 8.4(c), and 4.1(a). Lawyers may offer accurate legal information that does not materially mislead reasonable readers.[11] To avoid misleading readers, lawyers should make sure that legal information is accurate and current,[12] and should include qualifying statements or disclaimers that "may preclude a finding that a statement is likely to create unjustified expectations or otherwise mislead a

---

[7] These rules apply to "all information relating to the representation, whatever its source" including publicly available information. MODEL RULE 1.6 cmt. 3. The consent can be oral or written. Rules 1.6 and 1.9(c) require informed consent but do not require a written confirmation.

[8] See ABA Comm. on Eth. and Prof'l Resp., Formal Op. 09-455 (2009) (Disclosure of Conflicts Information When Lawyers Move Between Law Firms) (absent demonstrable benefit to client's representation, disclosure of client identifying information, including client's name and nature of matter handled, is not impliedly authorized under Rule 1.6(a)).

[9] MODEL RULE 7.2 cmt. [1] acknowledges that the "public's need to know about legal services can be fulfilled in part through advertising," a need that may be "particularly acute" in the case of persons who have not made extensive use of, or fear they may not be able to pay for, legal services.

[10] See, e.g., Vt. Advisory Eth. Op. 2000-04, supra note 3 (lawyer may use "frequently asked questions" format as long as information is current, accurate, and includes clear statement that it does not constitute legal advice and readers should not rely on it to solve individual problem).

[11] Rule 7.1 cmt. [2] provides that a "truthful statement is also misleading if there is a substantial likelihood that it will lead a reasonable person to formulate a specific conclusion . . . for which there is no reasonable factual foundation."

[12] ABA LAW PRACTICE MANAGEMENT SECTION, BEST PRACTICE GUIDELINES FOR LEGAL INFORMATION WEB SITE PROVIDERS 1 (Feb. 2003), *available at* **http://meetings.abanet.org/webupload/commupload/ EP024500/relatedresources/best_practice_guidelines.pdf** (website providing legal information should provide full and accurate information about identity and contact details of provider on each page of website, as well as dates on which substantive content was last reviewed).

prospective client."[13] Although no exact line can be drawn between legal information and legal advice, both the context and content of the information offered are helpful in distinguishing between the two.[14]

With respect to context, lawyers who speak to groups generally have been characterized as offering only general legal information. With respect to content, lawyers who answer fact-specific legal questions may be characterized as offering personal legal advice, especially if the lawyer is responding to a question that can reasonably be understood to refer to the questioner's individual circumstances. However, a lawyer who poses and answers a hypothetical question usually will not be characterized as offering legal advice. To avoid misunderstanding, our previous opinions have recommended that lawyers who provide general legal information include statements that characterize the information as general in nature and caution that it should not be understood as a substitute for personal legal advice.[15]

Such a warning is especially useful for website visitors who may be inexperienced in using legal services, and may believe that they can rely on

---

[13] MODEL RULE 7.1 cmt. 3. *See, e.g.*, ABA LAW PRACTICE MANAGEMENT SECTION, BEST PRACTICE GUIDELINES, *supra* note 12 at 2 (website providers should avoid misleading users about jurisdiction to which site's content relates, and if clearly state-specific, the jurisdiction in which the law applies should be identified).

[14] *See, e.g.*, Ariz. State Bar Op. 97-04, *supra* note 3 (because of inability to screen for conflicts of interest and possibility of disclosing confidential information, lawyers should not answer specific legal questions posed by laypersons in Internet chat rooms unless question presented is of general nature and advice given is not fact-specific); Cal. Standing Comm. on Prof'l Resp. and Conduct Formal Op. 2003-164, 2003 WL 23146203 (2003) (legal advice includes making recommendations about specific course of action to follow; public context of radio call-in show that includes warnings about information not being substitute for individualized legal advice makes it unlikely lawyers have agreed to act as caller's lawyer); S.C. Bar Eth. Advisory Comm. Op. 94-27 *2 (1995), 1995 WL 934127 (lawyer may maintain electronic presence for purpose of discussing legal topics, but must obtain sufficient information to make conflicts check before offering legal advice); Utah Eth. Op. 95-01 (1995), 1995 WL 49472 *1 ("how to" booklet on legal subject matter does not constitute practice of law).

[15] ABA Inf. Op. 85-1512 (1985) (Establishment of Private Multistate Lawyer Referral Service by Nonprofit Religious Organization), in FORMAL AND INFORMAL ETHICS OPINIONS: FORMAL OPINIONS 1983–1998, at 550, 551 (ABA 2000) (not unethical to prepare articles of general legal information for lay public, but may be prudent to include statement that information furnished is only general and not substitute for personalized legal advice); ABA Inf. Op. 85-1510 (1985) (Establishment of Multistate Private Lawyer Referral Service for Benefit of Subscribers to Corporation's Services), in FORMAL AND INFORMAL ETHICS OPINIONS: FORMAL OPINIONS 1983–1998, at 544, 545 (corporate counsel may author articles of general legal information for corporations' subscriber newsletter, but "good practice" to include a statement that information is only general in nature and not substitute for personal legal advice).

general legal information to solve their specific problem.[16] It would be prudent to avoid any misunderstanding by warning visitors that the legal information provided is general and should not be relied on as legal advice, and by explaining that legal advice cannot be given without full consideration of all relevant information relating to the visitor's individual situation.

C. Website Visitor Inquiries

Inquiries from a website visitor about legal advice or representation may raise an issue concerning the application of Rule 1.18 (Duties to Prospective Clients).[17] Rule 1.18 protects the confidentiality of prospective client

---

[16]*See, e.g.*, ABA LAW PRACTICE MANAGEMENT SECTION, BEST PRACTICE GUIDELINES, *supra* note 12 at 3 (websites that provide legal information should give users conspicuous notice that information does not constitute legal advice). Some state opinions also warn against providing specific or particularized facts in a lawyer's communication to avoid creating a client-lawyer relationship. *See also* Dist. of Columbia Bar Eth. Op. 316 (2002), *available at* **http://www.dcbar.org/for_lawyers/ethics/legal_ethics/opinions/opinion316.cfm** (online chat rooms and listservs); Md. State Bar Ass'n Comm. on Eth. Op. 2007-18 (2008) (lawyer conducting domestic relations law seminars for lay public); N.J. Advisory Comm. on Prof'l Eth. Op. 712 (2008) (Lawyer-Staffed Legal Hotline for Members of Nonprofit Trade Association), *available at* **http://lawlibrary.rutgers.edu/ethics/acpe/acp712_1.html** (lawyer staffing telephone hotline); N.J. Advisory Comm. on Prof'l Eth. Op 671, 1993 WL 137685 (1993) (Activities and Obligations of Pro Bono Lawyers), (lawyer-volunteer at abused women shelter); N.M. Bar Op. 2001-1 (2001) (Application of Rules of Professional Conduct to Lawyer's Use of Listserv-type Message Boards and Communications) (listservs); Wis. Prof'l Eth. Committee Op. E-95-5 (1995), *available at* **http://www.wisbar.org/AM/Template.cfm?Section=Legal_Research&Template=/CustomSource/Search/Search.cfm&output=xml_no_dtd&proxystylesheet=wisbar5&client=wisbar5&filter=1&start=0&Site=SBW&q=%22formal+opinion%22+E%2D95%2D5&submit=ethics** (lawyer-volunteer at organization that provides information about landlord-tenant law). The Model Rules defer to "principles of substantive law external to these Rules [to] determine when a client-lawyer relationship exists." Scope cmt. 17.

[17]*See, e.g.*, Ariz. State Bar Op. 02-04 (2002), *available at* **http://www.myazbar.org/Ethics/opinionview.cfm?id=288** (lawyer does not owe duty of confidentiality to individuals who unilaterally e-mail inquiries to lawyer when e-mail is unsolicited); Cal. Standing Comm. on Prof'l Resp. and Conduct Formal Op. 2001-155, *supra* note 3 (lawyer may avoid incurring duty of confidentiality to persons who seek legal services by visiting lawyer's website and disclose confidential information only if site contains clear disclaimer); Iowa Bar Ass'n Eth. Op. 07-02 (2007), *available at* **http://www.iowabar.org/ethics.nsf/e61beed77a215f6686256497004ce492/cb0a70672d69d8c1862573380013fb9d?OpenDocument** (message that encourages detailed response about case could in some situations be considered bilateral); N.H. Bar Ass'n Eth. Comm. Op. 20092010/1 (2009), *available at* **http://www.nhbar.org/legal-links/ethics1.asp** (when law firm's website invites public to send e-mail to one of firm's lawyers, it is opening itself to potential obligations to prospective clients); Ass'n of the Bar of the City of New York, Formal Op. 2001-1 (2001) (Obligations of Law Firm Receiving Unsolicited E-Mail Communications from Prospective Client), *available at* **http://www.abcny.org/Ethics/eth2001-01.html** (where firm website does not adequately warn that information transmitted will not be treated as confidential, information should be held in confidence by lawyer receiving communication and not disclosed to or used for benefit of another client even though lawyer declines to represent potential client); N.J. Advisory Comm. on Prof'l Eth. Op. 695, 2004 WL 833032 (2004) (firm has duty to keep information received from prospective client confidential); San Diego County Bar Ass'n Eth. Op. 2006-1

communications. It also recognizes several ways that lawyers may limit subsequent disqualification based on these prospective client disclosures when they decide not to undertake a matter.[18]

Rule 1.18(a) addresses whether the inquirer has become a "prospective client," defined as "a person who discusses with a lawyer the possibility of forming a client-lawyer relationship." To "discuss," meaning to talk about, generally contemplates a two-way communication, which necessarily must begin with an initial communication.[19] Rule 1.18 implicitly recognizes that this initial communication can come either from a lawyer or a person who wishes to become a prospective client.

Rule 1.18 Comment [2] also recognizes that not all initial communications from persons who wish to be prospective clients necessarily result in a "discussion" within the meaning of the rule: "a person who communicates information unilaterally to a lawyer, without any reasonable expectation that the lawyer is willing to discuss the possibility of forming a client-lawyer relationship, is not a prospective client."

For example, if a lawyer website specifically requests or invites submission of information concerning the possibility of forming a client-lawyer relationship with respect to a matter, a discussion, as that term is used in Rule 1.18, will result when a website visitor submits the requested information.[20] If a website visitor submits information to a site that does not specifically request or invite this, the lawyer's response to that submission will determine whether a discussion under Rule 1.18 has occurred.

A telephone, mail, or e-mail exchange between an individual seeking legal services and a lawyer is analogous.[21] In these contexts, the lawyer takes

---

(2006), *available at* **http://www.sdcba.org/index.cfm?Pg=ethicsopinion06-1** (private information received from non-client via unsolicited e-mail is not required to be held as confidential if lawyer has not had opportunity to warn or stop flow of information at or before the communication is delivered).

[18] Lawyers do not normally owe confidentiality obligations to persons who are not clients (protected by Rule 1.6), former clients (Rule 1.9), or prospective clients (Rule 1.18).

[19] For example, in ABA Committee on Ethics and Professional Responsibility, Formal Op. 90-358 (1990) (Protection of Information Imparted by Prospective Client), this committee considered the obligations of a lawyer who engaged in such a "discussion" in the context of a face-to-face meeting.

[20] Rule 1.18 cmt. 1.

[21] *See, e.g.*, Va. Legal Eth. Op. 1842 (2008), *available at* **http://www.vacle.org/opinions/1842.htm** (absent voicemail message that asks for detailed information, providing phone number and voicemail is an invitation only to contact lawyer, not to submit confidential information); Iowa State Bar Ass'n Eth. Op. 07-02 ("Communication from and with Potential Clients"), *available at* **http://www.iowabar.org/ethics.nsf/e61beed77a215f6686256497004ce492/cb0a70672d69d8c 1862573380013fb9d?OpenDocument** (telephone voicemail message that simply asks for contact details does not give rise to bilateral communication, but message that encourages caller to leave detailed messages about their case could be considered bilateral).

part in a bilateral discussion about the possibility of forming a client-lawyer relationship and has the opportunity to limit or encourage the flow of information. For example, the lawyer may ask for additional details or may caution against providing any personal or sensitive information until a conflicts check can be completed.

Lawyers have a similar ability on their websites to control features and content so as to invite, encourage, limit, or discourage the flow of information to and from website visitors.[22] A particular website might facilitate a very direct and almost immediate bilateral communication in response to marketing information about a specific lawyer. It might, for example, specifically encourage a website visitor to submit a personal inquiry about a proposed representation on a conveniently provided website electronic form which, when responded to, begins a "discussion" about a proposed representation and, absent any cautionary language, invites submission of confidential information.[23] Another website might describe the work of the law firm and each of its lawyers, list only contact information such as a telephone number, e-mail or street address, or provide a website e-mail link to a lawyer. Providing such information alone does not create a reasonable expectation that the lawyer is willing to discuss a specific client-lawyer relationship.[24] A lawyer's response to an inquiry submitted by a visitor who uses this contact information may, however, begin a "discussion" within the meaning of Rule 1.18.

---

[22]*See, e.g.*, Ariz. State Bar Op. 02-04 (2002), *available at* **http://www.myazbar.org/Ethics/opinion view.cfm?id=288** (lawyers who maintain websites with e-mail links should include disclaimers to clarify whether e-mail communications from prospective clients will be treated as confidential); Mass. Bar Ass'n Op. 07-01 (2007), *available at* **http://www.massbar.org/publications/ethics-opinions/2000-2009/2007/opinion-07-01** (lawyer who receives unsolicited information from prospective client through e-mail link on law firm website without effective disclaimer must hold information confidential because law firm has opportunity to set conditions on flow of information); S.D. Bar Eth. Op. 2002-2 (2002) (lawyer's website that invites viewers to send e-mail through jump site creates expectation of confidentiality).

[23]*See, e.g.*, Iowa State Bar Ass'n Eth. Op. 07-02, *supra* note 21 (web page inviting specific questions constitutes bilateral communication with expectation of confidentiality), and Va. Legal Eth. Op. 1842, *supra* note 21 (website that specifically invites visitor to submit information in exchange for evaluation invites formation of client-lawyer relationship).

[24]E-mails received from unknown persons who send them apart from the lawyer's website may even more easily be viewed as unsolicited. *See, e.g.*, Ariz. State Bar Op. 02-04, *supra* note 22 (e-mail to multiple lawyers asking for representation); Iowa State Bar Ass'n Eth. Op. 07-02, *supra* note 21 (website that gives contact information does not without more indicate that lawyer requested or consented to sending of confidential information); San Diego County Bar Assn. Op. 2006-1, *available at* **http://www.sdcba.org/index.cfm?Pg=ethicsopinion06-1** (inquirer found lawyer's e-mail address on state bar membership records website accessible to the public).

In between these two examples, a variety of website content and features might indicate that a lawyer has agreed to discuss a possible client-lawyer relationship. A former client's website communication to a lawyer about a new matter must be analyzed in light of their previous relationship, which may have given rise to a reasonable expectation of confidentiality.[25] But a person who knows that the lawyer already declined a particular representation or is already representing an adverse party can neither reasonably expect confidentiality, nor reasonably believe that the lawyer wishes to discuss a client-lawyer relationship. Similarly, a person who purports to be a prospective client and who communicates with a number of lawyers with the intent to prevent other parties from retaining them in the same matter should have no reasonable expectation of confidentiality or that the lawyer would refrain from an adverse representation.[26]

In other circumstances, it may be difficult to predict when the overall message of a given website communicates a willingness by a lawyer to discuss a particular prospective client-lawyer relationship. Imprecision in a website message and failure to include a clarifying disclaimer may result in a website visitor reasonably viewing the website communication itself as the first step in a discussion.[27] Lawyers are therefore well-advised to consider that a website-generated inquiry may have come from a prospective client, and should pay special attention to including the appropriate warnings mentioned in the next section.

If a discussion with a prospective client has occurred, Rule 1.18(b) prohibits use or disclosure of information learned during such a discussion

---

[25] *See, e.g.*, Iowa State Bar Ass'n Comm. Eth. Op. 07-02, *supra* note 22 (lack of prior relationship with person sending unsolicited e-mail requesting representation was one factor in determining whether communicator's disclosures were unilateral and whether expectation of confidentiality was reasonable); Ore. Eth. Op. 2005-146, 2005 WL 5679570 *1 (2005) (lawyer who sends periodic reminders to former clients risks giving recipients reasonable belief they are still current clients).
[26] *See, e.g.*, Va. Legal Eth. Op. 1794 (2004), *available at* **http://www.vacle.org/opinions/1794.htm** (person who meets with lawyer for primary purpose of precluding others from obtaining legal representation does not have reasonable expectation of confidentiality); Ass'n of the Bar of the City of New York Comm. on Prof'l and Jud. Ethics Formal Op. 2001-1 (2001), *available at* **http://www.abcny.org/Ethics/eth2001.html** ("taint shoppers," who interview lawyers or law firms for purpose of disqualifying them from future adverse representation, have no good faith expectation of confidentiality).
[27] *See, e.g.*, Mass. Bar Ass'n Op. 07-01, *supra* note 22 (in absence of effective disclaimer, prospective client visiting law firm website that markets background and qualifications of each lawyer in attractive light, stresses lawyer's skill at solving clients' practical problems, and provides e-mail link for immediate communication with that lawyer might reasonably conclude that firm and its individual lawyers have implicitly "agreed to consider" whether to form client-lawyer relationship).

absent the prospective client's informed consent.[28] When the discussion reveals a conflict of interest, the lawyer should decline the representation,[29] and cannot disclose the information received without the informed consent of the prospective client.[30] For various reasons, including the need for a conflicts check, the lawyer may have tried to limit the initial discussion and may have clearly expressed those limitations to the prospective client. If this has been done, any information given to the lawyer that exceeds those express limitations generally would not be protected under Rule 1.18(b).

Rule 1.18(c) disqualifies lawyers and their law firms who have received information that "could be significantly harmful" to the prospective client from representing others with adverse interests in the same or substantially related matters.[31] For example, if a prospective client previously had disclosed only an intention to bring a particular lawsuit and has now retained a different lawyer to initiate the same suit, it is difficult to imagine any significant harm that could result from the law firm proceeding with the defense of the same matter.[32] On the other hand, absent an appropriate warning, the prospective client's prior disclosure of more extensive facts about the matter may well be disqualifying.

Rule 1.18(d) creates two exceptions that allow subsequent adverse representation even if the prospective client disclosed information that was significantly harmful: (1) informed consent confirmed in writing from both the affected and the prospective client, or (2) reasonable measures to limit the disqualifying information, combined with timely screening of the disqualified lawyer from the subsequent adverse matter. Rule 1.18(d)(2) specifically would allow the law firm (but not the contacted lawyer) to "undertake or continue" the representation of someone with adverse interests without receiving the informed consent of the prospective client if the lawyer who initially received the information took reasonable precautions to limit the prospective client's initial disclosures and was timely screened from further involvement in the matter as required by Rule 1.0(k).

---

[28] Rule 1.18(b) allows disclosure or use if permitted by Rule 1.9. Rule 1.9(c)(2) and its Comment [7] in turn link disclosure to Rule 1.6, the general confidentiality rule, which requires client informed consent to disclosure.
[29] Rule 1.18 cmt. 4.
[30] Rule 1.18 cmt. 3.
[31] *See also* RESTATEMENT (THIRD) OF THE LAW GOVERNING LAWYERS § 15(2) (2000).
[32] Rule 1.18 cmt. 5 also allows lawyers to condition an initial conversation on the prospective client's informed consent to subsequent adverse representation in the same matter or subsequent use of any confidential information provided.

III. Warnings or Cautionary Statements Intended to Limit, Condition, or Disclaim a Lawyer's Obligations to Website Visitors

Warnings or cautionary statements on a lawyer's website can be designed to and may effectively limit, condition, or disclaim a lawyer's obligation to a website reader. Such warnings or statements may be written so as to avoid a misunderstanding by the website visitor that (1) a client-lawyer relationship has been created;[33] (2) the visitor's information will be kept confidential;[34] (3) legal advice has been given;[35] or (4) the lawyer will be prevented from representing an adverse party.[36]

---

[33] *See, e.g.*, N.M. Bar Op. 2001-1 (2001), *available at* **http://www.nmbar.org/legalresearch/ethics advisoryopinions.html** (appropriate disclaimers of lawyer-client relationship should accompany any response to listserv message board, but any response that would suggest to reasonable person that, despite disclaimer, relationship is being or has been established would negate disclaimer); N.C. State Bar Formal Eth. Op. 2000-3, 2000 WL 33300702 *2 (2000) (Responding to Inquiries Posted on a Message Board on the Web) (lawyers who do not want to create client-lawyer relationships on law firm message board should use specific disclaimers on any communications with inquirers, but substantive law will determine whether client-lawyer relationship is created); Ass'n of the Bar of the City of New York Comm. on Prof'l and Jud. Ethics Formal Op. 1998-2 (1998), *available at* **http://www.abcny.org/Ethics/eth1998-2.htm** (disclaimer that "if specific legal advice is sought, we will indicate that this requires establishment of an attorney-client relationship which cannot be carried out through the use of a web page" may not necessarily serve to shield law firm from claim that attorney-client relationship was established by specific on-line communications); Utah State Bar Eth. Advisory Op. Comm. Op. 96-12, 1997 WL 45137 *1 (1997) ("if legal advice is sought from an attorney, if the advice sought is pertinent to the attorney's profession, and if the attorney gives the advice for which fees will be charged, an attorney-client relationship is created that cannot be disclaimed by the attorney giving the advice"); Vt. Bar Ass'n Advisory Ethics Op. 2000-04 (2000), *supra* note 3 (despite website caveat and disclaimers, nonlawyer may still rely on information on website or lawyer's responses; disclaimer cannot preclude possibility of establishing client-lawyer relationship in an individual case).

[34] The Committee does not opine whether a confidentiality waiver might affect the attorney-client privilege. *See, e.g.*, Barton v. U.S. Dist. Ct. for the Cent. Dist. of Cal., 410 F.3d 1104, 1111–12 (9th Cir. 2005) (checking "yes" box on law firm website that acknowledged providing information in answer to questionnaire "does not constitute a request for legal advice and I am not forming an attorney-client relationship by submitting this information" did not waive attorney-client privilege because confidentiality was not mentioned in attempted disclaimer and questionnaires were nevertheless submitted in course of seeking attorney-client relationship in potential class action). *Cf.* Schiller v. The City of New York, 245 F.R.D. 112, 117–18 (S.D.N.Y. 2007) (although privilege may protect pre-engagement communications from prospective clients, it does not apply to person who completed questionnaires soliciting information from N.Y. Civil Liberties Union to allow it to "effectively advocate for change"). *See also* David Hricik, *To Whom It May Concern: Using Disclaimers to Avoid Disqualification by Receipt of Unsolicited E-Mail from Prospective Clients*, 16 ABA Professional Lawyer 1, 5 (2005) (agreement that waives all confidentiality tries to do too much and might destroy the ability of prospective client who eventually becomes firm client to claim privilege).

[35] *See* note 15 *supra*.

[36] Rule 1.18 cmt. 5.

Limitations, conditions, or disclaimers of lawyer obligations will be effective only if reasonably understandable, properly placed, and not misleading. This requires a clear warning in a readable format whose meaning can be understood by a reasonable person.[37] If the website uses a particular language, any waiver, disclaimer, limitation, or condition must be in the same language. The appropriate information should be conspicuously placed to assure that the reader is likely to see it before proceeding.[38]

Finally, a limitation, condition, waiver, or disclaimer may be undercut if the lawyer acts or communicates contrary to its warning.

---

[37] *See, e.g.*, Cal. Bar Comm. on Prof'l Resp. Op. 2005-168, 2005 WL 3068090 *4 (2005) (finding disclaimer stating that "confidential relationship" would not be formed was not enough to waive confidentiality, because it confused not forming client-lawyer relationship with agreeing to keep communications confidential).

[38] *See, e.g.*, District of Columbia Bar Ethics Op. 302 (2000), *available at* **http://www.dcbar.org/ for_lawyers/ethics/legal_ethics/opinions/opinion302.cfm** (lawyers may want to use "click-through" pages that automatically direct the reader to another webpage containing disclaimers to ensure that visitors are not misled and other devices such as confirmatory messages that clarify nature of relationship); Va. Legal Ethics Op. 1842, *supra* note 21 (approving of prominent "click-through" disclaimers that require readers to assent to terms of disclaimer before submitting information). Courts have refused to uphold disclaimers or licensing agreements that appeared on separate pages and did not require a reader's affirmative consent to their terms because they did not provide reasonable notice). *See, e.g.*, Sprecht v. Netscape Commc'ns Corp., 306 F.3d 17, 31–32 (2d Cir. 2002). On the other hand, courts have upheld website restrictions that provided actual knowledge by presenting the information and requiring an affirmative action (a click-through or "clickwrap" agreement) before gaining access to the website content. *See, e.g.*, Register.com v. Verio, 356 F.3d 393, 401–02 (2d Cir. 2004).

Glossary*

Active Directory
Active Directory (AD) is an implementation of Local Automatic Data Processing (LADP) directory services by Microsoft for use primarily in Windows environments. Its main purpose is to provide central authentication and authorization services for Windows-based computers. Active Directory also allows administrators to assign policies, deploy software, and apply critical updates to an organization. Active Directory stores information and settings in a central database. Active Directory networks can vary from a small installation with a few hundred objects to a large installation with millions of objects.

ActiveSync
ActiveSync is a synchronization program developed by Microsoft. It allows a mobile device to be synchronized with either a desktop PC or a server running Microsoft Exchange Server, PostPath Email and Collaboration Server, Kerio MailServer, or Z-Push.

Adware
Adware is any software package that automatically plays, displays, or downloads advertising material to a computer after the software is installed on it or while the application is being used. Some types of adware are also spyware and can be classified as privacy-invasive software.

AppleCare Protection Plan
Apple's warranty with a new product is 90 days' complimentary telephone support and a one-year hardware guarantee. These can both be

---

*This glossary was compiled from definitions available online at Wikipedia (**www.wikipedia.org**).

extended to a three-year (for computers) or two-year (for iPods and iPhones) warranty and telephone support (inclusive of the initial support) through the AppleCare Protection Plan packs, which can be purchased separately within the initial one-year warranty or simultaneously with new Apple products, mainly Macs, iPods, and iPhones.

ATA
Advanced technology attachment (ATA) is a standard interface for connecting storage devices such as hard disks and CD-ROM drives inside personal computers. The standard is maintained by X3/INCITS committee T13. Many synonyms and near-synonyms for ATA exist, including abbreviations such as IDE and ATAPI.

Auto Document Feeder
Auto document feeder (ADF) is a feature in multifunction or all-in-one printers, fax machines, photocopiers, and scanners that takes several pages and feeds the paper one page at a time into the scanner, allowing the user to scan (and thereby copy, print, or fax) multiple-page documents without having to manually replace each page.

Boot Camp
Boot Camp is a utility included with Apple's Mac OS X v10.5 Leopard operating system that assists users in installing Microsoft Windows XP or Windows Vista on Intel-based Macintosh computers. Boot Camp guides users through nondestructive repartitioning (including resizing of an existing HFS+ partition, if necessary) of their hard disk drive and using the Mac OS X Leopard disc to install Windows drivers. In addition to device drivers for the hardware, the disc includes a control panel applet for selecting the boot operating system while in Windows.

Byte
Byte (pronounced "bite," IPA: /ba_t/) is a unit of measurement of information storage, most often consisting of 8 bits. In many computer architectures it is a unit of memory addressing.

Category 5e Cable
Category 5e cable (Cat5e) is an enhanced version of Cat 5 that adds specifications for far-end crosstalk. It was formally defined in 2001 in the TIA/EIA-568-B standard, which no longer recognizes the original Cat 5 specification. Although 1000BASE-T was designed for use with Cat 5 cable, the tighter specifications associated with Cat 5e cable and connec-

tors make it an excellent choice for use with 1000BASE-T. Despite the stricter performance specifications, Cat 5e cable does not enable longer cable distances for Ethernet networks: Cables are still limited to a maximum of 328 ft. (100 m) in length (normal practice is to limit fixed ["horizontal"] cables to 90m to allow for up to 5m of patch cable at each end). Cat 5e cable performance characteristics and test methods are defined in TIA/EIA-568-B.2-2001.

Category 6 Cable
Category 6 cable (Cat6), commonly referred to as Cat 6, is a cable standard for gigabit Ethernet and other network protocols and is backward compatible with the Category 5/5e and Category 3 cable standards. Cat 6 features more stringent specifications for crosstalk and system noise. The cable standard provides performance of up to 250 MHz and is suitable for 10BASE-T/100BASE-TX and 1000BASE-T (gigabit Ethernet). It is expected to suit the 10GBASE-T (10 gigabit Ethernet) standard, although with limitations on length if unshielded Cat 6 cable is used.

Cathode Ray Tube
Cathode Ray Tube (CRT) is an evacuated glass envelope containing an electron gun (a source of electrons) and a fluorescent screen, usually with internal or external means to accelerate and deflect the electrons. When electrons strike the fluorescent screen, light is emitted.

CD-ROM
CD-ROM is a compact disc that contains data accessible by a computer. While the CD format was originally designed for music storage and playback, the format was later adapted to hold any form of binary data. CD-ROMs are popularly used to distribute computer software, including games and multimedia applications, though any data can be stored (up to the capacity limit of a disc).

Central Processing Unit
A central processing unit (CPU), or sometimes just processor, is a certain class of logic machines that can execute computer programs. This broad definition can easily be applied to many early computers that existed long before the term CPU ever came into widespread usage. However, the term itself and its initialism have been in use in the computer industry since at least the early 1960s (Weik, 1961). The form, design, and implementation of CPUs have changed dramatically since the earliest examples, but their fundamental operation has remained much the same.

Client Access License
A Client Access License (CAL) is a kind of software license, distributed by Microsoft, to allow clients to connect to its server software programs.

Code Division Multiple Access
Code division multiple access (CDMA) employs spread-spectrum technology and a special coding scheme (where each transmitter is assigned a code). In communications technology, there are only three domains that can allow multiplexing to be implemented for more efficient use of the available channel bandwidth, and these domains are known as time, frequency, and space. CDMA divides the access in signal space.

Computer Monitor
A computer monitor is a piece of electrical equipment that displays viewable images generated by a computer without producing a permanent record. The word *monitor* is used in other contexts, in particular in television broadcasting, where a television picture is displayed to a high standard. A computer display device is usually either a cathode ray tube or some form of flat panel, such as a thin film transistor liquid crystal display (TFT-LCD). The monitor comprises the display device, circuitry to generate a picture from electronic signals sent by the computer, and an enclosure or case. Within the computer, either as an integral part or a plugged-in interface, there is circuitry to convert internal data to a format compatible with a monitor.

Computer Virus
A computer virus is a computer program that can copy itself and infect a computer without permission or knowledge of the user. However, the term *virus* is commonly used, albeit erroneously, to refer to many different types of malware programs. The original virus may modify the copies, or the copies may modify themselves, as occurs in a metamorphic virus. A virus can only spread from one computer to another when its host is taken to the uninfected computer—for instance, by a user sending it over a network or the Internet or by carrying it on a removable medium, such as a floppy disk, CD, or USB drive. Additionally, viruses can spread to other computers by infecting files on a network file system or a file system that is accessed by another computer.

Contrast Ratio
Contrast ratio is a measure of a display system, defined as the ratio of the luminosity of the brightest color (white) to that of the darkest color (black) that the system is capable of producing. A high contrast ratio is a

desired aspect of any display, but with the various methods of measurement for a system or its part, remarkably different measured values can sometimes produce similar results.

DAT72 Backup Tapes
DAT72 stores up to 36GB uncompressed (72GB compressed) on a 170-meter cartridge. The Digital Audio Tape (DAT) 72 standard was developed by HP and Certance. It has the same form-factor and is backward compatible with DDS-3 and -4.

Database Application
A computer database is a structured collection of records or data that is stored in a computer system. A database usually contains software so that a person or program can use it to answer queries or extract desired information. The term *database* refers to the collection of related records, and the software should be referred to as the *database management system* (DBMS).

DDR2 SDRAM
DDR2 SDRAM, double-data-rate two synchronous dynamic random-access memory, is a random-access memory technology used for high-speed storage of the working data of a computer or other digital electronic device.

Digital Copier
In recent years, all new photocopiers have adopted digital technology, replacing the older analog technology. With digital copying, the copier effectively consists of an integrated scanner and laser printer. This design has several advantages, such as automatic image quality enhancement and the ability to "build jobs," or scan page images independently of the process of printing them. Some digital copiers can function as high-speed scanners; such models typically have the ability to send documents via e-mail or make them available on a local area network.

Digital Subscriber Line
Digital Subscriber Line (DSL) is a family of technologies that provide digital data transmission over the wires of a local telephone network.

Digital Visual Interface
Digital Visual Interface (DVI) is a video interface standard designed to maximize the visual quality of digital display devices such as flat-panel LCD computer displays and digital projectors. It was developed by an

industry consortium, the Digital Display Working Group (DDWG). It is designed for carrying uncompressed digital video data to a display.

Display Resolution
The display resolution of a digital television or computer display typically refers to the number of distinct pixels in each dimension that can be displayed. It can be an ambiguous term, especially as the displayed resolution is controlled by different factors in CRT and flat-panel or projection displays using fixed picture-element (pixel) arrays.

Domain Controller
On Windows Server Systems, the domain controller (DC) is the server that responds to security authentication requests (logging in, checking permissions, etc.) within the Windows Server domain.

Dots Per Inch
Dots per inch (dpi) is a measure of printing resolution, in particular the number of individual dots of ink a printer or toner can produce within a linear one-inch (2.54 cm) space.

DVD
DVD (also known as digital versatile disc or digital video disc) is a popular optical disk storage media format. Its main uses are video and data storage. Most DVDs are of the same dimensions as compact discs (CDs) but store more than six times as much data.

Email Spam
Email spam is the practice of sending unwanted e-mail messages, frequently with commercial content, in large quantities to an indiscriminate set of recipients.

Encryption/Decryption
Encryption/decryption is the process of transforming information (referred to as plaintext) using an algorithm (called cipher) to make it unreadable to anyone except those possessing special knowledge, usually referred to as a key. The result of the process is encrypted information (in cryptography, referred to as ciphertext). In many contexts, the word encryption also implicitly refers to the reverse process, decryption (e.g., "software for encryption" can typically also perform decryption), to make the encrypted information readable again (i.e., to make it unencrypted).

Enhanced-Definition Television

Enhanced- or extended-definition television, or EDTV, is a Consumer Electronics Association (CEA) marketing shorthand term for certain digital television (DTV) formats and devices. EDTV generally refers to video with picture quality beyond what can be broadcast in NTSC or PAL but not sharp enough to be considered high-definition television (HDTV). A DVD player with progressive output is considered the lower end of this class, when playing a progressively encoded disc. (The maximum EDTV frame rate of 60 per second is not possible from a DVD.) The common implementations of EDTV are 480- or 576-line signals in progressive scan, as opposed to 50–60 interlaced fields per second (see NTSC or PAL and SECAM). These are commonly referred to as "480p" and "576p," respectively. In comparison, a standard-definition television (SDTV) signal is broadcast with interlaced frames and is commonly referred to as "480i" or "576i." EDTV can also refer to a display device that has a maximum resolution of 480p or 576p.

Extensible Markup Language

Extensible Markup Language (XML) is a general-purpose markup language. It is classified as an extensible language because it allows its users to define their own elements. Its primary purpose is to facilitate the sharing of structured data across different information systems, particularly via the Internet. It is used both to encode documents and serialize data.

FireWire

FireWire is Apple's brand name for the IEEE 1394 interface (although the 1394 standard also defines a backplane interface). It is also known as i.LINK (Sony's name). It is a serial bus interface standard for high-speed communications and isochronous real-time data transfer, frequently used in a personal computer (and digital audio/digital video).

FireWire 400

FireWire 400 can transfer data between devices at 100, 200, or 400 Mbit/s data rates.

FireWire 800

FireWire 800 (Apple's name for the nine-pin "S800 bilingual" version of the IEEE 1394b standard) was introduced commercially by Apple in 2003. This newer 1394 specification (1394b) and corresponding products allow a transfer rate of 786.432 Mbit/s via a new encoding scheme termed beta mode. It is backward compatible to the slower rates and six-pin connectors of FireWire 400. However, while the IEEE 1394a and IEEE 1394b standards are compatible, FireWire 800's connector is different from FireWire 400's connector, making the legacy cables incompatible. A bilingual cable allows the connection of older devices to the newer port.

Gigabyte
A gigabyte (derived from the SI prefix giga-) is a unit of information or computer storage meaning either exactly 1 billion bytes (1000^3, or 10^9) or approximately 1.07 billion bytes (1024^3). It is commonly abbreviated as Gbyte or GB.

Global System for Mobile Communications
Global System for Mobile communications (GSM) is the most popular standard for mobile phones in the world. Its promoter, the GSM Association, estimates that 82 percent of the global mobile market uses the standard. GSM is used by over 2 billion people across more than 212 countries and territories. Its ubiquity makes international roaming very common between mobile phone operators, enabling subscribers to use their phones in many parts of the world. GSM differs from its predecessors in that both signaling and speech channels are digital call quality, and so it is considered a second generation (2G) mobile phone system. This has also meant that data communications were built into the system using the 3rd Generation Partnership Project (3GPP).

Hard Disk Drive
Hard disk drive, commonly referred to as a hard drive, hard disk, or fixed disk drive, is a nonvolatile storage device that stores digitally encoded data on rapidly rotating platters with magnetic surfaces. Strictly speaking, "drive" refers to a device distinct from its medium, such as a tape drive and its tape or a floppy disk drive and its floppy disk.

Hash Function
Hash function is a reproducible method of turning some kind of data into a (relatively) small number that may serve as a digital "fingerprint" of the data. The algorithm "chops and mixes" (i.e., substitutes or transposes) the data to create such fingerprints. The fingerprints are called hash sums, hash values, hash codes, or simply hashes.

High-Definition Multimedia Interface
High-definition multimedia interface (HDMI) is a licensable compact audio/video connector interface for transmitting uncompressed digital streams.

High-Definition TV
High-definition TV (HDTV) is a digital television broadcasting system with greater resolution than traditional television systems (NTSC, SECAM, PAL). HDTV is digitally broadcast because digital television (DTV) requires less bandwidth if sufficient video compression is used.

Hub
A hub is a device for connecting multiple twisted pairs or fiber optic Ethernet devices together, making them act as a single network segment. Hubs work at the physical layer (layer 1) of the OSI model, and the term *layer 1 switch* is often used interchangeably with hub. The device is thus a form of multiport repeater. Network hubs are also responsible for forwarding a jam signal to all ports if it detects a collision.

IEEE
The Institute of Electrical and Electronics Engineers, or IEEE (read i triple e), is an international nonprofit professional organization for the advancement of technology related to electricity. It has the most members of any technical professional organization in the world, with more than 360,000 members in around 175 countries.

Intel Core 2 Duo Processor
The Core 2 brand refers to a range of Intel's consumer 64-bit dual-core and MCM quad-core CPUs with the x86-64 instruction set and based on the Intel Core microarchitecture, which derived from the 32-bit dual-core Yonah laptop processor.

Intel Corporation
Intel Corporation (Intel) is the world's largest semiconductor company and the inventor of the x86 series of microprocessors, which are found in most personal computers.

Internet Information Services
Internet Information Services (IIS) is a set of Internet-based services for servers using Microsoft Windows. It is the world's second most popular web server in terms of overall websites, behind Apache HTTP Server.

Internet Protocol Address
An IP address (Internet protocol address) is a unique address that certain electronic devices currently use to identify and communicate with each other on a computer network utilizing the Internet protocol standard (IP)—in simpler terms, a computer address. Any participating network

device—including routers, switches, computers, infrastructure servers (e.g., NTP, DNS, DHCP, SNMP), printers, Internet fax machines, and some telephones—can have its own address that is unique within the scope of the specific network. Some IP addresses are intended to be unique within the scope of the global Internet, while others need to be unique only within the scope of an enterprise.

Intrusion Detection System
An intrusion detection system (IDS) is a piece of hardware that detects unwanted manipulations of computer systems, mainly through the Internet. The manipulations may take the form of attacks by crackers. An IDS is used to detect several types of malicious behaviors that can compromise the security and trust of a computer system. This includes network attacks against vulnerable services; data-driven attacks on applications; host-based attacks such as privilege escalation, unauthorized logins, and access to sensitive files; and malware (viruses, Trojan horses, and worms).

IPsec
IPsec (IP security) is a suite of protocols for securing Internet protocol (IP) communications by authenticating and/or encrypting each IP packet in a data stream.

iSight Camera
The iSight camera is a webcam developed and marketed by Apple. The iSight was sold retail as an external unit that connects to a computer via FireWire cable and comes with a set of mounts to place it atop any current Apple display, laptop computer, or all-in-one desktop computer. The term is also used to refer to the camera built into Apple's iMac, MacBook, and MacBook Pro computers.

Keyboard
In computing, a keyboard is a peripheral partially modeled after the typewriter keyboard. Physically, a keyboard is an arrangement of rectangular buttons, or keys. A keyboard typically has characters engraved or printed on the keys; in most cases, each press of a key corresponds to a single written symbol. However, to produce some symbols requires pressing and holding several keys simultaneously or in sequence; other keys do not produce any symbol but instead affect the operation of the computer or the keyboard itself.

Laser Printer

A laser printer is a common type of computer printer that rapidly produces high-quality text and graphics on plain paper. Like photocopiers, laser printers employ a xerographic printing process but differ from analog photocopiers in that the image is produced by the direct scanning of a laser beam across the printer's photoreceptor.

Light-Emitting Diode

A light-emitting diode (LED) is a semiconductor diode that emits incoherent, narrow-spectrum light when electrically biased in the forward direction of the p-n junction, as in the common LED circuit. This effect is a form of electroluminescence.

Linear Tape-Open

Linear tape-open (LTO or LTO2) is a magnetic tape data storage technology developed as an open alternative to the proprietary digital linear tape (DLT). The technology was developed and initiated by Seagate, Hewlett Packard, and IBM. The standard form-factor of LTO technology goes by the name Ultrium.

Liquid Crystal Display

A liquid crystal display (LCD) is a thin, flat display device made up of any number of color or monochrome pixels arrayed in front of a light source or reflector. It is often utilized in battery-powered electronic devices because it uses very small amounts of electric power.

Macintosh AirPort

AirPort is a local area wireless networking brand from Apple based on the IEEE 802.11b standard (also known as Wi-Fi) and certified as compatible with other 802.11b devices. A later family of products based on the IEEE 802.11g specification is known as AirPort Extreme. The latest family of products is based on the draft-IEEE 802.11n specification and carries the same name.

Macintosh/Macs

Macintosh—or, for newer models, Mac—is a brand name that covers several lines of personal computers designed, developed, and marketed by Apple Inc. The original Macintosh was released on January 24, 1984; it was the first commercially successful personal computer to feature a mouse and a graphical user interface (GUI) rather than a command line interface. Apple consolidated multiple consumer-level desktop models into the 1998 iMac, which sold extremely well. Current Mac systems are mainly targeted at the home, education, and creative professional markets. They are the aforementioned (though upgraded) iMac and the entry-level Mac mini desktop models, the workstation-level Mac Pro tower, the MacBook, MacBook Air and MacBook Pro laptops, and the Xserve server.

MagSafe Power Adapter
MagSafe power adapter is a power connector introduced in conjunction with the MacBook Pro at the Macworld Expo in San Francisco on January 10, 2006. The MagSafe connector is held in place magnetically. As a result, if it is tugged on—for instance, by someone tripping over the cord—it comes out of the socket safely, without damaging it or the computer or pulling the computer off its table or desk.

Media Access Control Address
Media access control (MAC) address is a quasi-unique identifier attached to most network adapters. It is a number that acts like a name for a particular network adapter, so, for example, the network interface cards (NICs, or built-in network adapters) in two different computers will have different names, or MAC addresses, as would an Ethernet adapter and a wireless adapter in the same computer and as would multiple network cards in a router.

Megabyte
A megabyte is a unit of information or computer storage equal to either 10^6 (1,000,000) bytes or 2^{20} (1,048,576) bytes, depending on context. In rare cases, it is used to mean 1000 x 1024 (1,024,000) bytes. It is commonly abbreviated as Mbyte or MB.

Message-Digest Algorithm 5 (MD5)
Message-digest algorithm 5 (MD5) is a widely used cryptographic hash function with a 128-bit hash value. As an Internet standard (RFC 1321), MD5 has been employed in a wide variety of security applications and is also commonly used to check the integrity of files. An MD5 hash is typically expressed as a 32-character hexadecimal number.

Microsoft Exchange Server
Microsoft Exchange Server is a messaging and collaborative software product developed by Microsoft. It is part of the Microsoft Servers line of

server products and is widely used by enterprises using Microsoft infrastructure solutions. Exchange's major features consist of electronic mail, calendaring, contacts and tasks, and support for the mobile and web-based access to information, as well as supporting data storage.

Microsoft SQL Server
Microsoft SQL Server is a relational database-management system (RDBMS) produced by Microsoft. Its primary query language is Transact-SQL, an implementation of the ANSI/ISO standard Structured Query Language (SQL) used by both Microsoft and Sybase.

Microsoft Windows
Microsoft Windows is the name of several families of software operating systems by Microsoft. Microsoft first introduced an operating environment named Windows in November 1985 as an add-on to MS-DOS in response to the growing interest in graphical user interfaces (GUIs). Microsoft Windows eventually came to dominate the world's personal computer market, overtaking Mac OS, which had been introduced previously. At the 2004 IDC Directions conference, IDC vice president Avneesh Saxena stated that Windows had approximately 90 percent of the client operating system market. The most recent client version of Windows is Windows 7. The current server version of Windows is Windows Server 2003. The successor to Windows Server 2003, Windows Server 2008, is currently being beta tested.

Modem
A modem (from modulator-demodulator) is a device that modulates an analog carrier signal to encode digital information and also demodulates such a carrier signal to decode the transmitted information. The goal is to produce a signal that can be transmitted easily and decoded to reproduce the original digital data.

Mouse
In computing, a mouse (plural mice or mouses) functions as a pointing device by detecting two-dimensional motion relative to its supporting surface. Physically, a mouse consists of a small case, held under one of the user's hands, with one or more buttons. It sometimes features other elements, such as "wheels," which allow the user to perform various system-dependent operations, or extra buttons or features that can add more control or dimensional input. The mouse's motion typically translates into the motion of a pointer on a display.

MP3
MPEG-1 audio layer 3, more commonly referred to as MP3, is a digital audio encoding format. This encoding format is used to create an MP3 file, a way to store a single segment of audio, commonly a song, so that it can be organized or easily transferred between computers and other devices, such as MP3 players.

Network Address Translation
Network address translation (NAT) is a technique of transceiving network traffic through a router that involves rewriting the source and/or destination IP addresses and usually also the TCP/UDP port numbers of IP packets as they pass through.

Network Card/Adapter
Network adapter, LAN adapter, or NIC (network interface card) is a piece of computer hardware designed to allow computers to communicate over a computer network.

Optical Character Recognition
Optical character recognition (OCR), usually abbreviated OCR, is the mechanical or electronic translation of images of handwritten, typewritten, or printed text (usually captured by a scanner) into machine-editable text.

Peripheral Devices
In computer hardware, a peripheral device is any device attached to a computer to expand its functionality. Some of the more common peripheral devices are printers, scanners, disk drives, tape drives, microphones, speakers, and cameras.

Personal Digital Assistants
Personal digital assistants (PDAs) are handheld computers but have become much more versatile over the years. PDAs are also known as small computers or palmtop computers. PDAs have many uses: for calculation; as a clock, calendar, and address book; to access the Internet and send/receive e-mails; for video recording, typewriting, and word processing; for making and writing on spreadsheets; to scan bar codes, use as a radio or stereo, play computer games, record survey responses, and as a Global Positioning System (GPS). Newer PDAs also have both color screens and audio capabilities, enabling them to be used as mobile phones (smartphones), web browsers, or portable media players. Many PDAs can access the Internet,

intranets, or extranets via Wi-Fi, or wireless wide-area networks (WWANs). Many PDAs employ touch-screen technology.

Portable Document Format
The Portable Document Format (PDF) is the file format created by Adobe Systems in 1993 for document exchange. PDF is fixed-layout document format used for representing two-dimensional documents in a manner independent of the application software, hardware, and operating system.

Private Branch Exchange
Private branch exchange (PBX) is a telephone exchange that serves a particular business or office, as opposed to one that a common carrier or telephone company operates for many businesses or for the general public.

PS/2 Connector
A PS/2 connector is used for connecting a keyboard and a mouse to a PC-compatible computer system. Its name comes from the IBM Personal System/2 series of personal computers, with which it was introduced in 1987. The PS/2 mouse connector generally replaced the older DE-9 RS-232 "serial mouse" connector, while the keyboard connector replaced the larger 5-pin DIN used in the IBM PC/AT design. The keyboard and mouse interfaces are electrically similar, with the main difference being that open collector outputs are required on both ends of the keyboard interface to allow bi-directional communication. If a PS/2 mouse is connected to a PS/2 keyboard port (or if a PS/2 keyboard is connected to a PS/2 mouse port), the mouse (or keyboard) will not be recognized by the computer.

Radio-Frequency Identification
Radio-frequency identification (RFID) is an automatic identification method that relies on storing and remotely retrieving data using devices called RFID tags or transponders. An RFID tag is an object that can be applied to or incorporated into a product, animal, or person for the purpose of identification using radio waves. Some tags can be read from several meters away and beyond the line of sight of the reader.

RAID 5
A redundant array of independent disks (RAID) 5 uses block-level striping with parity data distributed across all member disks. RAID 5 has achieved popularity due to its low cost of redundancy. Generally, RAID 5 is implemented with hardware support for parity calculations. A minimum of three disks is generally required for a complete RAID 5 configuration.

Random Access Memory
Random access memory (usually known by its acronym, RAM) is a type of computer data storage. Today it takes the form of integrated circuits that allow the stored data to be accessed in any order—i.e., at random. The word *random* thus refers to the fact that any piece of data can be returned in a constant time, regardless of its physical location and whether or not it is related to the previous piece of data.

Redundant Arrays of Independent Disks
Redundant arrays of independent disks (RAID) is the most common definition of RAID. Other definitions of RAID include "redundant arrays of independent drives" and "redundant arrays of inexpensive drives." RAID is an umbrella term for computer data storage schemes that divide and replicate data among multiple hard disk drives. RAID's various designs balance or accentuate two key design goals: increased data reliability and increased I/O (input/output) performance.

Remote Desktop Protocol
Remote desktop protocol (RDP) is a multichannel protocol that allows a user to connect to a computer running Microsoft Terminal Services. Clients exist for most versions of Windows (including handheld versions) and other operating systems such as Linux, FreeBSD, Solaris, and Mac OS X. The server listens by default on TCP port 3389. Microsoft refers to its official RDP client software as either Remote Desktop Connection (RDC) or Terminal Services Client (TSC).

Revolutions Per Minute
Revolutions per minute (abbreviated rpm, RPM, r/min, or $r \cdot min^{-1}$) is a unit of frequency: the number of full rotations completed in one minute around a fixed axis. It is most commonly used as a measure of rotational speed or angular velocity of some mechanical component.

Rootkits
A rootkit is a program (or a combination of several programs) designed to take fundamental control (in Unix terms, "root" access; in Windows terms, "administrator" access) of a computer system without authorization by the system's owners and legitimate managers. Access to the hardware (i.e., the reset switch) is rarely required, as a rootkit is intended to seize control of the operating system running on the hardware. Typically, rootkits act to obscure their presence on the system through subversion or evasion of standard operating system security mechanisms. Often they

are Trojans as well, thus fooling users into believing they are safe to run on their systems. Techniques used to accomplish this can include concealing running processes from monitoring programs or hiding files or system data from the operating system.

Router
A router is a piece of hardware that connects two or more different networks (e.g., LAN to WAN) to route data between them.

Scanning Resolution
Scanning resolution describes the detail of the scanned image. The term applies equally to digital images, film images, and other types of images. Higher resolution means more image detail.

Secure Sockets Layer
Secure Sockets Layer (SSL) is a cryptographic protocol that provides secure communications on the Internet for such things as web browsing, e-mail, Internet faxing, instant messaging, and other data transfers.

Serial Advanced Technology Attachment
A serial advanced technology attachment (SATA) is a computer bus primarily designed for transfer of data between a computer and storage devices (like hard disk drives or optical drives). The main benefits are faster transfers, ability to remove or add devices while operating (hot-swapping), thinner cables that let air cooling work more efficiently, and more reliable operation, with tighter data integrity checks than the older Parallel ATA interface.

Serial Attached SCSI
Serial attached SCSI (SAS) is a computer bus technology primarily designed for transfer of data to and from computer data storage devices such as hard drives, CD-ROM and DVD tape drives, and similar devices. SAS is a serial communication protocol for direct attached storage (DAS) devices. It is designed for the corporate and enterprise market as a replacement for parallel SCSI, allowing for much higher speed data transfers than previously available and is backward compatible with SATA drives.

Server
A server is an application or device that performs services for connected clients as part of a client-server architecture. A server application, as defined by RFC 2616 (HTTP/1.1), is "an application program that accepts

connections in order to service requests by sending back responses."
Server computers are devices designed to run such an application or
applications, often for extended periods of time, with minimal human
direction. Examples of d-class servers include web servers, e-mail servers,
and file servers.

Service Set Identifier
Service set identifier (SSID) is a name used to identify the particular 802.11
wireless LANs to which a user wants to attach. A client device will receive
broadcast messages from all access points within range advertising their
SSIDs and can choose one to connect to based on preconfiguration or by
displaying a list of SSIDs in range and asking the user to select one.

SHA Hash Functions
SHA hash functions are five cryptographic hash functions designed by
the National Security Agency (NSA) and published by the NIST as a U.S.
Federal Information Processing Standard. SHA stands for secure hash algorithm. Hash algorithms compute a fixed-length digital representation
(known as a message digest) of an input data sequence (the message) of
any length. The five algorithms are denoted SHA-1, SHA-224, SHA-256,
SHA-384, and SHA-512. The latter four variants are sometimes collectively
referred to as SHA-2. SHA-1 produces a message digest that is 160 bits
long; the number in the other four algorithms' names denote the bit
length of the digest they produce.

Shadow Copy
Shadow Copy (also called Volume Snapshot Service, or VSS) is a feature
introduced with Windows Server 2003 and available in all releases of
Microsoft Windows thereafter that allows taking manual or automatic
backup copies or snapshots of a file or folder on a specific volume at a specific point in time. It is used by NTBackup and the Volume Shadow Copy
service to back up files. In Windows Vista, it is used by Windows Vista's
backup utility, System Restore, and the Previous Versions feature.

Small Computer System Interface
Small computer system interface (SCSI) is a set of standards for physically
connecting and transferring data between computers and peripheral
devices. The SCSI standards define commands, protocols, and electrical
and optical interfaces. SCSI is most commonly used for hard disks and
tape drives, but it can connect a wide range of other devices, including
scanners and CD drives. The SCSI standard defines command sets for spe-

cific peripheral device types; the presence of "unknown" as one of these types means that in theory it can be used as an interface to almost any device, but the standard is highly pragmatic and addressed toward commercial requirements.

Smartphone
A smartphone is a mobile phone offering advanced capabilities beyond a typical mobile phone, often with PC-like functionality.

Spyware
Spyware is computer software that is installed surreptitiously on a personal computer to intercept or take partial control over the user's interaction with the computer without the user's informed consent. While the term *spyware* suggests software that secretly monitors the user's behavior, the functions of spyware extend well beyond simple monitoring. Spyware programs can collect various types of personal information but can also interfere with user control of the computer in other ways, such as installing additional software, redirecting web browser activity, accessing websites blindly that will cause more harmful viruses, or diverting advertising revenue to a third party. Spyware can even change computer settings, resulting in slow connection speeds, different home pages, and loss of Internet or other programs.

Stereophonic Sound (stereo)
Stereophonic sound, commonly called stereo, is the reproduction of sound, using two or more independent audio channels, through a symmetrical configuration of loudspeakers, to create a pleasant and natural impression of sound heard from various directions, as in natural hearing. It is often contrasted with monophonic (or "monaural," or just mono) sound, where audio is in the form of one channel, often centered in the sound field.

SuperDrive
SuperDrive is a term that has been used by Apple for two different storage drives: from 1988 to 1999, to refer to a high-density floppy disk drive capable of reading all major 3.5-inch disk formats, and from 2001 onwards to refer to a combined CD/DVD reader/writer. Once use of floppy disks started declining, Apple reused the term to refer to the (originally Pioneer-built) DVD writers built into its Macintosh models, which can read and write both DVDs and CDs. As of December 2006, SuperDrives are combination DVD ±R/±RW and CD-R/RW writer drives offering

speeds of 4x-36x and supporting the DVD-R, DVD+R, DVD+R DL, DVD±RW, DVD-9, CD-R, and CD-RW formats along with all normal read-only media.

Switch
A switch is a computer networking device that connects network segments. Low-end network switches appear nearly identical to network hubs, but a switch contains more "intelligence" (and comes with a correspondingly slightly higher price tag) than a network hub. Network switches are capable of inspecting data packets as they are received, determining the source and destination device of that packet, and forwarding it appropriately. By delivering each message only to the connected device it was intended for, a network switch conserves network bandwidth and offers generally better performance than a hub.

Tagged Image File Format
Tagged Image File Format (TIFF) is a container format for storing images, including photographs and line art. Originally created by the company Aldus for use with what was then called "desktop publishing," it is now under the control of Adobe. The TIFF format is widely supported by image-manipulation applications, by publishing and page layout applications, by scanning, faxing, word processing, OCR, and other applications.

Tape Drive
A tape drive is a data storage device that reads and writes data stored on a magnetic tape. It is typically used for archival storage of data on hard drives. Tape generally has a favorable unit cost and long archival stability.

Terminal Services
Terminal Services is a component of Microsoft Windows (both server and client versions) that allows a user to access applications and data on a remote computer over any type of network, although normally best used when dealing with either a Wide Area Network (WAN) or local area network (LAN). Ease and compatibility with other types of networks may differ and vary. Terminal Services is Microsoft's implementation of thin-client terminal server computing, where Windows applications, or even the entire desktop of the computer running terminal services, are made accessible from a remote client machine.

Time Machine
Time Machine is a backup utility developed by Apple that is included with Mac OS X v10.5.

Universal Serial Bus
Universal serial bus (USB) is a serial bus standard to interface devices. USB was designed to allow peripherals to be connected using a single standardized interface socket and to improve plug-and-play capabilities by allowing devices to be connected and disconnected without rebooting the computer (hot-swapping). Other convenient features include providing power to low-consumption devices without the need for an external power supply and allowing many devices to be used without requiring manufacturer specific, individual device drivers to be installed.

UNIX
UNIX is a computer operating system originally developed in 1969 by a group of AT&T employees, including Ken Thompson, Dennis Ritchie, and Douglas McIlroy, at Bell Labs. Today's Unix systems are split into various branches developed over time by AT&T as well as various commercial vendors and nonprofit organizations.

USB Thumb Drive
USB thumb (flash) drives are NAND-type flash memory data storage devices integrated with a USB connector. They are typically small, lightweight, removable, and rewritable.

Video Card/Graphics Adapter
The video card/graphics adapter, also referred to as a graphics accelerator card, display adapter, graphics card, and numerous other terms, is an item of personal computer hardware whose function is to generate and output images to a display.

Video Graphics Array
The term *video graphics array* (VGA) refers either to an analog computer display standard; the 15-pin D-subminiature VGA connector, first marketed in 1988 by IBM; or the 640 x 480 resolution itself. While this resolution has been superseded in the computer market, it is becoming a popular resolution on mobile devices.

Virtual Private Network

A virtual private network (VPN) is a communications network tunneled through another network and dedicated for a specific network. One common application is secure communications through the public Internet, but a VPN need not have explicit security features, such as authentication or content encryption. VPNs, for example, can be used to separate the traffic of different user communities over an underlying network with strong security features.

Web 2.0

Web 2.0 is a trend in web design and development and can refer to a perceived second generation of web-based communities and hosted services—such as social-networking sites, wikis, and folksonomies—which aim to facilitate creativity, collaboration, and sharing between users. The term gained currency following the first O'Reilly Media Web 2.0 conference in 2004. Although the term suggests a new version of the World Wide Web, it does not refer to an update to any technical specifications but to changes in the ways software developers and end-users use webs.

Wi-Fi

Wi-Fi is a wireless technology brand owned by the Wi-Fi Alliance intended to improve the interoperability of wireless local area network products based on the IEEE 802.11 standards. Common applications for Wi-Fi include Internet and VoIP phone access, gaming, and network connectivity for consumer electronics, such as televisions, DVD players, and digital cameras.

Wi-Fi Protected Access

Wi-Fi protected access (WPA) is a class of systems to secure wireless (Wi-Fi) computer networks. It was created in response to several serious weaknesses researchers had found in the previous system, wired equivalent privacy (WEP). WPA implements the majority of the IEEE 802.11i standard and was intended as an intermediate measure to take the place of WEP while 802.11i was prepared.

Windows Recycle Bin

Windows Recycle Bin is temporary storage for files that have been deleted in a file manager by the user but not yet permanently erased from the physical medium. Typically, a recycle bin is presented as a special file directory to the user (whether or not it is actually a single directory depends on the implementation), allowing the user to browse deleted files, undelete those that were deleted by mistake, or delete them permanently (either one by one or by the Empty Trash function).

Windows SharePoint Services
Windows SharePoint Services, or Windows SharePoint, is the basic part of SharePoint, offering collaboration and document management functionality by means of web portals by providing a centralized repository for shared documents, as well as browser-based management and administration. It allows creation of document libraries, which are collections of files that can be shared for collaborative editing. SharePoint provides access control and revision control for documents in a library.

Wired Equivalent Privacy
Wired equivalent privacy (WEP) is a deprecated algorithm to secure IEEE 802.11 wireless networks. Wireless networks broadcast messages using radio, so they are more susceptible to eavesdropping than wired networks. When introduced in 1999, WEP was intended to provide confidentiality comparable to that of a traditional wired network.

Index

Note: Page numbers in **bold** refer to glossary terms.

AbacusLaw (Abacus Data System), 109
ABA Model Rule 4.2, 210
ABA Model Rule 4.3, 210
Access Data, 121
Accounting software, 112–113
Active Directory (AD), **257**
ActiveSync, **257**
Adobe Acrobat
  as collaboration tool, 137–138
Adobe Acrobat 9.0 Standard software, 40, 125, 224
Adobe Acrobat X family, 91–94, 224
Advanced technology attachment (ATA), **258**
Advertisements, lawyers and, 211–212
Adware, **257**
Age of Instancy, 214–215
AIA Contract Documents, 129
AirCard, 149–150
AirPort, **267**
AirPort Express Base Station, 156
AirPort Extreme, 155–156, **267**
All-in-one security products, 147
Alternative fee arrangements (AFAs), 111–112, 240
American Power Conversion (APC) Back-UPS 50, 74
American Power Conversion (APC) Net-Shelter SX enclosures, 69
American Power Conversion (APC) Smart-UPS 1500VA, 75–76
Amicus Attorney, 104–106, 227
Amicus Premium Billing 2011, 118

Amicus Small Firm Accounting 2011, 118–119
Android, 79–80
Antispam protection, 100–101
AppleCare Protection Plan, **257–258**
Apple computers (Macs), 4–7
  desktop computers, 4–7
  laptops, 9–10
  software for, 159–163
Apple products
  AirPort, **267**
  AirPort Express Base station, 156
  AirPort Extreme, 155–156, **267**
  iCloud, 242
  increasing shift towards, 239
  iPad 2, 153–155, 240
  iPhone, 79–80, 79–82, 81–82
  iPod, 158–159
  iSight Camera, **266**
  iTunes, 162–163
  Magic Mouse, 157–158
  PGP Whole Disk Encryption software for, 162
  Thunderbolt Display, 157
  Time Capsule, 156
  wireless keyboards, 157
Apple software
  Intuit Quicken Essentials, 161
  iTunes, 162–163
  Microsoft Office 2008 for Macs Business Edition, 159–160
  Norton Internet Security, 160–161
  PGP Whole Disk Encryption 10 fo Mac OS X, 162
  QuickBooks 2011 for Macs, 161–162
  Toast 11 Titanium, 160

Auto document feeder (ADF), **258**
Autonomy iManage Worksite, 124, 225

Backup and disaster recovery devices (BDRs), 242
Backup solutions, 77–78
Battery backup devices, 74–76
Billing software. *See* Time and billing software
Billings software, 116
Bill4Time, 115
Blackberry smartphones, 79–80, 82, 238
Blogs, 192
Boot Camp, **258**
Box.net, 214
Brother IntelliFax-2920, 76–77
Burney, Brett, 239
Byte, **258**

Cabling, 69–70
Calloway, Jim, 235
Case management software
  about, 103–1104
  Amicus Attorney, 104–106
  Clio, 108
  Firm Manager, 109
  PracticeMaster, 107
  ProLaw, 109
  Rocket Matter, 108–109
  Time Matters, 106
Case organization programs, 121. *See also* Trial presentation programs
  LexisNexis CaseMap, 121
  LexisNexis Concordance, 121
  Sanction Solutions Verdical, 121
  West Case Notebook, 121
Category 6 cable (Cat6), **259**
Category 7 cabling, 70
Category 5e cable (Cat5e), **258–259**
Cathode Ray Tube (CRT), **259**
Cat6 standard cabling, 70
CD-ROM, **259**
Central processing unit (CPU), **259**
Cisco ASA 5500 Series Adaptive-Security Appliance, 67–68
Cisco 500 Series Secure Routers, 65–66
Client Access Licenses (CALs), 56, **260**
Client files, fragmented, 219
Clio, 108
Cloud computing, 215, 241–242
Code division multiple access (CDMA), **260**
Collaboration, 135

Collaboration tools
  Acrobat, 137–138
  Google Docs, 135–137
  Microsoft Word, 138
  Office 365, 139–140
  SharePoint, 138–139
Color network printers, 35–36
Computer monitors, **260**
Computer peripherals
  external storage devices, 26–29
  headphones, 30
  keyboards, 24–25
  mouse, 23–24
  speakers, 29–30
  wireless keyboard desktops, 25
Computers. *See* Personal computers
Confidentiality, social media and, 209–210
Contrast ratio, **260–261**
Copy2Contact, 180
Corel Suite, 88–89
Corel WordPerfect, 85
Cottam, Dale, 221–222, 232
Credenza, 175–176
Crispin v. Christian Audiger, Inc., 201–203
CRT monitors, 19

Database, **261**
Database application, **261**
Database/applications servers, 47–49
Database management system, **261**
DAT72 backup tapes, **261**
DBAN, 182
DDR2 SDRAM, **261**
Decryption, **262**
Dell computers
  Inspiron Mini 10, 11
  Latitude laptops, 7–9
  OptiPlex line, 1–4
  P2211H widescreen monitor, 20–21
  Professional P1911 flat-panel monitor, 20
  UltraSharp 3011 HD monitor, 21–22
Dell Mini 10 netbook, 11
Dell OptiPlex computers
  "Keep Your Hard Drive" program, 1–2
Dell PowerEdge T310 server, 44–49
Dell PowerEdge T710 server, 45–47
Dell UltraSharp 73011 monitor, 21–22
Desktop computers
  Apple computers (Macs), 4–7
  laptops, 7–10
  netbooks, 10–11
  personal computers, 1–4

Digital copier, **261**
Digital Subscriber Line (DSL), **261**
Digital Visual Interface (DVI), **261–262**
Discovery rules, 206–207
Display resolution, **262**
Document assembly software
  about, 127
  AIA Contract Documents, 129
  HotDocs, 127–128, 129
  ProDoc, 128–129
Documentation management systems
  about, 123
  Acrobat, 125
  Autonomy iManage Worksite, 124
  DocuShare, 123–124
  NetDocuments, 125–126
  plain folders for, 126
  searching, 126
  Web-based, 125–126
  Worldox, 124–125
Document management systems, 225–228
  Autonomy iManage Worksite, 225
  NetDocuments, 226
  PC Docs, 226
  Worldox GX2, 225
DocuShare, 123–124
Domain controller (DC), **262**
Dots per inch (dpi), **262**
Dragon Naturally Speaking 11.5, 95–96
DropBox, 214, 226
dtSearch, 174–175
DVD, **262**

EasyTime, 116
e-Discovery
  impact of social media on, 197–207
  social media and, 243
eDiscovery Assistant, 94–95
EEOC v. Simply Storage Mgmt., LLC, 200
802.11n standard, 72
Electronically stored information (ESI),
  social media as type of, 198
Electronic *vs.* paper files, advantages of, 232–234
Email spam, **262**
Encryption, 145, 148, **262**
Enhanced-defintion television (EDTV), **263**
Entry-level routers, 65–66
ESI. *See* Electronically stored information (ESI)
Evernote, 190

Extensible Markup Language (XML), 263
External hard drives, 26–27
  FireWire devices, 28–29
External storage devices
  external hard drives, 26–27
  thumb drives, 27–28
Eyejot, 178–179

Facebook, 191, 193–194, 239
FavBackup 2.0.2, 184
Fax machines, 76–77
Fire safes, 73–74
Firewall devices, 67
FireWire 400, **263**
FireWire 800, **263–264**
FireWire devices, 28–29, **263**
Firm Manager, 109
Flat-panel LCD monitors, 19–20
"Friends," social media sites and, 210–211
Fujitsu fi-5530C2 scanner, 40–41
Fujitsu 1100 scanner, 224
Fujitsu ScanSnap S1500M scanner, 40, 224
Fujitsu ScanSnap S1500 scanner, 40, 224

Gigabyte, **264**
Global System for Mobile (GSM) communications, **264**
Google+, 191, 195, 239
Google Docs, 135–137
Google Voice, 168
GoToMyPC, 142
GreenPrint, 177–178
Griffin v. State, 204

Hard disk drives, **264**
Hard drives, external, 26–27
Hasher program, 186
Hash function, **264**
Headphones, 30
Hewlett Packard (HP) Color LaserJet CP3525x printer, 35–36
Hewlett Packard (HP) LaserJet M4345x Multifunctional Printer, 34–35
Hewlett Packard (HP) LaserJet P2055dn printer, 33–34
Hewlett Packard (HP) LaserJet Pro P1606dn printer, 32
High-definition (HD) monitors, 21–22
High-definition multimedia interface (HDMI), **264**
High-defintion TV (HDTV), **265**
High-speed Internet, 170–171

High-volume networked printers, 34–35
High-volume scanners, 40–41
HotDocs, 127–128
Hub, **265**
Hyper-V virtualization system, 51

Ice Cream Sandwich, 82
iCloud, 242
IEEE (Institute of Electrical and Electronics Engineers), **265**
Instancy, age of, 214–215
Intel Core 2 duo processor, **265**
Intel Corporation (Intel), **265**
Intel Xeon processors, 50
Intermediate-level routers, 65–66
Internet Information Services (IIS), **265**
Internet protocol address, **265–266**
Intrusion Detection System (IDS), 66–67, **266**
Intrusion Prevention System (IPS), 66–67
Iomega UltraMax Plus External Hard Drive, 77–78
iPad, 240
iPad2, 153–155
iPad, trial presentation programs for, 121–122
iPhones, 79–82
iPod, 158–159
IPsec (IP security), **266**
IrfanView, 181–182
IronKey USB thumb drive, 27–28
iSight Camera, **266**
iTunes, 162–163

Karen's Power Tools, 186
Kaspersky Business Space Security software, 99–100
Kaspersky Internet Security 2012, 98
"Keep Your Hard Drive" program, Dell's, 1–2
Keyboards, 24–25, **266**
Kodner, Ross L., 235–236
Konica Minolta Bizhub C220 MFP device, 37

LaCie d2 Quadra Hard Disk, 29
Laptops
  Apple computers, 9–10
  Dell Latitutde line of, 7–9
Laser printer, **267**
Law firm networks, external attacks on, 240–241

Law firms
  social media and, 239
  virtual, 240
Lawyer videos, 240
Lawyer websites, ABA Formal Opinion 10-457, 245–256
Lee, Rob, 240, 241
LexisNexis CaseMap, 121
LexisNexis Concordance, 121
Light-emitting diode (LED), **267**
Linear tape-open (LTO), **267**
LinkedIn, 191, 194, 239
Linksys E3200 High-Performance Dual-Band N Router, 72
Linux-based operating systems, 62
Liquid crystal display (LCD), **267**
Litigation programs, 121–122
Livescribe Pulse Smartpen, 187–188
Logitech LS 21 speakers, 29–30
Logitech Wireless Wave Combo MK 550, 25
LogMeIn, 142–143
Low-volume networked printers, 33–34
Low-volume scanners, 40

MacBook Pro laptops, 9–10
Mac computers, 4–7, **267–268**. *See* Apple computers (Macs)
MAC (media access control) filtering, 71
Mac OS X operating system, 5
  version 10.5 (Leopard), 16, 61
  version 10.6 (Snow Leopard), 16–17, 61
  version 10.7 (Lion), 17
Magic Mouse, Apple, 157–158
MagSafe power adapter, **268**
Malware,1 Android devices and, 83–84
Manual generation, of time and billing, 112
Markey, Edward J., 194
Media access control (MAC) address, **268**
Megabyte, **268**
Message-digest algorithm 5 (MD5), **268**
Metadata Assistant, 186–187
Microsoft Comfort Mouse 3000, 24–25
Microsoft Exchange Server, **268–269**
Microsoft Natural Ergonomic Keyboard 4000, 24–25
Microsoft Office 2010, 85–88
Microsoft Office 2008 for Mac, 159
Microsoft Office for Mac 2011, 160
Microsoft Small Business Server 2011 (SBS 2011) Standard and Essentials, 60

Index

Microsoft SQL Server, 269
Microsoft Virtual Server 2005 R2SP2, 51
Microsoft Vista operating system, 3, 13–14
Microsoft Windows, **269**
Microsoft Windows 7, 3, 14–16, 239, **269**
Microsoft Windows Server 2003 Enterprise Edition, 56–57
Microsoft Windows Server 2008 Enterprise Edition, 59–60
Microsoft Windows Server 2008 R2, 57–58
Microsoft Windows Server 2003 Standard Edition, 55
Microsoft Windows Server 2008 Standard Edition, 59
Microsoft Windows Small Business Server (SBS) 2003 Standard and Premium Editions, 55–56
Microsoft Windows Small Business Server (SBS) 2008 Standard and Premium Editions, 58–59
Microsoft Windows XP operating system, 13
Microsoft Word, 85
  as collaboration tool, 138
MiniToolbar, 86
Mobile security. *see also* Security
  AirCard, 149–150
  all-in-one security products for, 147
  encryption and, 148
  public computers and, 151
  smartphones and, 151–152
  wireless, 148–149
Modem, **269**
Monitors
  CRT, 19
  flat-panel LCD, 19–20
  high-definition, 21–22
  widescreen, 20–21
Moreno v. Hanford Sentinel, Inc., 206
Motorola Droid Bionic phones, 82
Mouse, 23–24, **269**
MP3, **269**
Multifunctional printers (MFPs), 36–37
MySpace, 191, 194–195

Natural Ergonomic Keyboard 4000 (Microsoft), 24–25
Nelson, Sharon, 235, 237, 242
Netbooks, 10–11
NetDocuments, 125–126, 214–215, 226
NETGEAR ProSafe Unmanaged Desktop Switches, 64

Network address translation (NAT), **270**
Network card/adapter, **270**
Networked printers, 33–36
  color, 35–36
  high-volume, 34–35
  low-volume, 33–34
Networking hardware, 63–72
  cabling, 69–70
  entry-level and intermediate-level routers, 65–66
  firewalls/IDS/IPS devices, 65
  racks, 68–69
  switches, 63–64
  wireless networking devices, 70–72
Norton Internet Security, for Macs, 160–161

Office 365, 139–140
OmniPage Professional 18, 94–95
OpenOffice.org, 89–91
Open Systems Interconnection (OSI) model, 63–64
Operating systems. *See* Mac OS X operating system; Server operating systems
Optical character recognition (OCR), **270**
  software, 94–95
Outlook Send Assistant, 176–177

Paper, 215–216
Paper LESS
  backup-able advantage of, 234–235
  becoming, 216, 219–221
  bottom line of, 235–236
  quick tip, 225
  side benefit of, 221–222
Paper LESS cloud, 228–231
Paper LESS Office, 221
Paper MORE practices, cost of being, 216–219
PC Docs, 226
PCLaw, 116–117
Peer-to-peer networks, 52–53
Peripheral devices, **270**
Personal computers
  desktops, 1–4
  laptops, 7–9
  netbooks, 10–11
Personal digital assistants (PDAs), **270–271**
PGP Whole Disk Encryption software, for Macs, 162
Plantronics Audio 626 DSP headset/microphone system, 95

Portable Document Format (PDF), **271**
Postini, 100–101
PracticeMaster, 107
Presentation programs. *See* Trial presentation programs
Printers
   multifunctional, 36–37
   networked, 33–36
   stand-alone, 31–32
Private branch exchange (PBX), **271**
ProDoc, 128–129
Productivity software
   Adobe Acrobat, 91–94
   Corel Office Suite, 88–89
   Microsoft Office, 85–88
   OCR software, 94–95
   OpenOffice.org, 89–91
   voice recognition software, 95–96
ProLaw (Thomson Elite), 109, 119, 227
PS/2 connector, **271**
Public computer usage, 151

QuickBooks, 112–113
   for Macs, 161–162
Quicken, for Mac, 1661
QuickView Plus, 185

Racks, 68–69
Radio-frequency identification (RFID), **271**
RAID 5, **271**
Random access memory (RAM), **272**
Redundant arrays of independent disks (RAID), **272**
Remote access
   GoToMyPC, 142
   LogMeIn, 142–143
   TeamViewer Business Edition, 143
   tips for, 144–145
   virtual private networking, 141–142
Remote desktop protocol (RDP), **272**
Revolutions per minute, **272**
Ribbon, 86
Rocket Matter, 108–109
Romano v. Steelcase, Inc., 199
Rootkits, **272–273**
Routers, **273**
   entry-level, 65–66
   intermediate-level, 65–66

Saas (software as a service)
   advantages of, 133
   conclusions about, 133–134
   financial stability of provider and, 132

   security and, 131–132
   stability of communications network and, 132–133
   upgrades and, 132
Sam Spade, 185–186
Sanction Solutions Verdical, 121
Sanction (trial presentation program), 121
SanDisk Ultral USB flash drive, 27
Scanners, 220
   about, 39
   centralized and decentralized, 223–224
   effective use of, 222–223
   high-volume, 40–41
   low-volume, 40
   suggested models, 224
Scanning resolution, **273**
Seagate FreeAgent Desk external hard drive, 26–27
Secure Sockets Layer (SSL), **273**
Security. *See also* Mobile security
   increasing importance of, 238
   social media and, 242–243
Security software
   enterprise versions, 98–101
   stand-alone, 97–98
Serial advanced technology attachment (SATA), **273**
Serial attached SCSI (SAS), 273
Server operating systems, 55–62
   Linux-based, 62
   Mac OS X 10.7 "Lion," 61–62
   Mac OS X Server 10.5 "Leopard," 61
   Mac OS X 10.6 "Snow Leopard," 61
   Microsoft Small Business Server 2011 (SBS 2011) Standard and Essentials, 60
   Microsoft Windows Server 2003 Enterprise Edition, 56–57
   Microsoft Windows Server 2008 Enterprise Edition, 59–60
   Microsoft Windows Server 2008 R2, 57–58
   Microsoft Windows Server 2003 Standard Edition, 55
   Microsoft Windows Server 2008 Standard Edition, 59
   Microsoft Windows Small Business Server 2003 Standard and Premium Editions, 55–56
   Microsoft Windows Small Business Server 2008 Standard and Premium Editions, 58–59
   X64 operating systems, 60–61

Servers, **273–274**
　about, 43
　database/applications, 47–49
　peer-to-peer networks, 52–53
　small firm, 45–47
　solo, 43–45
　virtual, 49–52
Service set identifier (SSID), **274**
Shadow Copy, **274**
SHA has functions, **274**
SharePoint, 138–139
Shred 2, 183
SimplyFile, 183
Small computer system interface (SCSI), **274–275**
Small firm servers, 45–47
SmartDraw VP, 188–189
Smartpen, 187–188
Smartphone malware, 238
Smartphone policies, 238
Smartphones, 79–84, **275**
　security and, 151–152
　spam text messages and, 83
SnagIt, 184
SnippingTool, 184
Social media, 191
　advertisements and, 211–212
　confidentiality and, 209–210
　e-discovery and, 243
　"friends" and, 210–211
　impact of, on e-discovery, 197–207
　increasing importance of, 242
　law enforcement officials and trolling of, 207–208
　law firms and, 239
　lawyers and, 191–192
　security issues and, 242–243
　as type of ESI, 198
Social media discovery requests, responding to, 204–205
Social media effect, 196–197
Social media evidence
　admissibility of, 203–204
　discoverability of, 199–203
　ethics of obtaining, 205–207
Social media tools
　blogs, 192
　social messaging sites, 195–196
　social networking sites, 192–195
Social messaging sites, 195–196
Social networking, 133. *See also* Collaboration
Social networking sites, 192–195
　subpoenas to, 207

Solo servers, 43–45
Sony DR-BT101 Bluetooth wireless stereo headphones, 30
Speakers, 29–30
Spyware, **275**
Stand-alone printers, 31–32
State v. Bell, 203–204
Stereophonic sound (stereo), **275**
Subpoenas, to social networking sites, 207
Summation (Access Data), 121
SuperDrive, **275–276**
Switches, 63–64, **276**
Symbian-based phones, 79–80

Tabs3 billing package, 117–118
Tabs Practice Master, 227
Tagged Image File Format (TIFF), **276**
Tape Drive, **276**
TeamViewer Business Edition, 143
Terminal Services, **276**
Thumb drives, 27–28
Thunderbolt Display, Apple, 157
Time and billing software
　about, 111–112
　Amicus Premium Billing 2011, 118
　Amicus Small Firm Accounting 2011, 118–119
　integrated packages, 116
　for Mac computers, 115–116
　PCLaw, 116–117
　ProLaw, 119
　QuickBooks, 112–113
　Tabs3, 117–118
　Timeslips, 114–115
Time Capsule, 156
TimeMap, 189–190
Time Matters, 106, 227
Timeslips, 114–115
TinyURL, 181
Toast 11 Titanium, 160
Trend Micro Worry-Free Business Security, 100
Trial Director (trial presentation program), 121
TrialPad, 122
Trial presentation programs. *See also* Case organization programs
　defined, 121
　for iPad, 121–122
　Sanction, 121
　Trial Director, 121
　Visionary, 121
Trojan horses, 66

TweetDeck, 181
TwInbox, 180–181
Twitter, 191, 195–196

Unified messaging, 165–168
  Google Voice, 168
  high-speed Internet, 170–171
  Voice over Internet Protocol (VoIP), 168–170
Utilities
  Copy2Contact, 180
  Credenza, 175–176
  DBAN, 182
  dtSearch, 174–175
  Evernote, 190
  Eyejot, 178–179
  FavBackup 2.0.2, 184
  GreenPrint, 177–178
  Hasher program, 186
  IrfanView, 181–182
  Karen's Power Tools, 186
  Metadata Assistant, 186–187
  Outlook Send Assistant, 176–177
  QuickView Plus, 185
  Sam Spade, 185–186
  Shred 2, 183
  SimplyFile, 183
  SmartDraw VP, 188–189
  SnagIt, 184
  SnippingTool, 184
  TimeMap, 189–190
  TinyURL, 181
  TweetDeck, 181
  TwInbox, 180–181
  WinRAR, 190
  Winscribe, 178
  X1 program, 173–174
  YouMail, 188
  YouSendIt, 179–180

Virtualization, 49–50, 242
Virtual law firms, 240
Virtual private networking (VPN), 141–142
Virtual servers, 49–52
Viruses, 66, **260**
Visionary (trial presentation program), 121
VNware vSphere Hypervisor (ESXi), 52
Voice messages, 166–167. *See also* Unified messaging
Voice over Internet Protocol (VoIP) systems, 168–170
Voice recognition software, 95–96

Web-based documentation management systems, 125–126
Websites, lawyer, ABA Formal Opinion 10-457 for, 245–256
West Case Notebook, 121
Widescreen monitors, 20–21
Windows Phone 7, 79–80, 82–83
WinRAR, 190
Winscribe, 178
Wired equivalent privacy (WEP), 71
Wireless keyboard desktops, 25
Wireless keyboards, Apple, 157
Wireless networking devices, 70–72
WordPerfect Office X5, 88–89
Worldox, 124–125, 126, 215
Worldox GX2, 225, 226–227
Worms, 66

X1 program, 173–174

YouMail, 188
YouSendIt, 179–180
YouTube, 240

Zimmerman v. Weis Markets, Inc., 201

SELECTED BOOKS FROM  LAW PRACTICE MANAGEMENT SECTION
MARKETING • MANAGEMENT • TECHNOLOGY • FINANCE

The Lawyer's Guide to Collaboration Tools and Technologies: Smart Ways to Work Together
By Dennis Kennedy and Tom Mighell

Product Code: 5110589 / LPM Price: $59.95 / Regular Price: $89.95

This first-of-its-kind guide for the legal profession shows you how to use standard technology you already have and the latest "Web 2.0" resources and other tech tools, like Google Docs, Microsoft Office and Share-Point, and Adobe Acrobat, to work more effectively on projects with colleagues, clients, co-counsel and even opposing counsel. In *The Lawyer's Guide to Collaboration Tools and Technologies: Smart Ways to Work Together*, well-known legal technology authorities Dennis Kennedy and Tom Mighell provides a wealth of information useful to lawyers who are just beginning to try these tools, as well as tips and techniques for those lawyers with intermediate and advanced collaboration experience.

Google for Lawyers: Essential Search Tips and Productivity Tools
By Carole A. Levitt and Mark E. Rosch

Product Code: 5110704 / LPM Price: $47.95 / Regular Price: $79.95

This book introduces novice Internet searchers to the diverse collection of information locatable through Google. The book discusses the importance of including effective Google searching as part of a lawyer's due diligence, and cites case law that mandates that lawyers should use Google and other resources available on the Internet, where applicable. For intermediate and advanced users, the book unlocks the power of various advanced search strategies and hidden search features they might not be aware of.

The Lawyer's Guide to Adobe Acrobat, Third Edition
By David L. Masters

Product Code: 5110588 / LPM Price: $49.95 / Regular Price: $79.95

This book was written to help lawyers increase productivity, decrease costs, and improve client services by moving from paper-based files to digital records. This updated and revised edition focuses on the ways lawyers can benefit from using the most current software, Adobe® Acrobat 8, to create Portable Document Format (PDF) files.

PDF files are reliable, easy-to-use, electronic files for sharing, reviewing, filing, and archiving documents across diverse applications, business processes, and platforms. The format is so reliable that the federal courts' Case Management/Electronic Case Files (CM/ECF) program and state courts that use Lexis-Nexis File & Serve have settled on PDF as the standard.

You'll learn how to:

- Create PDF files from a number of programs, including Microsoft Office
- Use PDF files the smart way
- Markup text and add comments
- Digitally, and securely, sign documents
- Extract content from PDF files
- Create electronic briefs and forms

The Electronic Evidence and Discovery Handbook: Forms, Checklists, and Guidelines
By Sharon D. Nelson, Bruce A. Olson, and John W. Simek

Product Code: 5110569 / LPM Price: $99.95 / Regular Price: $129.95

The use of electronic evidence has increased dramatically over the past few years, but many lawyers still struggle with the complexities of electronic discovery. This substantial book provides lawyers with the templates they need to frame their discovery requests and provides helpful advice on what they can subpoena. In addition to the ready-made forms, the authors also supply explanations to bring you up to speed on the electronic discovery field. The accompanying CD-ROM features over 70 forms, including, Motions for Protective Orders, Preservation and Spoliation Documents, Motions to Compel, Electronic Evidence Protocol Agreements, Requests for Production, Internet Services Agreements, and more. Also included is a full electronic evidence case digest with over 300 cases detailed!

The Lawyer's Guide to Microsoft Word 2010
By Ben M. Schorr

Product Code: 5110721 / LPM Price: $41.95 / Regular Price: $69.95

Microsoft® Word is one of the most used applications in the Microsoft® Office suite. This handy reference includes clear explanations, legal-specific descriptions, and time-saving tips for getting the most out of Microsoft Word®—and customizing it for the needs of today's legal professional. Focusing on the tools and features that are essential for lawyers in their everyday practice, this book explains in detail the key components to help make you more effective, more efficient, and more successful.

The Lawyer's Guide to LexisNexis CaseMap
By Daniel J. Siegel

Product Code: 5110715 / LPM Price: $47.95 / Regular Price: $79.95

LexisNexis CaseMap is a computer program that makes analyzing cases easier and allows lawyers to do a better job for their clients in less time. Many consider this an essential law office tool. If you are interested in learning more about LexisNexis CaseMap, this book will help you:

- Analyze the strengths and weaknesses of your cases quickly and easily;
- Learn how to create files for people, organizations and issues, while avoiding duplication;
- Customize CaseMap so that you can get the most out of your data;
- Enter data so that you can easily prepare for trial, hearings, depositions, and motions for summary judgment;
- Import data from a wide range of programs, including Microsoft Outlook;
- Understand CaseMap's many Reports and ReportBooks;
- Use the Adobe DocPreviewer to import PDFs and quickly create facts and objects; and
- Learn how to perform advanced searches plus how to save and update your results.

TO ORDER VISIT **WWW.SHOPABA.ORG** OR CALL 1-800-285-2221

SELECTED BOOKS FROM

Virtual Law Practice:
How to Deliver Legal Services Online
By Stephanie L. Kimbro

Product Code: 5110707 / LPM Price: $47.95 / Regular Price: $79.95

The legal market has recently experienced a dramatic shift as lawyers seek out alternative methods of practicing law and providing more affordable legal services. Virtual law practice is revolutionizing the way the public receives legal services and how legal professionals work with clients. If you are interested in this form of practicing law, *Virtual Law Practice* will help you:

- *Responsibly deliver legal services online to* your clients
- Successfully set up and operate a virtual law office
- Establish a virtual law practice online through a secure, client-specific portal
- Manage and market your virtual law practice
- Understand state ethics and advisory opinions
- Find more flexibility and work/life balance in the legal profession

The Lawyer's Essential Guide to Writing
By Marie Buckley

Product Code: 5110726 / LPM Price: $47.95 / Regular Price: $79.95

This is a readable, concrete guide to contemporary legal writing. Based on Marie Buckley's years of experience coaching lawyers, this book provides a systematic approach to all forms of written communication, from memoranda and briefs to e-mail and blogs. The book sets forth three principles for powerful writing and shows how to apply those principles to develop a clean and confident style.

iPad in One Hour for Lawyers
By Tom Mighell

Product Code: 5110719 / LPM Price: $19.95 / Regular Price: $34.95

Whether you are a new or a more advanced iPad user, *iPad in One Hour for Lawyers* takes a great deal of the mystery and confusion out of using your iPad. Ideal for lawyers who want to get up to speed swiftly, this book presents the essentials so you don't get bogged down in technical jargon and extraneous features and apps. In just six, short lessons, you'll learn how to:

- Quickly Navigate and Use the iPad User Interface
- Set Up Mail, Calendar, and Contacts
- Create and Use Folders to Multitask and Manage Apps
- Add Files to Your iPad, and Sync Them
- View and Manage Pleadings, Case Law, Contracts, and other Legal Documents
- Use Your iPad to Take Notes and Create Documents
- Use Legal-Specific Apps at Trial or in Doing Research

Find Info Like a Pro, Volume 1: Mining the Internet's Publicly Available Resources for Investigative Research
By Carole A. Levitt and Mark E. Rosch

Product Code: 5110708 / LPM Price: $47.95 / Regular Price: $79.95

This complete hands-on guide shares the secrets, shortcuts, and realities of conducting investigative and background research using the sources of publicly available information available on the Internet. Written for legal professionals, this comprehensive desk book lists, categorizes, and describes hundreds of free and fee-based Internet sites. The resources and techniques in this book are useful for investigations; depositions; locating missing witnesses, clients, or heirs; and trial preparation, among other research challenges facing legal professionals. In addition, a CD-ROM is included, which features clickable links to all of the sites contained in the book.

How to Start and Build a Law Practice, Platinum Fifth Edition
By Jay G Foonberg

Product Code: 5110508 / LPM Price: $57.95 / Regular Price: $69.95

This classic ABA bestseller has been used by tens of thousands of lawyers as the comprehensive guide to planning, launching, and growing a successful practice. It's packed with over 600 pages of guidance on identifying the right location, finding clients, setting fees, managing your office, maintaining an ethical and responsible practice, maximizing available resources, upholding your standards, and much more. You'll find the information you need to successfully launch your practice, run it at maximum efficiency, and avoid potential pitfalls along the way. If you're committed to starting—and growing—your own practice, this one book will give you the expert advice you need to make it succeed for years to come.

Social Media for Lawyers: The Next Frontier
By Carolyn Elefant and Nicole Black

Product Code: 5110710 / LPM Price: $47.95 / Regular Price: $79.95

The world of legal marketing has changed with the rise of social media sites such as Linkedin, Twitter, and Facebook. Law firms are seeking their companies attention with tweets, videos, blog posts, pictures, and online content. Social media is fast and delivers news at record pace. This book provides you with a practical, goal-centric approach to using social media in your law practice that will enable you to identify social media platforms and tools that fit your practice and implement them easily, efficiently, and ethically.

TO ORDER VISIT **WWW.SHOPABA.ORG** OR CALL 1-800-285-2221

30-DAY RISK-FREE ORDER FORM

Please print or type. To ship UPS, we must have your street address. If you list a P.O. Box, we will ship by U.S. Mail.

Name

Member ID

Firm/Organization

Street Address

City/State/Zip

Area Code/Phone (In case we have a question about your order)

E-mail

Method of Payment:
❏ Check enclosed, payable to American Bar Association
❏ MasterCard   ❏ Visa   ❏ American Express

Card Number   Expiration Date

Signature Required

MAIL THIS FORM TO:
American Bar Association, Publication Orders
P.O. Box 10892, Chicago, IL 60610

ORDER BY PHONE:
24 hours a day, 7 days a week:
Call 1-800-285-2221 to place a credit card order.
We accept Visa, MasterCard, and
American Express.

EMAIL ORDERS: orders@americanbar.org
FAX: 1-312-988-5568

VISIT OUR WEB SITE: www.ShopABA.org
Allow 7-10 days for regular UPS delivery. Need it sooner? Ask about our overnight delivery options. Call the ABA Service Center at 1-800-285-2221 for more information.

GUARANTEE:
If—for any reason—you are not satisfied with your purchase, you may return it within 30 days of receipt for a refund of the price of the book(s). No questions asked.

Thank You For Your Order.

Join the ABA Law Practice Management Section today and receive a substantial discount on Section publications!

Product Code:	Description:	Quantity:	Price:	Total Price:
				$
				$
				$
				$
				$

Subtotal	$
*Tax:	$
**Shipping/Handling:	$
Yes, I am an ABA member and would like to join the Law Practice Management Section today! (Add $50.00)	$
Total:	$

**Shipping/Handling:

$0.00 to $9.99	add $0.00
$10.00 to $49.99	add $5.95
$50.00 to $99.99	add $7.95
$100.00 to $199.99	add $9.95
$200.00 to $499.99	add $12.95

*Tax:
IL residents add 9.75%
DC residents add 6%

TO ORDER VISIT **WWW.SHOPABA.ORG** OR CALL 1-800-285-2221

ABA WEBSTORE: WWW.SHOPABA.ORG

ITUNES: WWW.APPLE.COM/ITUNES

LAW PRACTICE MANAGEMENT
RESOURCES FOR THE DIGITAL AGE

LPM e-books are now available to read on your iPad, smartphone, or favorite e-reader! To download the **latest releases** in EPUB or Apple format, visit the ABA Webstore or iTunes today. LPM's digital library is expanding quickly, so check back often for new e-book availability. Purchase LPM e-books today and be only **one click away** from the resources your law practice needs.

FOLLOW LPM!

Stay current with the latest news about LPM Books, including discount offers, free excerpts, author interviews, and more.

- t   LPM Books Blog: http://lpmbooks.tumblr.com/
- t   @LawPracticeTips
- f   http://www.facebook.com/LawPracticeTips
- in ABA Law Practice Management Section Group

Join the ABA Law Practice Management Section Today!

Value is . . .

Resources that help you become a better lawyer:
- Up to 40% off LPM publications
- Six Issues of *Law Practice* magazine, both print and electronic versions
- Twelve issues of our monthly Webzine, *Law Practice Today*
- Your connection to Section news and events through *LawPractice.news*
- Discounted registration on "Third Thursday" CLE Teleconference Series and LPM conferences

Networking with industry experts while improving your skills at:
- ABA TECHSHOW
- ABA Law Firm Marketing Strategies Conference
- ABA Women Rainmakers Mid-Career Workshop
- LPM Quarterly Meetings

Opportunity given exclusively to our members:
- Writing for LPM periodicals and publications
- Joining ABA Women Rainmakers
- Becoming a better leader through committee involvement
- Listing your expertise in the LPM Speakerbase

Members of LPM get up to 40% off publications like this one. Join today and start saving!

www.lawpractice.org • 1.800.285.2221